Aeschylus' *Oresteia*

This is a fully revised new edition of Michael Ewans' 1995 English translation of the *Oresteia*, taking into account the extensive work published on the trilogy in recent years.

Accompanying this lucid, accurate and actable translation is a substantial introduction, outlining the festival setting of the plays, the original performance conditions and performance style, the form and meaning of the trilogy, the issues surrounding the act of translation, and finally a survey of some major productions since 1980. The text itself is a thoroughly competitive translation into modern English verse, now significantly revised in the light of recent scholarship on the Greek text. It is followed by a theatrical commentary on each scene and chorus, providing unique insights into how the plays might have been staged in ancient Athens and how they can be staged today. The book also includes notes on the translation, two glossaries of names and Greek terms, selected further reading, and a chronology of Aeschylus' life and times.

Aeschylus' Oresteia: *Translation and Theatrical Commentary* is the most comprehensive English edition of Aeschylus' masterpiece, and this new edition fully meets the needs of teachers, students and practitioners working on the trilogy as well as those interested in ancient Greek drama and literature more broadly.

Michael Ewans is Conjoint Professor of Drama in the School of Humanities, Creative Industries and Social Science at the University of Newcastle, Australia. His 12 books include two volumes each of translations of plays by Aeschylus, Sophocles and Aristophanes and a recent translation of Euripides' *Medea*, all with theatrical commentaries.

Aeschylus' *Oresteia*
Translation and Theatrical Commentary
Second Edition

Michael Ewans

To apply for permission to perform these translations,
contact ewansm7@gmail.com.

LONDON AND NEW YORK

Designed cover image: Maia Morgenstern and Adriana Moca in *Oresteia*.
Photo: Robbie Jack/Contributor/Getty Images

Second edition published 2024
by Routledge
4 Park Square, Milton Park, Abingdon, Oxon, OX14 4RN

and by Routledge
605 Third Avenue, New York, NY 10158

Routledge is an imprint of the Taylor & Francis Group, an informa business

© 2024 Michael Ewans

The right of Michael Ewans to be identified as author of this work has been asserted in accordance with sections 77 and 78 of the Copyright, Designs and Patents Act 1988.

All rights reserved. No part of this book may be reprinted or reproduced or utilised in any form or by any electronic, mechanical, or other means, now known or hereafter invented, including photocopying and recording, or in any information storage or retrieval system, without permission in writing from the publishers.

Trademark notice: Product or corporate names may be trademarks or registered trademarks, and are used only for identification and explanation without intent to infringe.

First edition published by J.M. Dent 1995

British Library Cataloguing-in-Publication Data
A catalogue record for this book is available from the British Library

Library of Congress Cataloging-in-Publication Data
Names: Aeschylus, author. | Ewans, Michael, 1946- translator, writer of added commentary.
Title: Aeschylus' Oresteia : translation and theatrical commentary / Michael Ewans.
Other titles: Oresteia. English
Description: Second edition. | Abingdon, Oxon ; New York, NY : Routledge, 2024. | Includes bibliographical references and index.
Identifiers: LCCN 2023044292 (print) | LCCN 2023044293 (ebook) | ISBN 9781032646985 (hardback) | ISBN 9781032646961 (paperback) | ISBN 9781032646992 (ebook)
Subjects: LCSH: Agamemnon, King of Mycenae (Mythological character)--Drama. | Orestes, King of Argos (Mythological character)--Drama. | Electra (Greek mythological figure)--Drama. | Aeschylus. Oresteia. | LCGFT: Drama. | Literary criticism.
Classification: LCC PA3827.A7 E93 2024 (print) | LCC PA3827.A7 (ebook) | DDC 882.01--dc23/eng/20231205
LC record available at https://lccn.loc.gov/2023044292
LC ebook record available at https://lccn.loc.gov/2023044293

ISBN: 978-1-032-64698-5 (hbk)
ISBN: 978-1-032-64696-1 (pbk)
ISBN: 978-1-032-64699-2 (ebk)

DOI: 10.4324/9781032646992

Typeset in Times New Roman
by SPi Technologies India Pvt Ltd (Straive)

Contents

List of Figures	*vii*
Preface	*viii*
Chronology of Aeschylus' Life and Times	*ix*

Introduction	1

A Text for Performance 1
Community and Festival at Athens 3
Performance Space 4
Choros and Actors 7
Orchēstra *and* Skēnē *9*
Form and Meaning in the Oresteia *11*
The Gods and Daemons 16
Politics 18
Translation 18
Some Modern Performances 21
Notes 24
Selected Further Reading 30
Notes on the Text, Translation and Commentary 31

Oresteia	35

BY AESCHYLUS

Agamemnon	37
Libation Bearers	79
Eumenides	109

vi   *Contents*

Theatrical Commentary   139

Agamemnon   141

Libation Bearers   168

Eumenides   192

Glossary   *217*
   Proper Names   *217*
   Greek words   *222*
Works Cited   *225*
Index   *232*

Figures

1   The Theatre of Dionysos at the time of the *Oresteia* (458 BCE)   5
2   Schematic diagram showing notation of positions in the *orchēstra*   33

Preface

These translations were originally published in 1995. I believe that, revised in the light of the latest textual scholarship, they stand up well in comparison with more recent versions, most of which do not aim, as this version does, to be both accurate and actable. I supply a comprehensive Introduction, Recommended Reading and two Glossaries – and also the unique feature of this edition, a Theatrical Commentary, which provides information and discussion which theatre practitioners, students and other readers will find valuable. All have been fully revised, and the Introduction much expanded, for this new edition.

This book would not exist without the devoted collaboration of the students and colleagues who took part in the premiere performances of the three translations. Although it is invidious to single out individuals from three large casts and production teams, I should especially like to thank my colleague Barry O'Connor (Agamemnon, Apollo), Vanessa Turton and Jan Hunt (Klytaimestra and Kassandra), Justin Collins and Dimity Raftos (Orestes and Elektra), Katherine Westbury (Athena), Ellen Caryanides (choreographer) and all the members of the three choroses. The productions were funded by the Drama Department and the Senate Research Committee of my University.

I was greatly aided by my appointment as a Visiting University Professor at Boston University in 1986–87; there I developed a first, rough draft of the commentary. Profs. Pat Easterling, Graham Ley and Gregory McCart provided valuable comments on the book before its 1995 publication; for this new edition, I am indebted to Prof. Marguerite Johnson and playwright Dr. Carl Caulfield for comments on the Introduction.

Michael Ewans
The University of Newcastle, Australia

Chronology of Aeschylus' Life and Times

Chronology of Aeschylus' Life			*Chronology of His Times*	
Year	*Age*	*Life*	*Year*	*Artistic and Historical Events*
			534	Peisistratos possibly initiated tragic performances
			528/7	Hippias succeeds Peisistratos as tyrant of Athens
525/4		Aeschylus born at Eleusis		
			c. 514	First Persian attempt to invade Greece thwarted by the Skythians
			514	Hippias' brother Hipparchos murdered by Harmodios and Aristogeiton
			510	Hippias expelled from Athens by the Alkmeonidai
			508/7	Constitutional reforms of Kleisthenes at Athens
			508–6	Defeat of attempts by Sparta and Boiotia to intervene in Athens' internal affairs
			505–01?	Performances of tragedy first incorporated into the Festival of Dionysos at Athens
499	26	Competes for the first time at the Festival of Dionysos	499	Ionia revolts from Persia, led by Miletos; Athens sends troops to assist
			494	Persians defeat Ionians at Lade; fall of Miletos and collapse of revolt
490	35	Fights at Marathon; his brother Kunegeiros is killed	490	First Persian invasion of Greece, repelled by Athenian victory at Marathon
484	41	Wins first prize in the competition for tragedy for the first time		

(*Continued*)

x   *Chronology of Aeschylus' Life and Times*

Chronology of Aeschylus' Life			Chronology of His Times	
Year	*Age*	*Life*	*Year*	*Artistic and Historical Events*
480	45	Fights at Salamis	480	Second Persian invasion under Xerxes
				Unsuccessful defence of Thermopylai by Spartan King Leonidas
				Sack of Athens by Persians
				Decisive Greek victory at Salamis led by Themistokles
				Withdrawal of Xerxes
479	46	Possibly fights at Plataia	479	Final defeat of Xerxes' lieutenant Mardonios by combined Greek army at Plataia
			478	Withdrawal of Sparta and allies from combined Greek league
				Athenians form Delian League
			474?	Pindar *Pythian* 11, giving his version of the Klytaimestra story
			476	Phrynichos wins tragedy competition with *Phoenikian Women* and other plays
472	53	Wins competition with a tetralogy which includes his first surviving drama, *Persians*		
470	55	In Syracuse. Re-stages *Persians* and produces *Women of Aitna* to celebrate the foundation in 475 of the city of Aitna by Hieron	470	Themistokles ostracized
				Pindar *Pythian 1*. His masterpiece, written for Hieron to celebrate his victory in the chariot race at Delphi and the foundation of Aitna
			469	Victory of League fleet at Eurymedon ends Persian threat to the Aigeian
468	57			Sophocles' first entry in the competition wins first prize

(Continued)

Chronology of Aeschylus' Life and Times   xi

Chronology of Aeschylus' Life			Chronology of His Times	
Year	_Age_	_Life_	_Year_	_Artistic and Historical Events_
467	59	Wins competition with Theban tetralogy: _Laios, Oidipous_, the surviving _Seven against Thebes_, and the satyr-play _Sphinx_		
			466–5	Themistokles condemned; flees to Persia
			465–3	Athens crushes attempted revolt by Thasos from the Delian League
463?	62	Wins competition with Danaid tetralogy, which included surviving play _Suppliants_		
			462	Ephialtes and Perikles curtail powers of the Areopagos
			462–1	Pindar _Pythians_ 4 & 5. Two of his greatest compositions, written for Arkesilas, king of Kyrene
			461	Ephialtes assassinated; Kimon ostracized; alliance between Athens and Argos
			460–45	War between Athens and Sparta, the 'First Peloponnesian War'
458	67	Wins competition for thirteenth and last time with the _Oresteia_		
458/7		Moves to Sicily		
456/5	69/70	Dies at Gela in Sicily	c. 456	Pindar _Isthmian_ 7, critical of Athens' expansionist foreign policy
			455	Euripides competes for the first time

Introduction

A Text for Performance

Aeschylus' *Oresteia* is one of the summits of drama, a tragic trilogy more than fit to be named in the same breath as *Hamlet* or *King Lear*. This saga of murder, revenge and ultimate resolution cries out for performance. But there are obstacles much harder to overcome than those accompanying a production of Shakespeare, not least the important role of music and dance. Aeschylus performed his trilogy in conditions very different from those of any modern society and in a performance space which, unlike most modern theatres, had spectators seated on three sides of the action. This edition therefore supplies a translation which aims to be both accurate and actable (a creative and fruitful tension), together with a Theatrical Commentary on each Scene and Choros[1] which elucidates the action and provides suggestions for how to solve the staging issues. These are based on the experience gained from my own productions of these translations, in a replica of the original performance space.[2]

Drama[3] means something enacted, not something written; the Greeks spoke of Aeschylus as the *poiētes*, the 'maker' or 'creator' of the *Oresteia* rather than its writer or author. This usage should make us constantly aware that '*The Oresteia*' meant far more to Aeschylus and his Athenian audience than just the spoken and sung words preserved in the script, which alone survives.

As a *poiētes*, Aeschylus was responsible for realizing, in each year that he was selected to compete at the festival, a new performance event which was displayed, on one occasion only, to his fellow-citizens and their guests. It consisted of three tragedies and a satyr-play – a short burlesque afterpiece with a choros of satyrs, followers of Dionysos and avid would-be consumers of sex and wine.[4] On several occasions, Aeschylus linked his three tragedies together to form a trilogy (only the *Oresteia* survives complete, though its satyr-play *Proteus* is lost); his successors generally preferred to offer three unrelated plays.

Aeschylus combined in his own person the roles which in the modern theatre we divide between the playwright, director, dramaturg, composer, choreographer and lead actor. In a Greek tragic performance, two complementary mixed media alternated as seamlessly as possible; the more emotional lyric mode, in which sung lyrics and choreographed dance unite to form a whole;

DOI: 10.4324/9781032646992-1

2   *Introduction*

and the more dialectical spoken mode, in which speech and freer, blocked movement unite to form a different whole. These were supported throughout by richly decorated costumes, a small number of very significant props, and the façade of a wooden building behind the acting area, with painted panels indicating the location of the action.

For Aeschylus, therefore, the script which we have valued for its literary genius was only one part – though a vital and major part – of the tetralogy composed in dialogue and song, in movement and in dance, with which he competed successfully for the prize for tragedy at the Festival of Dionysos in 458 BCE. The meaning of the *Oresteia* was enshrined in a close combination between verbal imagery and visual, between patterns of sound and patterns of movement. We possess the text, and we need to conduct research productions to explore how it might have been realized in performance – and how best to realize it today.

This is not a wholly subjective process. If the dramas are workshopped and performed in a replica of the Greek theatre shape, in a style faithful in the relevant aspects to what is known of Athenian dramatic conventions and theatre practice, we can recover some sense of how these dramas communicated with their original audience. Though many possible movements can be imagined by the armchair theorist, practical work with a scene from the script often yields only one overall pattern of blocking which is truly effective. Aeschylus knew only one theatre shape, and by the time he created the *Oresteia*, he had been using it to communicate with the Athenian audience for over 40 years; and although the *skēnē* building was relatively new, Aeschylus makes masterly use of it in this trilogy. The work contained in the Theatrical Commentary is the result of sustained reflection on practical staging alternatives through experiment during rehearsals in a half-size replica of the Greek playing space and with a half-sized *choros*. I tried to develop solutions to the plays' problems – and also to test which of the proposals made by scholars who are not also practitioners work in an actual production.[5] As Hornby wrote (1977: 171), in a living theatrical tradition:

> ...certain emotions become associated with certain spaces and certain patterns of movement and can be evoked by them. Performance is then...expressive of specific thoughts and feelings; the physical reality of the stage becomes metaphorical as well as tangible, in the same way that words, in a literary work, become metaphorical as well as literal. This is how effective staging can proceed from the playtext, even when not found in the text surface...Proper staging is in the text by implication. This does not mean that there is only one way of staging a script, but it does mean that, once variables of stage and actor are established, the script will suggest certain natural staging potentials.

The aim of this edition is to supply theatre practitioners and drama students with an accurate and actable translation, together with a suggested conception

Introduction 3

of how the plays worked in Aeschylus' own theatre space and can be successful in performance today, and to help students and other readers to imagine what the *Oresteia* was like for its original audience. I hope that this book, based on research productions and subsequent workshops, will enable performers to re-create for today's audiences the dynamism, intensity and realism which lay at the heart of the dramatic experience for Aeschylus, his acting company and his audience. Greek drama was designed to elicit empathy and a strong emotional as well as intellectual response, and those who produce it today must aim to do the same.[6]

Community and Festival at Athens

In Athens, tragedies, and later comedies, were performed at the festivals of Dionysos. Dionysos was 'first and foremost the god of wine and intoxication'[7]; but he was also a god of fertility and the god of *ekstasis* in general – of standing outside your normal self in an altered state, which could be created by wine, dancing and ritual. Dionysos, though terrifying if rejected and defied (see Euripides' *Bacchae*), had the power to augment the value of life through attainment of *ekstasis* by his worshippers; and most importantly for our purposes, this state could be achieved by the act of impersonation, the putting-on of a costume and mask and assumption of a personality other than your own, which is the essence of the new medium – drama. Tragic festival performances probably began in the last decade of the 500s (though some argue for an earlier date),[8] and the competition for comedy was added in 486.

The Great Festival of Dionysos was held in March, at the start of the sailing season, and thus attracted other Greek spectators to Athens as well as the domestic audience, which represented adult male citizens of all classes – farmers, city workers, intellectuals and aristocrats, together with resident aliens – and women and children at the back of the theatre.[9] This was therefore the largest and most inclusive gathering of the people of Attika, and it was a central event in the life of the *polis*.[10] There is no other known human culture in which a drama as serious and intense as ancient Athenian tragedy has commanded the close attention of a large portion of the community and dramatized for their collective judgement playwrights' visions of major issues, situations and problems affecting their society.

The Theatre of Dionysos was a purpose-built performance space 1.5 km from the city centre. The most modern estimate of its original seating capacity is about 6,000.[11] Three tragic playwrights, each presenting three tragedies and one satyr-play, were selected each year by the Eponymous Archon to be 'granted a choros' and provided with a sponsor (*chorēgos*) who financed, recruited and trained the choros. All parts were played by male citizens; the choros members were young aristocrats, who had the finely trained bodies and the leisure time to devote to the many rehearsals required for four plays. It is probable that tragic playwrights spent one year writing the text and music of their tetralogy and, if 'granted a choros', the following year putting it into production.

4   *Introduction*

From an unknown date, tragedies were also performed at the Lenaia, a winter festival of Dionysos. It is also certain that there were performances of plays in the towns and villages outside Athens in regional Attika, many of which had theatres of their own.[12] And during Aeschylus' lifetime, tragedy began to be exported to the Greek colonies in Sicily and southern Italy; he himself visited Syracuse in 470 to re-stage his *Persians* and present a festival play, *Women of Aitna*, to celebrate the new city of Aitna (situated at the base of the volcano). Aeschylus also returned to Sicily for the last two years of his life and died there at Gela.

Performance Space

The *Oresteia* was first performed in the Theatre of Dionysos, which the Athenians had hollowed out of the slope under the south-east end of the Acropolis. The theatre consisted of a *theatron*, an *orchēstra* and a *skēnē* building. The *theatron* seated tiers of spectators rising from level with the performance area to a considerable way up the hillside; it surrounded almost three quarters of a rectangular *orchēstra* ('dance floor') – the performance space used by both solo actors and choros.[13] Behind the *orchēstra*, from sometime before 458, lay the third component of the theatre, the *skēnē* – a single-storey wooden building on a tangent to the back of the *orchēstra*, extending across most of its width, and facing the centre block of the audience. The *skēnē* was up to 20 metres wide, 2–3 metres high, but not more than 3–4 metres deep, as the ground fell away steeply behind the rear of the theatre precinct, down to the temple of Dionysos. The *skēnē* had a practicable roof, a façade facing the audience which had one set of double doors at its centre-point (with a device, the *ekkuklēma* or 'rolling-out machine', to exhibit tableaux to the audience), and some windows. To this façade *skēnographia* panels could be attached – paintings which showed where the action was set – in the *Oresteia* a palace, open countryside, and a temple (Ley 1989) (Figure 1).[14]

The festival audience surrounded the performance area on three sides, looking down into it from rows of wooden benches which rose steeply up the hillside.[15] Though the acoustics were good, especially on the visually dominant line from the doors to the centre-point,[16] and anecdotes confirm that the audience paid close attention to the words, the Greek termed the area in which the audience sat not auditorium – hearing-space – as did the Romans, but *theatron*, 'seeing-space'. Let us examine what they saw. Facial expressions could have been seen only from the front rows. Masks, slightly larger than the natural head, were therefore worn. The Greek word for what we call a mask was *prosōpon* – literally 'face'; the *prosōpon* was designed not to conceal but to *reveal*, to make sure that all the spectators could identify the gender, age and status of the characters represented.[17] But there was more; the ancient Greek 'mask' was dynamic, and it could, in combination with movement and gesture, elicit emotional responses from the spectators.[18] Expressions could be read from (onto?) the mask according to the angle at which the wearer presented it, the words spoken and sung, and the movements of his body.

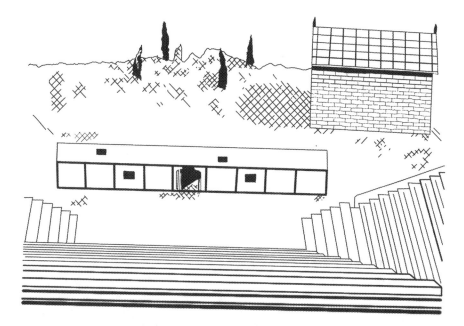

Figure 1 The Theatre of Dionysos at the time of performance of the *Oresteia*. Note the double doors in the centre of the *skēnē*, the windows, and the access to the practicable roof.
Sources: © Michael Ewans.

There were other reasons for the use of *prosōpa* by the Athenians, going back to before the construction of the large theatre. In Aeschylus' lifetime, the invention of dramatic representation in the West lay less than two generations in the past, and it is probable that acting a part was from the outset not regarded as possible without wearing a face other than the actor's own. An anecdote relayed in Plutarch's *Life of Solon* (Chapter 29) suggests that the very act of dramatic impersonation aroused suspicion and distrust in one of Greece's legendary wise men when Thespis invented drama, disguising his face – according to tradition – by smearing it with the lees of wine.

Although gesture was an important element in Greek drama, it is notable that in both tragedy and comedy moments in which detailed gestures are important are always narrated carefully in the spoken or sung text – presumably so that distant spectators, who might miss seeing them, could follow the action.[19] The size of the *theatron* makes it certain that the primary means of visual expression in Greek tragedy was not gesture but blocking – the grouping of actors and their patterns of movement.[20] What kind of space did they move in?

The Greek theatre was wholly unlike the proscenium arch theatre which has predominated in European cultures since the eighteenth century; it was more akin to the modern 'theatre in the round'. Our custom of physically separating actors and audience, and the frequent seclusion of VIPs in boxes,

6   Introduction

would have been alien to the Athenians.[21] So too would have been the separation of solo actors, playing the parts of named individuals, from the choros. However, modern proscenium arch–based conceptions of theatre have been very influential – with disastrous results for the understanding of Greek tragedy. Many scholars have conjectured that there was a raised stage behind the *orchēstra* and that the actors of the individual named parts almost always performed on it.

There is no archaeological evidence for a stage, and for arguments against it, see Pickard 1893 (decisive but ignored), Ley and Ewans 1985 and Wiles 1997: 63ff.[22] The presumed advantages do not exist once we abandon as inappropriate modern ideas of how theatre must work. In the Athenian performance space, a low raised stage would not give the solo actors any visual advantage over the choros, since the vast majority of the spectators looked down on the action from high up in a steeply raked *theatron*. Nor is there reason to suppose that there would have been any acoustic advantage in speaking from a stage behind the *orchēstra*, to compensate for the extra distance from most of the spectators.[23]

The decisive argument against a raised stage lies in the nature of Aeschylus' plays themselves. Unlike many subsequent Western forms of drama, Aeschylean tragedy is an art form in which individual characters are seen not in isolation but in a political and social focus; their fortunes are bound up with those of their *oikos* (household) and *polis* (city-state). Poems as diverse as Homer's epics and Pindar's victory odes show us that the classical Greeks invariably saw individual triumph or catastrophe not in isolation but in relationship to the wider focus of its impact on the community; Aeschylus embodies this way of seeing human life in the constant interaction between the solo actors and the choros, who play the part of the social group most affected by the action.[24]

The interplay between solo actor and choros is at the centre of every scene in Aeschylean drama, and the director's main task is to realize in the playing area the ebb and flow of the power relationships, which are central to the subtleties of the plays. Such sequences as Elektra's colloquy with the Libation Bearers as she first hesitates and then 'turns' Klytaimestra's offerings (*LB* Scene 2) or Apollo's confrontation with the Furies outside his temple (*Eu* Scene 2)[25] are constricted almost to the point of being unplayable if the solo actor is up on a raised stage, marooned in a separate playing area behind the choros; and even the scene where Klytaimestra appears in triumph and begins her first speech standing over the bodies of Agamemnon and Kassandra on the *ekkuklēma* in front of the *skēnē* doors (*Ag* 1379ff.; 'I stand just where I struck') gains very greatly both in force and in pathos if she soon comes forward into the *orchēstra* to challenge the Elders.[26] Workshopping scenes from Aeschylus, Sophocles and Aristophanes both with and without a raised stage has convinced me that in the fifth century there was no raised stage. The double doors at the front of the *skēnē* gave directly onto the back centre extremity of the *orchēstra*; solo actors and choros both used the whole of the *orchēstra*, and it was the sole acting area (apart from brief, exceptional uses of the roof of the *skēnē*, as in *Ag* Scene 1).

Introduction 7

Choros and Actors

A misunderstanding of the role of the choros in Greek tragedy began early in the nineteenth century, with the German philosopher Friedrich Schlegel's influential claim that the chorus was an 'ideal spectator' whose function is to mediate between an action performed by solo actors and the audience, bringing a detached wisdom to the contemplation of that action.[27] The misunderstanding goes so deep that it even affects the way in which the choros part almost invariably appears on the printed page – with their speeches and songs prefixed 'Chorus'.[28]

The twelve men who made up the choros in Aeschylus' time play the part of, and represent in the drama, a collective character: in the *Oresteia* successively the Elders of Argos, the Libation Bearers, and the Furies. Their speeches and songs should be prefixed by these designations. The only differences from named characters are that choros members collectively represent and play the part of a group, do not normally make long speeches, and must give the illusion that they are a more passive character than the individuals – but only the illusion; in *Agamemnon*, they have more lines than any of the solo characters, and in *Libation Bearers* and *Eumenides*, the choros character is highly involved in the action (cf. also Aeschylus' *Suppliants*, where the choros plays the main character).[29]

The choroses of the *Oresteia* do not mediate between actors and audience; together with the solo actors, they are surrounded on three sides by the audience. Their choral odes do provide moments of reflection on the course of the action up to that point; but this reflection is not vague metaphysical speculation; rather, it is a precise reaction to the dramatic situation as it evolves, sung and danced by a group of people who experience that situation from the inside, as active participants in and passive sufferers of the events.

The modern consensus about the choros is expressed, for example, by Gagné and Hopman: 'the chorus oscillates between two identities, an intra-dramatic identity as a fictional group of slaves, soldiers or captive women, and an extra-dramatic identity as a ritual, civic and institutionalized collective performing in the festival of Dionysus'.[30] Laura Swift has shown that the choral odes of Greek tragedy include or allude to several kinds of extra-dramatic choral performances such as the *epineikion* or victory-song and the paean[31]; nonetheless, in the *Oresteia*, the choros has an entirely intra-dramatic identity; it performs in character as Elders, Libation Bearers and Furies throughout, including in the choral odes. Athena's 'foundation speech' (681ff.) in *Eu* is explicitly addressed to her future citizens (i.e., the theatre audience); but while some choral lyrics (e.g. *Eu* Choros 3, Choros 4 and in the Finale 995ff.) have direct relevance to the audience, in none of these instances are the actors performing out of character or out of the action of the play. Griffith (1999: 42) presents a valuable perspective:

> it is primarily through the Chorus' privileged, yet utterly powerless and dependant, subject position that the stage action, and the impact of the 'hero/ine's' sufferings, are experienced by the audience. Thus, even as we

8 *Introduction*

shift back and forth during the course of the play between this and that point of view, we are strongly inclined to relapse (intermittently, and especially at the play's end) into a subject position quite closely aligned to that of the play's main internal audience, the Chorus.

It is very often assumed that the members of the choros were normally silent (as well as motionless!) during the spoken scenes of Greek tragedy except for one spokesman called the 'Chorus Leader'. I have not seen a single modern production of a Greek tragedy prepared to countenance the assumption of a single spokesman.[32] No director tolerates the incongruity of having eleven individuals totally silent except during the odes, while a twelfth is overburdened by having to deliver all their dialogue. And Wilson rightly remarks (unfortunately in an endnote) that: 'The basis in ancient sources for the modern editorial practice is virtually non-existent. Even the habit of assigning the lines of spoken dialogue to an individual leader rather than the whole group rests on no more than an assumption about the collective's need for a "spokesman"'.[33] The idea of a spokesperson is a very frequent modern misunderstanding (e.g., Sommerstein 2010: 24) of the meaning of the Greek word *koryphaios*, which actually means the man who initiates choral movement by giving a cue to the *parastatai*, the next in line.[34] After Agamemnon's death-cry at *Ag* 1343ff., it is obvious that the dialogue *must* have been divided between the twelve individual Elders; so why not elsewhere?

During Aeschylus' lifetime, the Athenians had rapidly evolved an innovative, highly participatory democracy. That is the reason why the choros character's speeches and songs alternate naturally between 'I', expressing an individual member's particular point of view, and 'we', spoken by an individual to express what he or she takes to be the overall view of the group.[35] If we regard Aeschylus' choroses as playing the parts of twelve individuals who collectively form a group, their lines can even be assigned in such a way as to bring out a particular temperament or attitude in each of them, which is suitable to the individual actor and can be developed over the duration of a drama. This makes for very exciting theatre!

This idea has been resisted because it disturbs the authoritarian assumption that the name-role solo actor is far more important and interesting than the anonymous group – just as the raised stage was imported to separate the solo actor from that group, and the choros' responses to the action were misread as spectatorial reflections to deny them their true role as participants in that action. But under the test of production, the old orthodox scholarly view collapses. The effect of dividing between several individual choros members moments such as the edgy dialogue between Klytaimestra and the Elders which opens Scene 2 of *Agamemnon*, or the cross-examination of Orestes and Apollo by the Furies in the trial scene of *Eumenides*, has to be seen to be believed. At once, a balance and an impetus to dramatic flow are given to an action which is lame and halting if only one person speaks for the choros. Hence, in this translation, all choral dialogue is assigned, for example, to '1 ELDER', with

Introduction 9

the expectation that directors and actors will decide which individual choros members will speak each line – just as Aeschylus himself doubtless did. And, of course, the members of the choros interact with the solo actors, responding fluidly to their speeches with movement and gesture – and, in modern unmasked performances, with facial expression.

The consensus about choral singing is equally vehement. We have been told that all ancient Greek choral music was normally sung in unison; so too therefore were the choral lyrics of tragedy. There are, however, good reasons to challenge this view as well. There are three places in the trilogy where the choral lyrics patently must have been divided between different singers.[36] There are also several places where it would be very advantageous to divide a choral lyric between the members' individual voices (e.g. the first four stanzas in the Finale of *Eumenides*); and there is no choral ode in the trilogy where some subdivision, at the discretion of the director and company, is not valuable. Compare especially *Ag* 782ff.; the four variations on 'I agree' in Agamemnon's response at 830ff. make theatre sense only if directed to four different individual Elders who chanted 788ff., 795ff., 799ff. and 805ff.

Orchēstra and *Skēnē*

Athenian dramas were set outdoors primarily because in classical Greece (unlike Northern Europe and North America) significant action and interaction took place outdoors, and indoor events are pertinent only in their impact on the community outside. Aeschylus' works are immediate, precise dramas. The participants created before the audience events familiar from real life; homecomings, prayers and offerings, the arrival of messengers and suppliants, a new dawn at Delphi and a trial for homicide. These events happen, as they all did in ancient Greece, outdoors, anchored in the context of a specific place and political and social situation. Athenian society was defined by a fundamental set of parallel binary polarities; between the public life of an individual as a citizen and his private life; between the male-dominated outdoors and the mostly female-dominated indoors; between the realm of logical, word-based reason and the realm of emotional persuasion; in short, between *polis* and *oikos*. These polarities were reflected in the theatre by the division between the outside world of the *orchēstra* and the indoor world represented by the *skēnē*. When the *skēnē* represents a building, the doors can pull the focus of the action back from the centre-point of the *orchēstra*. This sets up a dialogue between the *orchēstra*, which represents a public arena, and the *skēnē*, which represents the often sinister indoors. Compare Padel (1990: 344): 'Conflict in the dramas between male and female, public and private, knowledge and imagination, is intricately related to the theatre's physical contrast between real and imagined, seen and unseen space.'[37]

Aeschylus makes powerful and effective use of the *skēnē* in the *Oresteia* – the first extant plays since its construction. The trilogy opens with a speech

10   *Introduction*

delivered from the roof. Aeschylus then frequently employs the central double doors, which permitted sudden entries (especially with Klytaimestra's role in *Agamemnon*; see Theatrical Commentary); the threshold is of critical importance in Scene 4 of that play, when Agamemnon is induced to enter his house trampling on expensive, blood-red robes; and the first two plays both reach a climactic revelation exploiting the *ekkuklēma* to display a tableau of murdered bodies. (Dale 1969: 103ff. convincingly demonstrated that only one doorway is required for performances of all the surviving fifth-century tragedies and comedies; compare Taplin 1977a: 344 and 349–51. I have directed full productions of ten tragedies and three comedies, and conducted workshops on scenes from many other fifth-century plays, and found only one doorway to be necessary.[38]) Finally, the doorway's literal liminality becomes a metaphorical liminality in *Ag* Scene 6 and *Eu* Scene 1, where the dark interior becomes a place of terror.

There was also a three-way dialogue between the three means of entrance and exit from the playing space; the (actor) left *eisodos*, leading to downtown of the city in which the play is set; the *skēnē* doorway; and the (actor) right *eisodos*, leading to the countryside and (in *Agamemnon*) to the sea. As Wiles remarks (1997: 144): 'The opposition of wilderness (= audience left) versus civilization (audience right) is, I would suggest, a characteristic device of Greek culture'. Aeschylus makes clearly demarcated use of the polarity between the two open-air entrances, such as in *Libation Bearers*, when Orestes and Pylades come from Phokis (right *eisodos*) and meet Elektra and the Libation Bearers, coming from the palace (left *eisodos*). But, in *Agamemnon*, the Elders enter and exeunt from downtown, and Klytaimestra controls the threshold. Then the Herald and Agamemnon both enter from the harbour (right *eisodos*), while by contrast Aigisthos enters by the left *eisodos* from the city to celebrate his victory. In this way, there is a three-way dialogue between the three entrances, which is replicated in the second half of *Libation Bearers*.[39]

An *orchēstra*, surrounded on three sides by the audience, requires a way of interacting between characters which is wholly different from the upstage/ downstage antithesis of the modern proscenium arch stage. Actors predominantly face each other and must not be grouped towards the back of the *orchēstra* facing the central block of the audience. The proscenium arch theatre encourages this acting style, but in a production of a Greek tragedy, the result is often that the players do not directly face each other, even during crucial scenes of confrontation. In an arena production, turning one's back on part of the audience is perfectly acceptable, provided there is frequent movement so that all spectators are given a chance to relate to each of the individual faces.

This must have been the case in the original productions since the Greek theatre shape positively invites movement[40] and makes stillness a powerful statement – especially the stillness of the choros, who must be moved to the front perimeter of the *orchēstra*, and preferably made to kneel or lie down as well, on the rare occasions (e.g. *LB* Scene 5) on which they take absolutely no part in the action and need to be withdrawn from focus.[41] Athenian tragedy was a vital, vigorous, intense and dramatic medium, which Aeschylus used primarily

Introduction 11

for the representation of emotional, social and personal conflict and its resolution.[42]

Vickers and Walcot are totally convincing in their insistence that what some of us – with criteria for realism derived from the psychological, naturalistic style of middle-period Ibsen, Chekhov, and much twentieth-century drama – might regard as a stylized form of theatre was nothing of the kind to the Athenians.[43] My practical experience has encouraged agreement with Walcot (1976: 51) that the acting style, though obviously large-scale, was fundamentally realistic and designed to involve the emotions of the audience.[44] This basic insight has not been successfully challenged in the fifty years since they wrote (cf. Ewans 2023: 32–4). Arnott (1989: 20) correctly insists that the Greek theatre shape, with its steeply raked *theatron*, was an intimate one; it is a false assumption that a large auditorium and 'masks' imply a remote, distant actor–audience relationship.

Form and Meaning in the *Oresteia*

Aeschylus created this trilogy for an audience which was closely familiar since childhood with a number of previous versions of the 'myth', the old story of the house of Atreus. He did not, of course, expect them to clear their minds of all memory of those versions while watching the *Oresteia* – that would negate the whole purpose of basing new tragedies on old stories. The audience was to presume, in general, that one or more of the 'standard versions' of each story was being followed, unless it was specifically contradicted. But they had to hold that knowledge in a special relationship to the new plays. It must not be allowed to rush in actively and fill gaps with incidents deliberately omitted by the playwright; and it must never be allowed to obliterate new variants, even when they departed from central, near-canonical parts of the traditional versions.

The audience's provisional knowledge of how the story is likely to turn out was a passive field, so to speak, for the Greek dramatist to play on. The audience 'knew' more than the human characters who, except Kassandra, are placed in our normal situation of having no certain knowledge about the future. Since the outlines of what would happen could be guessed from the tradition, the Athenian playwrights were largely saved from the burden of exposition and could concentrate primarily on showing the interactions of people, gods and events which explain *why* they happen. Aeschylus had, of course, to make plain what is going on where he innovates in the *Oresteia* – as, for example, with the new reason for the sacrifice of Iphigenia.[45] But elsewhere, allusion sufficed to carry even the most central points.[46]

Some of Aeschylus' changes to myth would appear to be very substantial, even making allowance for our scanty knowledge of previous versions of the story. For example, legend provided a wealth of past crimes in the House of Atreus: the reckless ambitions of Tantalos; the murders of Oinomaos and Myrtilos by Pelops; Thyestes' adultery and Atreus' appalling revenge for it – all

12   *Introduction*

provided ample material for a playwright who wished to see Agamemnon as accursed, doomed to disaster by the violence of his ancestors. And many of the early Greeks believed that the gods exact payment from the descendants of men whose deeds go unrequited in their own lifetime.[47]

Aeschylus does not employ that belief in the *Oresteia*. Of all these horrors from the past, he refers only to the Thyestean banquet – but not until *Ag* Scene 6 and only to explain the presence of Aigisthos as Klytaimestra's fellow-conspirator. By presenting his new account of the reasons for Artemis' anger, Aeschylus ensured that Agamemnon's own situation and character explain both his self-dooming action at Aulis and his consent to walk on the robes in Scene 4.

There are other striking innovations. Aeschylus was almost certainly the first *dramatist* to have placed the murders of their kindred by Klytaimestra and Orestes unequivocally at the centre of the story. Homer had told of an all-too-feminine Klytaimestra, chaste and at first unwilling, but seduced by a powerful, noble Aigisthos into complicity in his vengeance on Agamemnon, which he took himself.[48] Orestes then kills Aigisthos, with no mention of any vengeance against Klytaimestra, merely a statement that she had died (perhaps by suicide?).[49] Aeschylus, by contrast, develops the version of the story told by Stesichoros of Himera in his sixth-century poem *Oresteia*: Klytaimestra murdered Agamemnon because he had killed her daughter; she dreamt of a snake – as at the beginning of *Libation Bearers*, though in Stesichoros, the dream was that it had a gory head out of which sprang a prince, a descendant of the Pleisthenidai (probably Orestes emerging from the treacherous death of Agamemnon). Elektra's recognition of Orestes by a lock of hair (presumably at Agamemnon's grave, as in *LB*) is also from Stesichoros, in whose poem Apollo gave Orestes a bow to protect himself from Klytaimestra's Furies – so Stesichoros' version involved matricide. It is uncertain how Stesichoros brought the story to an end.[50]

Aeschylus presents a strong, masculine-spirited Klytaimestra who does the murder herself by treachery and so in turn invites personal vengeance on her by her son. These changes enable Aeschylus to use the story to confront head-on in *Libation Bearers* the issue of matricide and the prospect of endless bloodshed (both studiously avoided by Homer, who wished to use Orestes as an example to Telemachos); they also place gender conflict at the centre of the trilogy.[51]

However, Aeschylus works most of his alterations gently into the texture. There are in *Ag* Choros 1 the twin shocks that Iphigenia is not saved from death and that Agamemnon kills her himself.[52] But the portrait of Klytaimestra's masculine powers is elaborated gradually over the whole first half of *Agamemnon*, from the Watchman's hint (11) through to her triumph over Agamemnon in persuading him to walk over the robes. The fact that Agamemnon is to return without his army is introduced and developed with equal care, from Klytaimestra's first fears for the safety of the returning fleet (338ff.) through the Herald's confirmation that the Greeks destroyed the shrines of the gods in the sack of Troy (527) – and were punished for it by a catastrophic storm during their return (648ff.) – to the moment when the king arrives alone in his carriage (except for his concubine Kassandra) and is therefore vulnerable to Klytaimestra. And in another innovation, she kills him alone; in Stesichoros and much iconography, Aigisthos and Klytaimestra murdered Agamemnon together.

Aeschylus does not employ the sudden reversals of audience expectation which play a large part in the work of Euripides, in the late plays of Sophocles and in Aristotle's theory of drama.[53] There is surprise in *Agamemnon*, but it is carefully directed into two impressive *coups de théâtre* – Klytaimestra's use of the robes in Scene 4 and Kassandra's prophecies in Scene 6 – which themselves advance the action powerfully towards the climax. The same is true of the sequence after Orestes arrives at the palace doors in *LB* and the remarkable opening scene of *Eumenides*.

Each of the three dramas of the *Oresteia* builds up to a moment of acute tension whose outcome, far from being a surprise, fulfils the audience's deepest expectations. The *moira* of the characters increasingly takes shape until the moment when Agamemnon must and will die; Orestes will succeed in his plan and must kill Klytaimestra; the Athenians will acquit Orestes and yet escape retribution. (*Moira* means a person's lot in life; it is the nearest Greek word to 'destiny', but it is not predetermined; cf. Ewans 2023: 53–57.) The audience's knowledge of previous versions of the legend makes each outcome a strong possibility from the earliest moments, and Aeschylus organizes the subsequent action so that this possibility is slowly but inexorably converted into certainty.[54] But it was Aeschylus who combined the legend of Orestes' purification at Delphi with that of his acquittal at Athens, so creating the plot of *Eumenides*, which accordingly would have involved more suspense than the original audience would have experienced in *Agamemnon* or *Libation Bearers*.[55]

The act of violence at the climax of each of the first two dramas is elevated to tragic stature, simply because by the time when it takes place Aeschylus has shown it to be in retrospect inevitable. (But nothing in Aeschylus is predetermined; his characters are not puppets of gods or of an omnipotent Fate.[56]) For all their horror, the deaths of Agamemnon and Klytaimestra bring a profound sense of relief, together with pity for characters who are trapped in the web of their unfolding *moira* when it has achieved its final, tragic form. The power of these dramas lies in the fact that their ever-growing suspense leads to a climax which is a surprise in terms of the exact moment when it happens but in every other way has grown to be deeply expected.

Aeschylus concentrates constantly on the twin axes of expectation and fulfilment, hope and fear. Throughout the first two-thirds of *Agamemnon*, there is a sustained dialogue between the growing fear that Agamemnon will be murdered and the increasingly futile hope that good will prevail. The pattern is then continued in the development through the even bleaker world of the second drama to the Finale of the third, the moment when the Furies accept Athena's offer and the Athenians' hopes finally cease to be qualified by fears.[57]

14   *Introduction*

This glorious ending to the saga of revenge does not imply that situations like those which caused the tragic events of the first two dramas will never recur. The order of the universe ruled by Zeus does not evolve or change its nature in the *Oresteia*.[58] Zeus and the world-order have many times been said to evolve in the course of the trilogy[59]; but this is not the case. Wallace (2023: 24) is perhaps the most recent writer to reject 'the old-fashioned view that the *Oresteia* ends with the establishment of universal justice'; as he notes, the gods remain capricious (and self-interested) throughout.

John Jones argued conclusively, over 60 years ago, against any such interpretation that '[Aeschylus] is not looking down from a position of superior enlightenment on the urgencies of the *Oresteia*' (1962: 112). Aeschylus was well aware that no law court could solve a dilemma like Orestes' or prevent such terrible acts of revenge as Klytaimestra's. Kindred murder still happened in fifth-century Athens, as it does in our supposedly more 'civilized' societies – and for compelling reasons. Lloyd-Jones rightly noted the *Oresteia*'s place in the continuity of Greek social practice:

> The cliché we have heard repeated all our lives, that the *Eumenides* depicts the transition from the vendetta to the rule of law, is utterly misleading. Even in the *Iliad*, the blood feud is regulated by the justice of Zeus administered through kings; even in the law of the Athenian *polis* in the fifth century, the blood feud and the Erinyes (Furies) have their allotted place.[60]

More recent writers have endorsed this reading. For example, Naiden writes that 'to extract from the play some evolution from vengeance to a generous notion of *dikē* is...problematic', even though the foundation of the Areopagos creates 'a permanent, constitutional response to murder [at Athens]'.[61] The view that in the *Oresteia* the divine order presided over by Zeus is harsh, dependant on 'might is right' and never becomes benevolent was well argued by Cohen (1986).[62]

However, there is clearly a difference between the way in which actions beget consequences in *Eu* and that in the two preceding dramas. This difference is due to the differences in moral stance between the three agents involved in the three decisive and climactic actions: Klytaimestra, Orestes and the Athenian jury (see below, p. 16). The *Oresteia* presents four paradigms of human action under extreme stress (for Agamemnon at Aulis is the first to be confronted with a terrible choice which will have inevitable consequences). We have people who perform acts of kindred murder among us today – and making headlines for their deeds; so all three plays of the trilogy are true for all time but anchored in Aeschylus' own time and place by the hope, and the warning against civil war, extended to his fellow-citizens in the trial scene and the Finale of *Eumenides* (see below, p. 18 ff.). It is Athens, nowhere else, that has the opportunities given by the alliance struck between Athena and Klytaimestra's Furies; Athens has founded a court which will provide the necessary element of fear that will ward off crime and civil war (*Eu* 697ff.); and Athens has deserved the domestic peace and prosperity which the Solemn Goddesses will provide, by its equally divided vote which means acquittal but not vindication for Orestes the mother-murderer.

For his entry in at least five of the 13 festivals at which he competed, Aeschylus chose to create a connected sequence in which his three tragedies were linked together and told three chronologically successive parts of one single myth.[63] Of these sequences, only the *Oresteia* survives intact. The word 'trilogy' is often loosely applied to almost any work of drama or prose fiction which consists of one story together with two sequels which continue its narrative. The *Oresteia*, of course, includes this basic design; but Aeschylus goes much further. All three tragedies move single-mindedly from the opening situation towards one main event which occurs two-thirds of the way through the play; the remaining third is then devoted to exploring the consequences of the event and its implications for the future of the principal character (in *Eumenides*, characters). Each of the first two dramas is therefore linked closely to the events which open the action of its successor. Furthermore, *Libation Bearers* and *Eumenides* are not just sequels which explore the consequences of the events of *Agamemnon*; they are also parallel in action and in structure.

The sequence is set in motion by Agamemnon's sacrifice at Aulis, which the Elders relive in Choros 1. Agamemnon found himself faced with a choice which was also no choice at all, when Artemis demanded that he sacrifice Iphigenia to stop the adverse winds which forced the Greeks to wait at Aulis:

> Then the elder king said this:
> 'Heavy my fate to disobey
> but heavy if I slaughter my own child,
> the glory of our household,
> and pollute with virgin blood
> my hands – a father's hands – beside
> the altar. Which of these courses lacks its evil?
> How can I desert the ships,
> abandoning the expedition?
> No; her demand, her utter and insensate rage
> for sacrifice of virgin blood
> to stop the winds
> is right. May all be well.'
>
> And when he put upon himself the harness of necessity...
> (203ff.)

He recognizes the justice of Artemis' demand and freely choosing ('put on') but nonetheless accepts the (inevitable) 'harness of *necessity*'.[64] He must lead the expedition against Troy, since he goes as the agent of Zeus to avenge the abduction by Paris of Menelaos' wife Helen; that violated the ties of *xenia* between

16 *Introduction*

guest and host, which were overseen by Zeus himself. But in sacking Troy to avenge Paris' deed, the Greeks whom Agamemnon commands will destroy many innocent lives; for that action, the goddess Artemis, protectress of the young and innocent, demands her price. Agamemnon must sacrifice to her his own innocent daughter – and by committing this horrendous crime, he will bring about his own death at the hands of Iphigenia's mother Klytaimestra.

Agamemnon's act at Aulis is the paradigmatic situation which underlies the action of the rest of the *Oresteia*. The main action portrays three different agents in parallel dilemmas, all of whom come to find, like Agamemnon at Aulis, that they have to choose between two alternatives. Either choice threatens disastrous consequences – and in the ethics of Aeschylus' time, responsibility for action is absolute; diminished responsibility cannot be successfully pleaded because of external pressures, even from the gods; but each of the agents comes to realize that only one of the dire alternatives is truly possible.

The climaxes of the three dramas – the murder of Agamemnon, the death of Klytaimestra and the acquittal of Orestes – are to be seen in parallel as well as in sequence. Klytaimestra when she murders her husband, Orestes when he kills his mother, and Athena and her fellow-Athenians when they judge Orestes are all remaking Agamemnon's traumatic moment of decision and attempting to purge society of its consequences. And it is the agent's degree of insight into the past and the future, their moral stance as they embrace the action which they must inevitably perform, which determines what ultimately happens to them. Klytaimestra kills her husband exultantly and deserves death herself; Orestes kills her reluctantly and is conscious that he himself is doing wrong (*LB* 930), so he eventually does not deserve the same fate; the Athenians reach a verdict which does not vindicate Orestes and so deserve not to be blighted by the anger of the Furies (*Eu* 973–5); indeed, the Athenians deserve to be bonded with them in a relationship which will bring great blessings to both parties.

Aeschylus expressed his meaning not simply through imagery or ideas, which though very important are incorporated into the drama,[65] but by unfolding the pattern of the story through the action as it is shaped by the theatrical forms in which he chose to dramatize it, in an alternating, unfolding sequence of Scenes and Choroses.

The Gods and Daemons

Aeschylus unfolds a vision of our world as a place where people choose freely, but every act has far-reaching implications, and everyone ultimately receives his or her deserts. He offers us a fierce, tragic but ultimately affirmative view of humankind; the contrast is stark between this harsh but comforting assurance and the bleaker image presented by the patterns of action in most of the surviving dramas of Sophocles and Euripides.[66] In the often tortured vision of the later fifth century, gods and goddesses could no longer be imagined as interacting on Homeric or even Aeschylean terms with human beings. For Aeschylus,

Introduction 17

the gods and daemons are immanent forces in a universe which is completely animate, surrounding and interpenetrating human nature and accomplishing or fulfilling the implied consequences of human actions. So Klytaimestra is personally responsible for the murder of Agamemnon, but the daemon of the accursed house of Tantalos is acting through her (*Ag* 1468ff.), and she is the avenger of the banquet of his children's flesh set by Atreus before Thyestes (*Ag* 1500ff.); also, she is the agent of Ares, God of War (*Ag* 1509ff.). Orestes murders his mother because Apollo has predicted ghastly tortures, and pursuit by his father's Furies, if he does not do the deed (*LB* 270ff.), but also, in practical human terms, his motive is to regain his inheritance and liberate Argos from the tyrants Aigisthos and Klytaimestra (*LB* 298ff.). Apollo's intense pressure does not relieve Orestes from responsibility for matricide: as Orestes himself says in his last words to Klytaimestra, 'You killed, and it was wrong; now suffer wrong' (*LB* 930). In *Eumenides*, the dilemma caused by Orestes' arrival at Athens is too big for either human beings alone or Athena alone to resolve it, since Orestes is a pure suppliant, and the Furies have a valid duty too. Athena therefore decides to found a court, in which she and 'the best of all my citizens' will sit in judgment together (*Eu* 470ff.).

Each of the Olympian and chthonian gods and goddesses represents powers that influence human action; in ancient Greek life, they required worship, through cults, sacrifices and ritual, to propitiate them. Most of them have multiple responsibilities; Artemis, for example, is the goddess of hunting and of innocence and virginity but also of childbirth. The Glossary provides brief notes on the spheres of influence of each god and goddess named in the *Oresteia*; for more detail, a good resource is the *Oxford Classical Dictionary* (4th ed.).

Humans in Aeschylus are influenced not only by gods but also by daemons; for example, if a man has 'kicked into oblivion/the great altar of Justice':

> Fearful Persuasion forces him,
> unbearable child of the plans of Ruin.
> All cure is in vain…
>
> (Ag 383ff.)

Daemons are what we would now call personifications of forces which act on human beings; they are much more prominent in Aeschylus' universe than in that portrayed by his successors. Together with the gods, they reinforce the strong feeling that Aeschylean humanity is surrounded by divine powers. Indeed, Apollo, the Furies and Athena manifest themselves as characters in *Eumenides*, and by this means Aeschylus can dramatize a conflict which no modern playwright could stage (cf. below, p. 195). The presence in early to mid-fifth-century belief of the element of *to theion* – the Greek term which means 'divine' but by the same token signifies all that is wonderful, marvellous and strange in our world – is the distinctive feature of the culture of his time and place which made Aeschylean tragedy possible.[67]

18   *Introduction*

Politics

Eumenides locates the final actions of the trilogy firmly in two aspects of contemporary Athenian policy: foreign and domestic. In inter-*polis* relationships, Aeschylus celebrates the break from the pro-Spartan policies of the right-wing aristocrat Kimon and his supporters; Orestes promises that his city, Argos, will become an ally of Athens for all time (*Eu* 754ff.). The alliance of Athens with democratic Argos was made in 461 and led to a drawn-out war between Athens and Sparta (459–45; the 'First Peloponnesian War').[68] Note that Athena enthusiastically urges the Athenians to fight wars with foreigners (864ff.; cf. 914–5, 1009); in the year of the *Oresteia*'s performance, Athens was in fact engaged in simultaneous combat with Persia (in Egypt), Sparta, Corinth (in defence of Megara) and Aigina.

On the domestic front, Athena's foundation of the Areopagos at *Eu* 681ff. bought into a hotly contested issue. In 462, Ephialtes and Perikles had successfully trimmed down the powers of this court and diluted its membership, which had hitherto been wholly aristocratic – making it a more democratic court and restricting its powers largely to cases of homicide and malicious wounding. Ephialtes was assassinated, doubtless by aristocrats and perhaps by supporters of Kimon, because of these reforms; but they were not overturned. Opinions differ on Aeschylus' attitude to the events of 461: Forrest concluded that Aeschylus was pronouncing in favour of the democrats who had reformed the Areopagos, and he was followed by Wiles.[69] On the other hand, Athena's warning against 'allow[ing] polluted flows of muddy waters in' (694) might imply that Aeschylus opposed the reforms (Rosenbloom 2023: 383). The modern consensus is that he deliberately did not slant Athena's comments towards endorsing or criticizing the reformers but made her words ambiguous; what matters is that the Areopagos can become a bulwark against on the one side anarchy and on the other side tyranny; in short, it will be a bastion of Athenian democracy.[70] The key point is that both Athena (858ff.) and the Furies (976ff.) vehemently oppose civil strife such as occurred in 461, and this above all seems to be the 'message' of *Eumenides* to the citizens about domestic politics.[71]

Translation

Reading the *Oresteia* for the first time in 1816, Goethe described Aeschylean drama as 'a primaevally gigantic form of monstrous shape, which shocks and overwhelms us'.[72] Throughout the nineteenth century, Aeschylus was read and admired as a Gothic or Romantic artist, a poet of rugged, awe-inspiring grandeur and spectacular theatrical effects.[73] There is no justification for holding this view today. Aeschylus' dramas may have seemed bombastic or obscure to some spectators and (increasingly) readers during and after the late fifth century (as the caricature of him in Aristophanes' *Frogs*, 405, attests); but they were not so to their original audience in 458, who gave the *Oresteia* first prize and who were steeped in a tradition of popular entertainment by rich and

Introduction   19

complex dramatic and choral verse; accordingly, these plays must be translated lucidly for modern audiences. But their essential 'foreignness' must to an extent be preserved; the *Oresteia*, after all, comes from a very different society now 2,482 years in the past.

George Steiner's massive essay on language and translation, *After Babel*,[74] demands that good translation should attempt the impossible – a synthesis of literal fidelity to the source text and literate expression in the target language. The challenge of these tragedies is to be as *accurate* as possible while providing *actable* versions which enable a verse drama to be played before audiences which possess no live tradition of poetic plays. Accuracy and actability are both very important; it is no service to Aeschylus or to the modern audience to present free adaptations, implying that the specific content of his work is unimportant if the 'version' makes 'good theatre'.[75] The role of translator has often been devalued in British productions of Greek tragedy when 'a literal translation is reworked by a poet/dramaturg/playwright'[76]; conspicuous examples would include Ted Hughes' 'version' of the *Oresteia* and Ben Power's of Euripides' *Medea*, both presented by the National Theatre of Great Britain and published by the prestigious house of Faber and Faber.[77]Another danger to avoid is domestication, 'a specific Anglo-American tendency to reduce the source text to target language cultural values',[78] as opposed to keeping some sense of its foreignness. Ideally, the result will be 'a text which, in the name of theatricality, has not erased the asperity, strangeness, and ambiguities of the original'.[79] While I have tried to live up to this ideal by being as accurate as possible, I have found this impossible to achieve fully in the case of the *Oresteia*; such are the richness and especially the occasional deliberate ambiguity of Aeschylus' verse – and the need of a live audience for *clarity*.

For this translation, I attempted to find a language that would match the feel of the text as I experience it, which would work effectively in my productions, and would communicate with the audiences of today. The act of translation was closely tied to my work as dramaturg and subsequently as director; I modified the translations during rehearsals when actors encountered difficulty with their draft lines. I wanted to present Aeschylus' meaning as clearly as possible, responding closely to the tone of each subsection of the dramas and to the flow and shape of the language and syntax. At times (e.g. *Ag* 1208, *LB* 423ff.), this demanded a slight simplification; at others, a decision had to be made between different interpretations of the original (e.g. *LB* 583). And there are many places where the manuscript text of the Greek is corrupt, and the translator must choose between the emendations offered by editors.

Aeschylus' language has an extraordinary range – from the colloquial to the elevated, from clarity to complexity and sometimes ambiguity, from simplicity and sometimes shocking directness to delicate understatement. There is also the contrast between almost comic moments – the dignified Priestess in *Eumenides* re-entering on all fours, Kilissa's musing on baby Orestes' uncontrolled need to pee, and above all Orestes having to knock three times on his own door before a grumbling servant answers him and then slams it in his

20   *Introduction*

face – and the high tragic mode which predominates in, for example, *Ag* Scenes 6 and 7 (the initial comic dithering of the Elders excepted) and *LB* Scenes 1 and 2. I have therefore not hesitated to bring out the humour of the script where the tone of the Greek justifies this.

Since rhyme was not used in Greek verse (except in some drinking songs) and has a distancing effect on modern audiences, blank verse is employed. No attempt has been made to re-create in English the metrical forms or strophic responsion of the original; the source and target languages are too different from each other to justify such a procedure. This is unfortunate, since Wiles (1997: 96ff.) made a strong case for the dance movements of *strophe* and *antistrophe* to have been identical to match and illuminate the identical metrical patterns of the verse in the original.[80] A sharp differentiation is, however, made between the five- to seven-beat line into which the Greek *iambic trimeter* and *trochaic tetrameter* spoken dialogue is rendered and the much shorter lines, matching those of the original, in the *anapaestic* (chanted) and lyric sections.[81] Lines which were originally lyric or anapaestic are double-indented in this translation. And special care has been taken to ensure that the lyric sections can be sung if a director desires this.

Particular care has also been taken in the handling of the divine forces and powers known as daemons and of value-words. No translation can hope to bridge completely the gap between our culture and Aeschylus', in which the personified powers whom I capitalize (though, of course, this cannot come through in performance) such as Persuasion and Ruin denoted living daemonic forces. Nor can the translator convey (though he or she can imply) how the word *miasma* ('pollution') denotes a single entity combining physical dirt and psychic taint. Equally, it is very hard to express the ways in which as simple a word as *agathos* ('good') denoted for the Greeks a set of values and qualities very different from those denoted by the English word in our society.[82] And the word *dikē*, central to the meaning of the trilogy, can connote (sometimes simultaneously) retribution, revenge, punishment, penalty, case, right and (often) justice.[83] However, this translation carefully avoids importing concepts for which there is no equivalent in Aeschylean Greek; 'guilt' and 'sin', for example, both suggest a Judaeo-Christian world-order totally alien to the polytheistic culture of fifth-century Athens.

I have sometimes replaced a god's obscure alternative title by his or her more familiar name or included in the translation the name of a person or god who is alluded to but not named in the original Greek; Aeschylus naturally presumed in his audience a level of familiarity with myth and cult which almost all modern spectators do not possess.

It should go without saying that this translation presents Aeschylus' text uncut. I do not believe that directors should abbreviate these marvellous, precisely structured plays; but that is, of course, their right. And I have kept rigorously to the lines of the original; Aeschylus' concision needs to be matched by concise English.[84]

Introduction 21

All translation necessarily involves some loss – and no wise translator would pretend to render all of Aeschylus' rich verse into English; but at least we can choose, carefully, what to keep.[85] Let us learn to see and hear Aeschylus as a poet of lucidity – though also of complexity and richness – and as a playwright whose action is filled with human depth and emotional vividness. All of these qualities are easily discovered in rehearsal.

Some Modern Performances

I hope I have shown that Aeschylus' *Oresteia* was a complex blend of multiple media, with plots and action which address acute moral dilemmas, powerful both through the vigorous music and dance of its performance and through the richness of its poetic imagery and fascinating in its vision of humankind. It was also a finely balanced theatrical event, in which choral and sometimes actor lyrics alternated with spoken dialogue scenes to create a totally involving experience for the spectators. To fail to realize in a modern production any of its essential components is inevitably to fail to transmit some of Aeschylus' meaning(s) to a modern audience – to create a different and inferior play.

The four blockbuster productions of the early 1980s and early 1990s all attempted to do justice to Aeschylus. Karolos Koun in Greece (1980), Peter Stein in Germany (1980), Sir Peter Hall in England (1981) and Ariane Mnouchkine in France (1990–92) all titled their productions 'Aeschylus: *Oresteia*' – except for Mnouchkine, who added in Euripides' *Iphigenia at Aulis* as a prequel to her presentation of the trilogy and entitled her production *Les Atrides*. And all made serious attempts to present Aeschylus' trilogy to modern audiences as opposed to offering modern reworkings or 'adaptations'.[86]

There were unfortunately weaknesses in all four of these productions. Karolos Koun had the great advantage of working in an actual ancient Greek theatre, at Epidaurus. His production was effective and sometimes emotionally moving, though given the large *orchēstra* at his disposal, it was disappointing that Agamemnon and Kassandra did not enter in a carriage but simply stood on a platform. The actors wore half-masks and 'ancient' costumes with long flowing robes for the women. Various means were used to present the choral odes, with some spoken over instrumental accompaniment and some sung; these were in general very effective. But there were many stylized gestures and limited movement in some passages (none whatever in *Eu* Scene 2, which cries out for movement!); and a fatal mistake was made in the Finale, where Apollo and Athena were both placed on pedestals at the back, overlooking the Furies in the *orchēstra* below. Apollo should not be there at all,[87] and Athena should be in the *orchēstra*, close to the Furies whom she is seeking to persuade.[88]

Peter Stein's production was in his own German prose translation, which was fluent and colloquial. He had worked extensively with translations and commentaries and created a long script in which variants from several of the translated versions were incorporated; in consequence of this, and some

22   *Introduction*

non-verbal vocalisation from the chorus, the performance lasted for nine hours (including two one-hour intervals). There was no singing or dancing and no musical accompaniment. All characters except Athena wore modern dress. The performance space made no attempt to reconstruct ancient Greek conditions, except for the use of an *ekkuklēma* at the climaxes of *Ag* and *LB*; but the rituals in *LB* were performed with scrupulous accuracy. There was a raised stage, but most of the action of the first two plays was performed in the auditorium, in the wide aisle between the two sections of the spectators; a table for the Elders, in suits and hats, to sit at was placed in the front of this area for *Ag* and the tomb for *LB*. The passionate acting, especially of Edith Clever as Klytaimestra, evoked critical acclaim. At the end, the jurors counted and re-counted votes, suggesting a resonance to the contemporary politics of West Germany, which Stein saw as a fragile democracy comparable to Athens in 461–58. But the absence of verse, music and choreography inevitably placed limits on the production's ability to present the full power of Aeschylus' vision.[89]

In London, Sir Peter Hall appointed Oliver Taplin as dramaturg and worked with the latter's *The Stagecraft of Aeschylus* (1977a) as a guide; but Hall was hamstrung by some of his own decisions. He followed Athenian conventions in having an all-male, masked group of actors – but these fifth-century conventions, the gender dictated by Athenian patriarchy and the 'mask' by the need for clarity of a character's age and sex in a very large open-air theatre, served in the much smaller indoor space of the National Theatre's Olivier auditorium[90] only to distance the modern audience from the emotional and intellectual content of Aeschylus' trilogy, which revolves around a gender conflict best shown today by having unmasked actresses playing female characters. There was an alliterative and rhymed translation by Tony Harrison – brilliant but intent on 'foreignization' of the text and heavy with coined words and odd compounds – and unnecessary cuts, some of significant material[91]; and an abrasive, percussive score by Harrison Birtwhistle, which often intruded into the spoken dialogue. A raised stage was used for some of the action, and the blocking was largely static with limited movement; also, speakers in dialogue often faced away from each other, so losing emotional power. This was a quasi-ritualistic, stylized and non-naturalistic vision of Greek tragedy which I found simply depressing. Nonetheless, its season was extended by demand, and it was subsequently performed at Epidaurus.[92]

Ariane Mnouchkine did not use masks, but she made her actors' faces just as static with elaborate make-up derived from the Indian Kathakali tradition. Kathakali (in *Iphigenia* and *Ag*) and in *LB* Kabuki elements were included in the production, as Mnouchkine looked to Asia for sources of a viable dance idiom for the plays today. This was a successful decision, though for obvious reasons of cultural appropriation, it is problematic. However, the inclusion of *Iphigenia at Aulis* caused problems, as Euripides' vision and dramaturgy in 406 were very different from those of Aeschylus in 458; and in *Eumenides* the striking physicality of mass dancing choruses in Eastern styles, very impressive in

Introduction 23

the first three plays, was abandoned; Aeschylus' dancing choros of twelve Furies was replaced with three European old bag-ladies and a pack of dogs, and Orestes was offstage for the binding song (!). (The preparation for *Eu* was less thorough than for the earlier plays because of funding concerns which foreshortened the time available: Marshall 2023: 502.) There was no reference of any kind to the ancient Greek performance space in Mnouchkine's use of a playing area resembling a blood sports arena. Music inspired by Balkan idioms accompanied the extended dancing of the Choroses, and improvised music accompanied all spoken dialogue. All text was spoken, in the case of the Choroses by one person chanting stanzas between dance sequences, which often dominated over the text so much that it had 'little impact'.[93] Like Stein's, this was a long show; when all four plays were finally performed together, the running time (including intervals) was ten hours.

The National Theatre of Great Britain returned to the *Oresteia* in 1999; Katie Mitchell directed in the much smaller Cottesloe theatre at the South Bank arts complex. She was handicapped by a self-indulgent free verse 'version' of Aeschylus by poet Ted Hughes. And there was little choreography; the Elders of *Agamemnon* were bemedaled war veterans in wheelchairs. But she delivered a powerful feminist interpretation of *Agamemnon*; a memorable image was that the robes over which the king walked in Scene 4 were a collage of bloodstained little girls' dresses, symbolizing both the sacrifice of Iphigenia and the many other innocents slaughtered in the sack of Troy. Indeed, Iphigenia overshadowed the production, appearing as a silent ghost during the action of *Agamemnon*. Mitchell later admitted (2009: 3) that she had involved herself too much with the figure of Iphigenia, and this affected her ability to focus properly on the second and especially the third play of Aeschylus' trilogy, where she failed to capture the optimistic vision of Aeschylus' Finale.[94]

Over the years 2014–2021 (the latest for which reviews have been published), there were four productions of the *Oresteia* reviewed in *Didaskalia*: an Aeschylus *Oresteia* in two parts, split between two different directors with mixed results, at Syracuse in 2014[95]; an Israeli adaptation in 2018 of Robert Icke's *Oresteia*[96]; and in 2019 both an extensive reworking, with many cuts and a few additions, 'Ellen McLaughlin's *The Oresteia*', at the Shakespeare Theater Company in Washington, DC,[97] and a US performance of Icke's *Oresteia*.[98]

Icke's work was a 2015 'new adaptation' of the trilogy which premiered at the Almeida Theatre in Islington under the author's direction and later transferred to the West End. The whole play seems to be a dream-sequence, conjured up by an Orestes who is in therapy. The Greek gods are abolished; Calchas calls on the One God by his many names in the opening invocation. Gone too is the choros; this is a modern play of individuals, who sit round a dining-room table and talk banal, everyday prose that is totally inadequate to the horrific situations dramatized by Aeschylus. This is not an adaptation but a brand-new play, loosely evoking elements of the original plot. A whole first Act leads up to the death of Iphigenia; after the action paralleling *Agamemnon* gets under way in Act 2, some lines from Aeschylus are paraphrased, especially

24 *Introduction*

at crucial moments – their powerful imagery shining out in Icke's relatively unimpressive contemporary dialogue. The trial of Orestes takes place in a court, with the Kassandra actress playing Athena as judge and the Kilissa actress becoming the (one) Fury (with very little to say). Athena finds Orestes to be innocent with a casting vote, and the play ends with him repeating 'What shall I do?' into emptiness.

Though it has attracted some admiration, Icke's *Oresteia* falls firmly under the critique already mounted by George Steiner (1961: 326) of similar attempts in the twentieth century to 'have it both ways, combining the resonance of the classic theme with the savour of the new'. This cannot be done on a level of truly serious intent, even in our post-modern world.

For my own productions, I had modest resources and only one professional actor – the rest of the casts were just very enthusiastic drama students. I was translator, dramaturg and director. A few parts of the Choroses were sung, and the rest declaimed to instrumental accompaniment. Music was used always and only when Aeschylus wrote in lyric verse. All lyrics were choreographed simultaneously with, and to illuminate, the speaking or singing of the words; dance was not divorced from text as in *Les Atrides*. The audience sat on three sides of a circular *orchēstra* 10 metres in diameter (these productions were created before the more recent archaeological evidence that the original space was rectangular). Modern dress was used, except in the first play to be produced, *LB*, where 'classical' dress was attempted. The essential realism of Aeschylus' action was brought out; dance and song were media as natural to the Athenians as was spoken verse. There were no masks in the intimate space of the Drama Studio, and there was lots of movement to illuminate the dialogue scenes. The accurate verse translations published here were used, with no cuts or additions to the Aeschylean text. So in several ways, these humble productions were nearer to conveying the essence of Aeschylus' *Oresteia* to a modern audience than some of the high-impact performances described above.[99]

Notes

1 I use the Greek spelling throughout to remind readers that the role of the choros in Greek tragedy is very different from that of the chorus of a modern opera or musical.
2 For a full consideration of the issues involved in performing Greek tragedy and comedy today, compare Ewans 2023.
3 All italicized words are defined in the Glossary.
4 Satyrs were men in bearded masks who were naked except for furry shorts with an erect phallus protruding at the front and a horse-like tail from the rear. Only one satyr-play survives complete, Euripides' *Cyclops*. There is also a substantial fragment of Sophocles' *Trackers*; for a translation, see Ewans (ed. and tr.) 2000. On Aeschylus' satyr-plays, compare Griffith 2002 and Coo and Uhlig 2019. The few fragments (in Ewans ed. and tr. 1996) support the ancient view that Aeschylus was a master of satyr-play.
5 Taplin 1977a is the foundation work for study of Aeschylus' stagecraft; but it contains, beside many brilliant insights, some suggestions which are simply impractical. See references in the Theatrical Commentary.

Introduction 25

6 Meineck 2017, drawing on cognitive science, analyses in detail the various ways in which Greek tragedy was a medium designed to evoke an empathetic response from the audience.

7 Heinrichs 2012: 62.

8 All dates in this book, except, of course, for references to modern scholarship, are BCE. On the commencement date of tragic performances at the festival, compare Connor 1990, arguing for a date after the liberation from tyranny and the reforms of Kleisthenes; however, Osborne 1993: 27–8 and 36 believes that competitions for tragedy began earlier, during the tyranny of Peisistratos or Hippias (531?), as does Sourvinou-Inwood 1994: 275ff. Owing to insufficient evidence, the issue really cannot be settled.

9 The presence of women has been contested, but the issue seems to me to be settled by Aristophanes *Peace* 960ff., a joke which is simply incomprehensible if they were not present and seated at some distance from the performance area. Compare Olson 1998: 254–5 *ad loc*, with references, and Henderson 1991. *Pace* Storey and Allan 2013: 39, an ingenious but unsuccessful attempt to reinterpret these lines.

10 For details of the festival events, compare Rehm 2017: 3–21.

11 For example, Meineck 2017: 59.

12 Csapo and Wilson 2021 is an account of theatres in Attika (part III) and the remainder of the Greek world (part IV). At least seven Attic towns had theatres and celebrated the Dionysia in the fifth century, and this number increased in the fourth century (Csapo and Wilson IIIA 8).

13 The shape of the fifth-century *orchēstra* at Athens is contested, as the remains are slight and concealed under subsequent re-buildings. Recent archaeologists, including Goette 2007 and Papastamati-von Mook 2015, have identified remains which point to a rectangular shape; but the long-held view that it was circular continues to be maintained by some scholars. However, Hughes 2011: 61 (cf. 59) notes that there is no circular *orchēstra* extant anywhere before the mid-fourth century (either the 'Lycurgan' reconstruction of the Theatre of Dionysos or the theatre at Epidaurus, whichever came first); but there are several examples of rectangular or trapezoidal theatres from the fifth century. Rehm 2002: 39–41 strongly rejects the circular *orchēstra*; Mitchell-Boyask 2009: 37 assumes a circular shape without argument. What matters, however, is that regardless of the shape the audience surrounded the action on three sides.

14 Ley 1989 is a very important article though largely ignored (cf. Ley 2006: 23–4). Wiles 1997: 161–2 accepts that there was scene-painting, but only of a fixed façade, on the grounds that changing panels between plays (or, in *LB*, *Eu* and Sophocles' *Aias* between two locations in one tragedy) would have been too much trouble. Why? It would have provided a valuable, added visual dimension, and Greek tragedies are always set in a definite location. Mastronade 1990: 253 writes of 'light, moveable panels'.

15 Even at this early stage of development, there may have been marble seats in the first row for VIPs. In the mid-fourth century, the theatre was reconstructed to include curved rows of marble seating.

16 Wiles 1997: 69.

17 Wiles 2000: 151.

18 Compare Meineck 2017: 110.

19 Arnott 1989: 74. Compare Aristophanes' *The Women's Festival* 634–51 for a striking example. Taplin 1978 and Arnott 1989 both provide good discussions of the use of gesture in Greek tragedy – but isolated from the context of the overall patterns of movement in the *orchēstra*.

20 Compare Wiles 2000: 110–12.

21 Walcot 1976: 4–5; cf. Arnott 1989: 11. Baldry 1971: 15 draws a parallel with the *agora*, where political debates were held. He makes the vital point (see below) that

26   *Introduction*

Athens' political assembly lacked the customary modern practice of elevating speakers above their audience to enhance their status as figures of authority. (The same is true of the Pnyx.) Speaking well did not require standing still in political or legal debate or when reciting epic or iambic poetry. So also, I suggest, in tragedy. Compare Pickard-Cambridge 1968: 171–6 against Taplin 1977a: 20; and for the central role of performance and competition in Athenian culture, compare Rehm 2017: 3–12. Plato (*Laws* 654a) condemned as uneducated any citizen who was *achoreutos* – unable to dance in a choros.

22   Compare also Ewans 2023: 11–4 and Ley 2006: ix ff. *Contra* Goldhill 2007: 8, Raeburn 2016: 4 and Dunbar and Harrop 2018: 154. Sommerstein 2010: 22 cites passages from Aristophanes (*Wasps* 1341–4) and Euripides (*Elektra* 489–92) to argue that a raised stage was in place by c. 420; but in both cases, the 'ascent' is easily presented by moving up-*orchēstra*, towards the *skēnē* door, while miming difficulty in 'climbing'. This was undoubtedly the case with the sequence after the entrances of the two half-choroses in Aristophanes' *Lysistrata* (411); cf. Ewans 2010: 234. And the stage for a comic actor on an Attic chous from around the same date should not be taken to reflect actual practice in the Theatre of Dionysos; the scene looks like a private performance.

23   The experiments conducted by Hunningher 1956 demonstrated that the visual focus of the theatre – the centre of the *orchēstra* – was also the acoustic focus.

24   Compare Macleod 1982: especially 142–4 on the social significance of individual misfortune in the *Oresteia*.

25   For an analysis of possible patterns of movement for *Eu* Scene 2 in an *orchēstra*, compare Ewans 2023: 27–32.

26   See Theatrical Commentary on *Ag* Scene 7, p. 159ff. The names of the three tragedies in the *Oresteia* are abbreviated *Ag*, *LB* and *Eu* in this book.

27   This view is justly condemned by Rehm, 1985: 42. It had an extreme manifestation in J. Michael Walton's concept of a choros miming, out of character, as an accompaniment, like the orchestra in an opera, to the mood suggested by the speeches of the principals rather than responding to them in their own character (1980: 182–3 and 1984: 69–70, 81, 90 and 92). 'There is no adequate evidence for the assumption' (Pickard-Cambridge 1968: 252).

28   The sole exception known to me before my own publications was Postgate 1969. But compare now Ewans (tr.) 1996, 2010, 2011 and 2021 and Ewans (ed. and tr.) 1999 and 2000.

29   The solo actors were termed *hypokritai* – 'responders'; appropriately, in view of the central importance of the choros in Aeschylean drama.

30   2013; 27. Compare Calame in their volume, 46, who claims that there are three voices of the choros; as character, *qua* actor and ritual performer, and in between 'the emotive, choral voice'; and Murnaghan 2013: 175 citing Heinrichs for a 'double identity' of the choros as 'character' and 'choral identity'. Compare also Lehmann 2016: 215–6.

31   Swift 2010.

32   In David Rudkin's adaptation of *Hippolytus* (1980), the whole of the chorus part, including the originally sung lyrics, was spoken by one individual. This made for a very intimate version of the play, in which the public focus provided by the Greek choros was effectively abolished.

33   Wilson 2000: 353.

34   Aristotle *Politics* 1277a: 11–2.

35   It is a bad mistake in Hinds and Cuypers 2017 to eliminate this distinction and translate all choral 'I's as 'we'. The usage of singular and plural was studied in depth in Kaimio 1970.

36   *Ag* 475ff. (despite Fraenkel's attempt – 1950: II. 245ff. – to bully his opponents into submission) and *Eu* Choroses 1 and 2, where if you accept that the choros

Introduction 27

members entered individually to begin the dance, you cannot sensibly deny that the first few lines were sung by soloists as they entered in ones and twos.

37 For an overview, see Wiles 1997: 161ff.

38 Their arguments are not damaged by Hammond 1972: 438, Walton 1980: 116–8 or Bain 1981: 56ff. Sommerstein 2010: 168–9 wrongly supposes that two doors are needed for *LB* Scene 6 (see Theatrical Commentary, p. 191 n.45). He also claims (2010: 22) that a few words preserved from the comic playwright Eupolis' *Autolykos* (frag. 48) imply that the three doors which were needed for late fourth-century Menandrian comedy were already present by around 420; but the fragmentary reference to three houses no more implies the presence of three doors in the *skēnē* than the scene near the close of Aristophanes' *Acharnians* where Dikaiopolis and Lamachos order servants to bring out items for their use implies two. The three doors were doubtless installed in the mid-fourth-century 'Lycurgan' reconstruction of the theatre (cf. Papastamati-von Mook 2014).

39 In *Eu*, all three entrances are use in the section set at Delphi; when the scene has changed to Athens, the *skēnē* is not in use. On the three-way dialogue between entrances/exits, see further Ewans 2002 on Sophocles' *Antigone*.

40 Sir Peter Hall's controversial 1981 production of the *Oresteia* provided very little movement. In *Ag* Scene 7, his Klytaimestra moved once, to distance herself from the body of Agamemnon; by contrast, there were 34 movements for Klytaimestra in the premiere production of this translation, to reflect the complex ebb and flow of the confrontation between her and the Elders; see the Theatrical Commentary on this scene.

41 These moments with a 'parked' choros cause problems in an end-on theatre. Compare Ewans 2023: 140–7.

42 Played (as they were) in loose costumes and light, low-heeled shoes and boots, with a fluid physical interaction, the dramas do not move at the slow and solemn pace which is sometimes regarded as appropriate for classical tragedy. The uncut first performances of this translation played for 97, 63 and 65 minutes respectively.

43 Vickers 1973: 53–4, Walcot 1976: 6–7.

44 Compare Taplin 1977a: 28–39 and Seale 1982: 19–20.

45 *Ag* 105ff. In one probably early version, Artemis demanded the sacrifice because Agamemnon had shot a sacred stag and boasted that 'not even Artemis could shoot so well' (cf. Apollodorus *Library, Epit.* 3.21). Euripides invented yet another variant in his *Iphigenia among the Taurians* (c. 413), 16ff.; Agamemnon had vowed to sacrifice to Artemis the fairest creature born in a particular year and that was Iphigenia.

46 The special relationship between a Greek audience and myth is discussed, in contrast with nineteenth-century and subsequent perspectives, in Ewans 1982b: Chapter 2, especially 56ff.

47 Compare Solon 13 and Theognis 731ff. This belief is explicitly opposed by the Elders at *Ag* 750ff.

48 Homer, *Odyssey*: 1. 29ff, 3. 234–5, 262–310, 4. 519–37, 11. 405ff. – where, however, Agamemnon's 'sluttish wife' helped Aigisthos to murder him. (She herself killed Kassandra; 11. 421–5.)

49 Homer, *Odyssey* 3. 304ff.

50 For a fuller discussion of Aeschylus' relationship to his predecessors, compare Sommerstein 2010: 136ff. On Stesichoros' *Oresteia*, compare Swift 2015: 127–32, Finglass 2023. Pindar *Pythian* 11 (474 or possibly 454 and so after Aeschylus) told of Klytaimestra murdering Agamemnon and speculates whether it was because of the death of Iphigenia or her adulterous liaison with Aigisthos.

51 Aeschylus' rejection of Homer's use of the Orestes myth in the *Odyssey* is well discussed by Goldhill 1992: 46ff. See also Sommerstein 2010: 136ff.

52 In many versions (e.g. Euripides *Iphigenia among the Taurians* 28ff.), Artemis substituted a hind for Iphigenia at the last moment; in Hesiod's *Catalogue of Women*,

28 Introduction

a phantom in Iphigenia's shape was sacrificed and she herself became immortal. In Stesichoros, Artemis probably saved Iphigenia, and she became the goddess Hekate. Iphigenia's death is final in Pindar *Pythian* 11, but in no other version before Euripides' *Iphhigenia among the Traurians* (c.419-13) does Agamemnon himself wield the knife to sacrifice Iphigenia, as he does in Aeschylus (*Ag* 1417).

53 Aristotle, *Poetics* 1452a-b, 1454a-b. This book (which neglects Aeschylus) has been studied and related to the actual surviving fifth-century tragedies since its rediscovery during the Renaissance; but Aristotle's focus on the words of the text, rather than the theatrical experience as a whole, is justly criticized by Lehmann 2016: 19–24. It has been far too influential on more recent theorists of tragedy, as Lehmann proceeds to demonstrate; 24–38. Meineck, however (2017), taking a cognitive approach, finds value in Aristotle's categorization.

54 Aristotle, *Poetics* 1452a: 18ff., states that in tragedy the events must form a sequence which is 'either necessary or probable'; Aeschylus always structures his plot so as to tend towards the former, stricter requirement. This aspect of Greek tragedy is discussed, in relation to Shakespeare and to modern concepts of tragedy, in Ewans 1995.

55 Compare Sommerstein 2010: 145.

56 The unfolding progress of the action in each play of the *Oresteia* towards a climax which has by then become inevitable is analysed in Ewans 1980.

57 See further the section on Dramatic Structure at the beginning of the Theatrical Commentary on each play; pp. 141–3, 169–70 and 192–5.

58 Nor in any other surviving drama by Aeschylus. The different picture possibly presented in the Prometheus plays is one of the arguments against their authenticity, added to the stylistic features analysed by Griffith 1977. Compare Ewans 1996: liv–lx.

59 Compare, for example, Thomson 1966: I. 55ff. (a Marxist interpretation), Winnington-Ingram 1983, Herington 1986, Conacher 1987, Sommerstein 1989 and 2010 (especially 198–9, 274ff.), Burian in Burian and Shapiro 2003: 3–27.

60 Lloyd-Jones 1971: 94–5. Compare Neuburg 1981: 75ff. and 183ff.

61 Naiden 2023: 370.

62 Compare also Griffith 1995: 105ff.

63 Compare Sommerstein 2010, 32ff. In those years, Aeschylus used the satyr-play, in which players and audience relaxed after the three serious dramas, to treat in farce and burlesque a related aspect of the same myth. *Proteus*, which followed *Eumenides*, dramatized an episode during Menelaos' delayed and roundabout return from Troy.

64 It is Artemis' demand, not that of the chieftains, who are shown as grieving about the sacrifice, very far from being in 'utter and insensate rage' for it. (199–200). For this interpretation of the passage, see Ewans 1975, endorsed by Winnington-Ingram 1983: 85. Compare Neuburg 1981: 36ff.

65 The imagery, ideas and language of the *Oresteia* have been studied by many classical scholars (imagery since Lebeck 1971, a pioneering book, though she virtually ignores the second half of *LB* and is relatively weak on *Eu*); but a recurring problem is that they have often been studied in isolation from the action. Rehm's chapter on the *Oresteia* (Rehm 2017: 91–123) is an excellent exception, integrating the patterns of imagery with the action. And Sommerstein 2010: 171ff. has a useful section on imagery. Compare also Goward 2005: 91–108 on *Agamemnon*.

66 On the difference, compare Ewans 2023: 46–58. Traditional readings of Sophocles' often bleak worldview as 'comfortable' were rightly attacked by Kells 1973, Winnington-Ingram 1980 and Segal 1981.

67 Compare Herington 1986 especially Chapter 1.

68 Thucydides 1. 102. Compare Sommerstein 1989: 26ff. and Podlecki 1989: 19–20.

Introduction 29

69 Forrest 1966: 214–5, Wiles 2000: 58. Against them Podlecki 1966: 80–100 and 1989: 17–21 and Lloyd-Jones 1979: 75–7.
70 Sommerstein 1989: 31–2 and 2010: 309, Hall 2010: 226 and Burian 2023: 141.
71 For a thorough and excellent further discussion of the political dimensions of *Eu*, compare Sommerstein 2010: 281ff or 2008: xv–xxi.
72 Cited in Ewans 1982b: 26.
73 In part, this view is a result of Aristophanes' wicked caricature of 'Aeschylus' in *Frogs* and the clear preference of Aristotle for Sophocles. Hellenistic and Roman critics, for whom the style and content of Euripides were more congenial, also played a part. The false ascription to Aeschylus of *Prometheus Bound*, dramatically static but rhetorically and scenically grandiose, influenced many, including Shelley, who composed a sequel, *Prometheus Unbound*.
74 Steiner 1975: Chapter 4 *passim*, especially 313–6 on Aeschylus.
75 Compare Ewans 1989: 120–1; Hinds and Cuypers 2017: 12.
76 Marinetti 2013: 31–2.
77 For a critique of Hughes' *Oresteia*, see Ewans 2023: 65–9.
78 Nigri 2013: 99.
79 Besson 2013: 156.
80 See pp. 146–8 below for an example of the ways in which words in the lines of a *strophe* and *antistrophe* are parallel in meaning and invite responding choreography, drawn from *Ag* Choros 1. Wiles offers a similar analysis of *LB* Choros 7 (2000: 139–41).
81 Hinds and Cuypers 2017 is a recent translation which also aims at accuracy and actability (12), and their *Agamemnon* was actually performed before publication (which is surprisingly rare). Their *Oresteia* has many felicities but falls down for me by reducing all of the text to short iambic lines, whereas Aeschylus alternates between longer lines in spoken dialogue and shorter lines in the lyrics. Accordingly, their translation does not reflect a very important feature of the original and is freer from the Greek than that offered in this book.
82 Awareness of the need to study value-terms carefully was initiated by Adkins 1960.
83 Marshall 2017: 10. Compare Foley 1998: xxxii and Burian 2023: 130–1.
84 Shapiro, in Burian and Shapiro 2003, takes (for example) 1217 lines to translate Aeschylus' 1076 in *L B*. I do not think this is acceptable.
85 Compare Ewans 1989 *passim*, especially 138.
86 On all four productions, compare Marshall 2023.
87 Compare Theatrical Commentary, p. 209, with quotation from Taplin 1978: 39.
88 On this production, see further Ewans 2023: 184–6. It is available on YouTube; enter "Ancient Greek Theatre Performance – *Oresteia* Aeschylus".
89 On this production, see the detailed analysis by Fischer-Lichte, 2017: 294–312.
90 Fairly large by modern standards, as it seats 1150 spectators in a quasi-arena shape (whose potential Hall strangely left mostly unfulfilled, often directing forwards as if for a proscenium arch theatre).
91 See Taplin 2005: 240 on 'foreignization'. His chapter is an eloquent defence of the 'Harrison Version' which for me departs far too far from the Greek.
92 Hall's production was justly criticized by Rehm 1985. Compare Ewans 2023: 74 and 183–4. It is available on YouTube in four parts: *Oresteia* Agamemnon Part One 1983 and Part 2 1983, Aeschylus Choephori (*sic*) (Libation Bearers), and *Oresteia*: Eumenides (The Furies) by Aeschylus.
93 Foley 1998: xlii. Compare Macintosh 1997: 319. Dance extracts from *Les Atrides* are available to view on YouTube.
94 Compare Michael Billington, *The Guardian*, 3 December 1999.
95 *Didaskalia* 11.04, 2014.
96 *Didaskalia* 15.12, 2019.

30   *Introduction*

97 *Didaskalia* 15.09, 2019.
98 *Didaskalia* 15.07, 2019.
99 Video recordings, of relatively poor quality due to the limited equipment then at our disposal, may be found at https://uoncc.wordpress.com/2014/03/20/ewansarchive/
100 See *LB* endnote 10 p. 108 and *Eu* endnote 24 p. 215.

Selected Further Reading

Greek Tragedy

Ewans, M. (2023) *Staging Ancient Greek Plays: A Practical Guide*. London: Bloomsbury. Methuen Drama. Close analysis of issues facing directors and actors, including detailed discussion of *Ag* Scenes 4 and 6 and *Eu* Scene 2.

Hall, E. (2010) *Greek Tragedy: Suffering under the Sun*. Oxford: Oxford University Press. Chapters 1–4 provide an excellent, wide-ranging introduction to Greek tragedy. But it needs complementing by Rehm, Taplin and/or Wiles (see below) to add the performative dimension.

Rehm, R. (2017) *Understanding Greek Tragic Theatre*. Abingdon: Routledge. A very good introduction to the nature and context of Greek tragic performance; it includes an analysis of the *Oresteia*.

Storey, I. and Allan, A. (2013) *A Guide to Ancient Greek Drama* (second edition). Oxford: Blackwell. A good introductory text, aimed primarily at classics students.

Taplin, O. (1978) *Greek Tragedy in Action*. London: Methuen. This book provides discussion of gestures, props, tableaux and other important aspects of the subject, covering among nine plays all three dramas of the *Oresteia*.

Wiles, D. (2000) *Greek Theatre Performance: An Introduction*. Cambridge: Cambridge University Press. A relatively short but comprehensive book; as its title suggests, it is constantly aware of the performative dimension which was central to Athenian drama.

Aeschylus

Sommerstein, A. (2010) *Aeschylean Tragedy*. London: Bristol Classical Press. A fine book which includes a detailed analysis of the *Oresteia*, and a thoughtful final chapter on the relevance of Aeschylus' plays today.

Oresteia

(See also Rehm and Sommerstein, described above.)

Goldhill, S. (1992) *Aeschylus: The Oresteia*. Cambridge: Cambridge University Press. A short introduction designed for the general reader.

Goward, B. (2005) *Aeschylus: Agamemnon*. London: Bloomsbury. The first of three Duckworth monographs on the individual plays of the trilogy. Her chapter on language and imagery is particularly good.

Marshall, C. (2017) *Aeschylus: Libation Bearers*. London: Bloomsbury.

Mitchell-Boyask, R. (2013) *Aeschylus: Eumenides*. London: Bloomsbury. Very good on the gender conflicts and issues in the play; less so on staging.

Introduction 31

Vickers, B. (1973) *Towards Greek Tragedy*. London: Longman. This stimulating book still offers a very good interpretation of the *Oresteia* (347ff.).

Notes on the Text, Translation and Commentary

Editions of the Greek text

In revising this translation, I have worked closely with the most recent edition of the trilogy, the text and literal translation by Alan Sommerstein (2008). I have also consulted Brown's edition of *Libation Bearers* (2018). However, following West (1990), Sommerstein has a practice of diagnosing lacunas (allegedly missing lines) in the text as transmitted by our manuscripts. In my opinion, few of these are justified, and what has occurred is more likely to be corruption than omission. In any case, a text with lacunas is unperformable, and with one exception (*Eu* 1026), I have been reluctant to compose lines of my own to fill these gaps. I therefore present a continuous text, reconstructing where the text transmitted by the manuscripts is obviously damaged and noting these passages in the notes to the text.

These two editors also make substantial transpositions which are hard to justify as repairing scribal errors. There are some transpositions which need to be made, but in many other instances, these are entirely unnecessary; the logic of the transmitted text, which they question working in their studies, is perfectly clear in performance.[100]

Lyric and Spoken Verse

The interplay between lyric and spoken verse is marked in this edition by double-indenting all verses that were sung or chanted in the original Greek plays.

The notations A1, A2, B1, B2 and so on beside the lyrics denote groups of 'strophic' responding stanzas, 1 stanzas being *strophes*, and 2 stanzas with the same letter their corresponding *antistrophes*. Each new system inside an ode or lyric interaction with soloists is marked A, B and so on; inside each system, the 2 stanza had in the original an identical metrical structure to the 1 stanza and was probably choreographed to similar movements. (No attempt has been made to match in my English translation the patterns of long and short syllables in the original Greek verse, as this would unacceptably constrict the options for expressing Aeschylus' meaning.) In some systems, the pattern of first and second stanza, *strophe* and *antistrophe*, is completed either by an intervening *mesode* in a related metre, here numbered A1a and so on, or by an *epode* after stanza 2, here numbered A3 and so on.

Punctuation

This is for actors. A comma, semi-colon, and full stop each indicate a greater pause.

32 *Introduction*

Line Numbering

For uniformity in referencing, all scholars use the numbering of one of the early editions of Aeschylus. This numbering sometimes diverges from the actual number of lines in the text; the layout of this translation follows modern editions of the Greek text which incorporate scholars' insights into the line-divisions of Aeschylus' lyric stanzas.

Stage Directions

There are no stage directions in our Greek texts of Aeschylus. The stage directions in this translation are justified, where there is dispute, in the Theatrical Commentary. Stage directions are for a theatre shaped like the ancient Athenian one, though consideration is given to the problems of producing Greek tragedy in an end-on theatre shape.

Theatrical Commentary

Modern directors will, of course, not adhere to all of the suggestions in the Commentary, but the principal ones for exit and entrance, and those which are strongly derived from the spoken or sung words, should be followed. The Theatrical Commentary reconstructs many features of the action and will be a useful guide not only for directors and actors but also for students and other readers seeking to imagine the *Oresteia* in performance while reading the text.

Structure

I have not used the technical terms found in the possibly spurious Chapter 12 of Aristotle's *Poetics*, *prologos* (speech before entry of choros), *parodos* (entrance song of choros), *epeisodion* (scene), *stasimon* (choral interlude) and *exodos* (exit song of choros). I have simply numbered all Scenes and Choroses in two consecutive sequences starting with 1. Short choral odes which do not separate scenes but are embedded in one have their number in brackets, such as (Choros 2) in *LB* and *Eu*.

Spelling and Notation

I have used Greek spellings rather than Roman (so Klytaimestra not Clytemnestra), with a few exceptions which include the name of the playwright (Aeschylus not Aischylos).

All directions for exit and entry left and right are from the actor's viewpoint standing at EBC (discussed below), not the audience's. They reflect the Athenian convention that, as in actual reality, entry actor right is from overseas or from the countryside, while entry actor left is from downtown of the city near which the action is located.

Positions in the playing space are notated not by the modern system of upstage, downstage and so on but by combinations of the following letters:

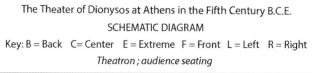

So, for example, EBC denotes a position at the extreme back of the playing space, right in front of the central doors in the *skēnē* façade. EBL denotes a position next to the left entrance (*eisodos*), while CL denotes a position on the central cross-axis but to the (actor's) left of the centre spot, in between C and ECL, which is a position on the left edge of the playing space on that same cross-axis. BC is halfway between the doors and the centre of the playing space, FC halfway from the centre to the extreme front centre (EFC). See the schematic diagram in Figure 2.

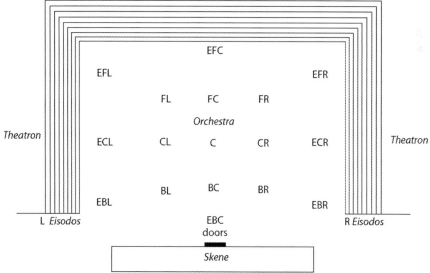

Figure 2 Schematic diagram showing notation of positions in the *orchēstra*.

Oresteia

By

Aeschylus

Agamemnon

CAST (IN ORDER OF APPEARANCE)

Watchman
Elders of Argos
Klytaimestra, queen of Argos
Herald
Agamemnon, king of Argos
Kassandra, a Trojan prophetess
Aigisthos, cousin of Agamemnon and lover of Klytaimestra

Silent characters: Maidservants attendant on Klytaimestra, Bodyguards attendant on Aigisthos.

38   Oresteia

Behind the playing space is the palace of Agamemnon at Argos, with one set of double doors at the centre and a practicable roof.
  Preset the Watchman *on the roof.*

Scene 1

Watchman: I beg the gods, release me from these sufferings,
        this year-long watch that I have lain
        huddled upon the house of Atreus' sons, just like a dog.
        I've come to know the mass of stars assembled in the night,
        and those bright overlords who bring to mortal men
        winter and summer – stars that shine clear in the sky
        both when they set and when they rise.
        So now I'm watching for the torch-signal,
        a beam of fire to bring from Troy the news
        the city's fallen: that is how she's used her power –   10
        the hopeful woman who plans like a man.
        But when I try to rest at night, now here, now there,
        covered in dew, no dreams watch over me;
        instead of sleep, Fear stands beside my bed
        and stops my eyes from closing safely into sleep;
        but if I feel I'd like to sing or hum a tune,
        pricking myself with song as antidote to sleep,
        then I cry out in mourning for this household, once
        tended with care and labour – now no more.
        But I still long for good luck, for release from suffering –   20
        fire, shining out of darkness as the messenger of joy.

        Flame in the night, I greet you! You bring us
        the light of day, and you command
        that all of Argos sing and dance to celebrate.
        Hey! Hey!
        By this shrill cry I signal Agamemnon's wife to rise
        quick as she can, and raise a cry of greeting for this light
        throughout the household, if the Trojan citadel of Ilion
        has fallen, as the beacon tells so vividly.   30
        And I myself will dance the prelude to their song;
        for I shall place the pieces for my master's lucky throw,
        since this my beacon-watch has landed triple six.
        But…may it only happen; may he come home, and let me clasp
        my well-loved master's hand in mine.
        I'll say no more; upon my tongue
        a great ox sits. The house itself, could it take voice,
        would tell most clearly. I prefer to speak only for those
        who'll understand; to those who don't, I haven't said a word.

Exit Watchman, *down into the palace.*

Agamemnon 39

Choros 1

Enter the Elders of Argos, *left.*

Elders:	This is the tenth year since Priam's	40

This is the tenth year since Priam's   40
great opponents,
Menelaos the king and Agamemnon,
two sons of Atreus,
firm in their partnership of power,
twin-throned, twin-sceptred by the gift of Zeus,
put to sea from this land
an Argive fleet of a thousand ships,
an army of men to fight for their cause.
And they cried out with all their hearts
for mighty War,
like vultures with their nestlings gone
and crazed by grief,
who circle eddying   50
on high above the nest,
when they have seen the toil
of nurturing their young all gone for nothing.
And on the heights above some god – Apollo, say,
or Pan, or Zeus – hears these strange residents
of heaven crying shrill in mourning,
and sends down on the victims' ruthless enemies
a late-avenging Fury.
Just so does Zeus, great god   60
who watches over guests and hosts, send out
the sons of Atreus against Paris
for a wanton woman's sake, and lays
many contests, as the knee is bent in the dust
and the spear is snapped as the rites begin,
on Greeks and Trojans alike.
Whatever's happening will be fulfilled
right to the destined end;
not by burnt offerings, nor pouring out
libations can you soothe   70
the stubborn angers of the gods.
With our old muscles
we were judged unfit for service;
they left us behind
to wait, guiding our child-like strength
with walking staffs; the marrow which commands
a young boy's breast is like an old man's – Ares
is not yet in his place; advanced old age,
its leaves already withering, goes on its way   80

40 Oresteia

three-footed, and no stronger than a child
wanders, a dream-image by day.

But you, daughter
of Tyndareus, Queen Klytaimestra,
what need of us? What is the news? What
have you heard, what message has persuaded you
to send and order sacrifice?
For all the gods – the city guardians,
the gods above, those of the underworld, the household
and the market-place –   90
the altars blaze with offerings;
the flare of torches rises everywhere
as high as heaven,
charmed by the soft and harmless aid
of sacred unguents
taken from the royal store.
Tell us what you can, and what is right to tell,
of this; consent, and be the healer
of our deep anxiety –
for now I'm sometimes full of desperate thoughts   100
and sometimes from the sacrificial offerings
that you have made to blaze comes Hope,
preventing me from utter misery,
the grief that wears away the heart.

(A1) I have authority to tell the generals' power
that ruled with friendly omen when the troops set out;
Persuasion still breathes down on me from heaven, and
my age is suited to a song –
how a fierce, warlike bird-omen sent
the twin-throned power of the Achaians,
the single-minded leaders of the youth of Greece   110
with spear and with avenging hand to Troy,
the king of birds for the king of ships,
the black-tailed eagle and the white,
appearing near the household on the spear-hand side,
perched in full view,
feasting upon a mother-hare pregnant with young;
her race was over, she would never come to term.   120
Cry sorrow, sorrow – yet may good prevail!

(A2) The army's prophet saw the portent, and the two devourers
of the hare,

Agamemnon 41

who sent the army on its way, his wisdom knew to be
the two Atreidai, diverse in their temperaments. He spoke,
       reading the omens:
'In time this expedition captures Priam's city-state
and Destiny will kill all of their livestock,
caught outside the citadel.   130
Only – may no god's anger darken this great curb on Troy
by striking it beforehand, as the troops assemble: Artemis
       the pure
is jealous of the wingèd hounds of Zeus
in pity for the wretched, cowering thing they sacrificed
with all its young before their birth;
she hates the eagles' feast.
Cry sorrow, sorrow – yet may good prevail!

(A3) For she, the Fair One, dearly loves   140
       the savage lion's helpless cubs
       and she takes pleasure in the suckling young
       of all the animals that roam the wild;
       now she demands the portent be fulfilled.
       I judge the omens are part good, part bad.
       I call in grief upon the god of healing; beg your sister
       not to stop the ships, not to delay us with contrary winds
       in eagerness to bring about another sacrifice, bereft
           of flute and feast,   150
       building strife inside the royal house, beyond
       the fear of any man; for she awaits, and will arise
           – a terrifying, treacherous
       house-guardian, an unforgetting Wrath which will avenge
           the child.'
Such were the fearful happenings Kalchas proclaimed (with many
       blessings too)
as fated by the roadside portent for the royal house;
in harmony with them,
Cry sorrow, sorrow – yet may good prevail!

(B1) Zeus – whoever he is,   160
       if this name pleases him,
       I use it as I call on him;
       when I take stock,
       there's nothing to refer to
       except Zeus, if I'm to cast away the burden of
       these futile thoughts once and for all.

42   Oresteia

(B2)   The one who once was great,
       bursting with never-conquered might,
       men now forget that he once lived.   170
       The next great power both came and went,
       thrown to the floor by Zeus
       the Conqueror; if you shout gladly for him by this name,
       you'll hit the target of good sense –

(C1)   the god who keeps us on the road to wisdom,
       he who made it law that men
       will learn through suffering.
       But still, in sleep the pain
       of memory drips down beside the heart; the calm   180
       of reason comes even to those who do not want it.
       I think the favours of the gods who sit on sacred thrones
       are gifts that hurt.

(C2)   Just so, then, was the elder leader
       of the ships of Greece,
       not blaming any prophet,
       breathing along with the winds of fate
       until the food ran out
       and all the Greeks were suffering because they could not sail,
       were forced to wait upon the shore
       across the flowing tides from Chalkis, at a place   190
       called Aulis.

(D1)   The winds blew in from Strymon, winds
       of harmful idleness, of hunger, evil anchorage,
       driving men mad,
       wearing away both ships and cables,
       doubling and redoubling time –
       and crushed the flower of Argos into pieces.
       Then against the bitter weather Kalchas shouted out
       another remedy, proclaiming Artemis –
       a cure more heavy on the chieftains than
       the cause itself, and one to make the sons of Atreus   200
       strike with their royal sceptres at the earth and weep
       beyond control.

(D2)   Then the elder king said this:
       'Heavy my fate to disobey
       but heavy if I slaughter my own child,
       the glory of our household,

Agamemnon 43

and pollute with virgin blood
my hands – a father's hands – beside   210
the altar. Which of these courses lacks its evil?
How can I desert the ships,
abandoning the expedition?
No; her demand, her utter and insensate rage[1]
for sacrifice of virgin blood
to stop the winds
is right. May all be well.'

(E1) And when he put upon himself the harness of necessity
his mind veered on a course
impious and unholy; then   220
he changed, and all his thoughts were reckless.
For shameful are the counsels of that wretched mania
which gives men courage to embark upon a chain
         of miseries.
And so he dared to sacrifice
his daughter for a war
fought to avenge one woman, as
a sending-off rite for the fleet.

(E2) Thirsting for war, the chieftains set
at nothing all her prayers, her cries of 'Father!'
or her youth and her virginity;   230
after the prayer her father told
the servants, as she lay
clasping his robes with all her heart,
to lift her up above the altar like a goat,
face down, and bind
her lovely mouth – so that she might
not make a sound and curse the royal house –

(F1) by force, and with a bridle silence her.
Her saffron robe poured down towards the earth,
and her eyes struck each minister of sacrifice   240
with piteous glance, her silhouette
just like a figure in a painting as she tried
to speak to them by name, since often in
her father's halls she'd sing a paean
for them, and with pure voice she,
a maiden not yet brutalized by man,
had paid this honour to the last libation of the feast
for her dear father.

44 Oresteia

(F2) What happened after that I did not see, nor will I speak of it;
      but Kalchas' prophecies are never unfulfilled.
      The scales of Justice tilt – and some men learn   250
      from suffering. As for the future –
      when it happens, then you'll hear about it; till then let it go;
      don't weep before it's time;
      all will come clear when the day breaks.
      Only, may the outcome now be good;
      such is our wish, the sole and closest guardians
      of Argos.

Scene 2

Doors open. Enter Klytaimestra, *from the palace.*

1 Elder: Klytaimestra, I come in reverence for your power;
      it is the custom to esteem the ruler's wife
      when he, the male, is absent from the throne.   260
      And if you've heard good news, or have not,
      but ordered sacrifice in hope of happiness, I would
      be glad to hear it – but could not protest if you refuse.
Klytaimestra: May this dawn, coming from its mother Night,
      break full of happiness just as the proverb says.
      Now learn of joy greater than all our hopes:
      the Argives occupy King Priam's citadel.
1 Elder: What did you say? Your words have lost me: I cannot believe.
Klytaimestra: Troy is now Greek. Do I speak clear enough?
1 Elder: Joy starts to creep up on me, and evokes a tear.   270
Klytaimestra: Yes, now your eyes give witness of your loyal heart.
1 Elder: What has convinced you? Have you proof of this?
Klytaimestra: Of course, how could I not? – unless a god deceived me.
1 Elder: Has a mere image in a dream persuaded you?
Klytaimestra: I would not trust the vision of a sleeping mind.
1 Elder: I hope no fledgling rumour's swollen up your hopes?
Klytaimestra: You scoff at me as though my mind was still a child's.
1 Elder: And how long is it since the city's fall?
Klytaimestra: I'll tell you – the same night that gave birth to this dawn.
1 Elder: What messenger could possibly have come so fast?   280
Klytaimestra: The god of fire dispatched his blaze from Ida's peak:
      beacon sent beacon on to here; Hephaistos was
      my courier. He leapt from Ida to the rock of Hermes
      in Lemnos; from that island Zeus' peak, the Mount
      of Athos, was the third to take the mighty blaze:
      then, rising up to skim the sea,
      the travelling torch passed on;

the golden pine-tree gleaming like the sun
came and announced its radiant joy at Makistos.[2]
The man on watch there was not lazy, nor did he neglect   290
his task as messenger, bemused by sleep; from far away
the beacon's light across the streams of Euripos
told of its coming to the guardsmen of Messapion.
They lit their pyre in answer, sent the message on
by lighting up a pile of agèd heather. Then
the light did not grow dim, but full of strength
it leapt across the plain of Asopos, just like
the shining moon, to reach the rock of Kithairon
and wake a new relay of beacon-fire.
Nor did the men on duty there reject   300
the distant fire, but kindled even more than what was asked;
the light then darted down across the lake of gorgon eyes
and reached the mountain of the roving goats,
rousing the guard there to respect the fire's command.
They did not stint their strength, but sent it further on,
igniting a great beard of flame, which passed
beyond the promontory that looks down upon
the Gulf of Saron; then it darted ever on, and came
to Mount Arachneion, the lookout nearest to our city;
from there the fire leapt down to this, the house of Atreus –   310
a true descendant of the blaze on Ida.
So the commands I gave my light-bearers were all
fulfilled, as each took over from the one before;
and victory belongs to every one, the first as well as last.
Such is the proof and token which I give to you,
sent by my husband here to me from Troy.
1 Elder: Lady, I shall give thanks in due course to the gods;
for now, I long to hear this story as a whole
and marvel; would you tell it once again?
Klytaimestra: Today the Greeks hold Troy. And I would say   320
that in the city sounds are heard that do not blend.
Put oil and vinegar in one bowl, and they fight
so that you'd call them anything but friends.
Just so you'd hear the cries of conquerors
and conquered, very different as befits their fates:
the women falling to embrace the bodies of their men –
husbands and brothers; children at the side
of agèd fathers; throats that are no longer free
cry out in anguish for the fate of those they loved.
The others, weary from wandering after the battle stopped,   330
hunger drives them to breakfast on the city's food,
not taking turns according to their rank,
but as each drew the lot of chance.

46   Oresteia

Now they are lodged in captured Trojan homes;
they've won release from frost and dew
under the open sky; like prosperous men
they sleep securely through the night.
And if they reverence the city gods
of their new-captured land, and the gods' shrines,
then they, the captors, won't be taken in their turn.   340
But still I fear; may no desire fall on the troops
to ravage sacred places, overcome by love of gain;
for they still need a voyage home,
a safe return along the course's second leg.
And if the army comes without offence against the gods,
the sufferings of the dead might be appeased,[3]
unless some unexpected harm lands its blow first.

Well, there is all that I, a woman, have to say;
yet may the good prevail – and clearly, for us all to see;
I want to enjoy that more than all other blessings now.   350

Exit Klytaimestra *into the palace; doors close.*

1 Elder: Lady, you've spoken graciously and wisely, like a man;
And I, since I have heard trustworthy proof from you,
will now prepare a fitting address to the gods;
great is the favour granted in return for pain.

Choros 2

Elders: O Zeus our lord
and wonderfully ornamented Night,
our friend because you cast
over the towers of Troy your covering
mesh, so that not one, however great or young,
could overset it and escape
the mighty, all-embracing net   360
of slavery;
I reverence Zeus, great god of guests and hosts,
who took this as his price, and aimed his bow
at Paris long ago, so that the shot would not
be wasted, falling below the mark
or far above the stars.

(A1)   They have been struck by Zeus –
that much we can track out;
he did as he decreed. Once someone said
the gods don't think it worth their while   370

Agamemnon   47

to be concerned with men who trample on
the beauty of a sacred thing; but he was impious.
Suffering falls on those to come
for deeds beyond all daring, done by men
proud past the bounds of Justice,
living in homes that teem with riches,
far beyond what's best. Let wealth
be free from pain, enough to satisfy
men of good sense.   380
For there is no defence
against excess, when once a man
has kicked into oblivion
the great altar of Justice.

(A2) Fearful Persuasion forces him,
unbearable child of the plans of Ruin.
All cure's in vain – his wound
cannot be hidden, but shines out with dreadful gleam;
and like bad bronze   390
that's rubbed away and knocked around
he has his blackness deep ingrained
when he is brought to justice, since
he is a child chasing a bird upon the wing,
bringing unbearable affliction on his city.
None of the gods will hear his prayers;
the man familiar with such things
Justice destroys.
Just so was Paris, when he came
to the house of Atreus' sons   400
and shamed the table shared by guest and host,
stealing another's wife.

(B1) Leaving her city's people
a tumult of shielded warriors,
ambush and sea-borne armament,
she brought to Troy instead of dowry
death and destruction, as
lightly she passed between the gates
daring to do what nobody should dare.
The palace seers
loudly cried out, and said:
'Disaster for the rulers of the house,   410
disaster in the marriage-bed and everywhere she used to go
loving her husband. You can see him sitting there
dishonoured, silent, unable to curse or pray;
in his desire for her beyond the sea

48   Oresteia

Helen's ghost will seem to rule the house,
and now the husband hates the beauty of
her graceful statues;
in their empty eyes
all his desire is lost.

(B2)   Mournful images appear   420
in dreams, and bring
an unreal joy;
unreal because when someone sees a promised good
the vision swerves and slips
out of his hands, and never afterwards
accompanies on wings the paths of sleep.'
These were the griefs at home, beside the hearth –
these, and much more;
and all through Greece a woman waits at home
with patient sorrow in her heart   430
for each of those who went to Troy.
Many things touch their feelings:
each one knows the person she sent out;
instead of him
a pot of ashes comes back home.

(C1)   The god of War's a money-changer, dealing in bodies;
he lifts the scales in the combat of spears
and from the funeral fires of Ilion   440
he sends the relatives
the heavy dust for which they'll weep
cramming the urns with ashes
easily stowed
in place of men.
Then they lament; this one
they praise – he was well skilled in fighting;
this one died nobly, as the battle raged –
but all for someone else's wife;
that's what they snarl under their breath,
and grief-tinged anger creeps up on   450
the leaders of this cause, the sons of Atreus,
while Greeks in all their beauty
lie around the walls
in Trojan graves; a hostile soil
covers the men who won it.

(C2)   The city's angry words are dangerous;
they pay the debt due for the people's curse.

I'm waiting anxiously to hear
the truth the murky night conceals: 460
the gods unfailingly mark out
those who've killed many, and the black
Furies in time cast into darkness anyone
who's built success by unjust means;
they turn his fortune round and wear his life away –
and then when he has gone among the shades
there is no help. To be praised very much
is dangerous; a thunderbolt from Zeus
is cast down on the house. 470
I seek prosperity with no such jealousy;
may I not be a sacker of cities,
nor eat away my life
slave to another.

1 Elder: The beacon's good news sent
swift Rumour through
the city; but who knows if
it's true, or a deception sent us by the gods?

1 Elder: Who'd be so childlike or crazed
to let his heart be set on fire 480
by this new message from the beacon-flare, and then
be upset when the tale is changed?

1 Elder: It's typical of female leadership
to praise the favour of the gods before it's come.

1 Elder: It is just like a woman in command
to ordain thanks before the news is sure.
A woman's rule is too persuasive; it is quick to flourish –
but then quickly fades away.
A rumour trumpeted by woman vanishes.

Scene 3

1 Elder: We'll soon know now about the torches bearing light,
relays of beacon-watching and of fire – 490
whether they're true, or like a dream
this joyful light has robbed us of our wits;
I see a Herald coming from the shore, his forehead crowned
with wreath of olive. And the thirsty dust,
sister and closest relative of mud, assures me that
he will not make signs to us by the smoke of fire,
voicelessly kindling flames from mountain wood;
he'll either tell us clearly that we can rejoice,
or else…but I do not desire to hear the opposite.
Good things have come to us so far; let's have more good. 500

50   Oresteia

If anyone prays for the city otherwise than us,
may he himself reap all the fruit of his perverted thoughts.

Enter Herald, *right.*

Herald: Land of our fathers, soil of Argos!
I've come to you in this, the tenth year's light.
One hope has stayed intact when many hopes were broken:
I never did believe that I would die
back in this land of Argos, and be buried here.
I greet the earth, I greet the sunlight,
Zeus, our lord on high, and the great god of Delphi.
Do not shoot your arrows at us any more;   510
you were our enemy more than enough at Troy;
now change your aspect, and become our saviour and our healer,
Lord Apollo. And I now address the gods
of the assembly-place, especially my own protector,
Hermes the herald-god, whom heralds love and honour most,
and all the heroes who once sent the army out; I pray to you
welcome back kindly all that's left of us.

Halls of our kings, dearest dwelling-place,
and sacred thrones and gods who face the sun,
if ever you did once, with gladness shining in your eyes,   520
receive the king with honour fitting after all this time –
for he returns, bearer of light in darkness
for you and all those here to share, Agamemnon the king.
Welcome him truly, as he well deserves,
who dug down Priam's city to the ground
with Zeus' avenging pickaxe. Nothing stands upon the plain of Troy;
the altars and the shrines of gods are all destroyed,
and all the seed has perished from the land.
Such is the yoke he's cast on Troy – and now
the elder king, the son of Atreus, comes home   530
a man blest by the gods; of all those living on the earth
most worthy of esteem. Paris and Troy
must now admit that what they did
is less than what they've suffered. He was convicted both of robbery
and theft; he's forfeited his booty, and has reaped the harvest in
total destruction of his fathers' house and land.
So Priam's sons have paid a double penalty for crime.

1 Elder: I greet you, herald of the army of the Greeks.
Herald: I'm happy, but would consent now if the gods demand my death.

1 Elder:	Did longing for your native land exhaust you so?	540
Herald:	Yes, my eyes are filled with tears of joy.	
1 Elder:	You were then struck by a most pleasant malady.	
Herald:	What do you mean? Teach me, so I may master what you say.	
1 Elder:	You longed for those who longed for all of you.	
Herald:	You mean they missed the army here, as we missed them?	
1 Elder:	So that I often groaned, my heart clouded by darkness.	
Herald:	How did this gloomy misery attack the people here?	
1 Elder:	Since long ago silence has been my remedy for grief.	
Herald:	What? While the kings were absent was there someone whom you feared?	
1 Elder:	So much that now – to use your words – death would be joy.	550
Herald:	Yes. The outcome has been good. Over a span of time	

you'd say some things have fallen well –
and others badly. Who except the gods
lives through his lifetime free of pain?
Suppose I told you of our sufferings – bad quarters,
narrow gangways, lousy bedding – what did we not
complain about? Each day brought every form of misery.
Then when we landed things were even worse:
we had to sleep close under hostile walls;
and from the heavens and the meadowland   560
dew drizzled down on us, a constant plague
making our woollen garments verminous.
And then the winter, death to all bird life,
intolerable cold brought by the snows of Ida –
or scorching heat, when the sea fell asleep,
a noon siesta without wind or wave.
What reason to lament all that? The pain has gone!
It's gone for us, and for the dead
there is no fear they'll ever have to rise again,   569
while for what's left of all the Argive troops   573
the gains are won, and not outweighed by sufferings.   574
Why should we count the number of the dead like votes,   570
why should the living grieve that Fortune wounded them?   571
Myself, I want to bid a fond farewell to misery,   572
since we can rightly boast here, in the sun's bright gleam,   575
words that will soar on wings above both land and sea:
'We are the Argive force that once took Troy;
these are the spoils we nailed, throughout the length of Greece,
upon their temple walls as everlasting glory for the gods.'
When men hear this, their duty is to honour both   580
this city and its generals; so we will pay our debt to Zeus,
whose favour gave this prize to us. That's all I have to say.

52 Oresteia

1 Elder: Your words have won me over – and I'm glad;
old men are always young enough to learn.
But this is news which should especially concern the house
and Klytaimestra – though I also gain.

Doors open. Enter Klytaimestra *from the palace, perhaps with two* Attendants.

Klytaimestra: I raised my cry of joy some time ago,
when the first messenger of fire by night
came telling of the capture and the sack of Troy.
Then some reproached me, saying: "D'you believe   590
just from these beacons in the fall of Troy?
How typical of female empty hopes.'
Such speeches made me seem a lunatic;
but still I sacrificed, and as we women do
we raised a cry of ecstasy through all
of Argos, lulling at the altars of the gods
the incense-laden, fragrant flames.
So now, why should you tell me any more?
I'll hear the story whole, from my own lord.
I must be active now, to welcome back
as well as possible the husband I revere;   600
can you imagine any sweeter light for woman to behold
than that of opening the doors, after the gods have brought
her man back safe from war? This is my message; tell my husband he
must come quick as he can – the darling of his city;
here he will find a faithful wife
just as he left her, watchdog of the house,
loyal to him, an enemy to those who wish
him harm, and as she was in every way; through all
this time she's broken not one seal.   610
Of pleasure from another man, or rumoured scandal,
I know less than how to temper steel.
Such is my boast, brimful of truth –
and one a noble woman may proclaim without disgrace.

Exit Klytaimestra *and* Attendants *into the palace. Doors close.*

1 Elder: That speech was pleasing to the ear, but for
a clear interpreter her words have only surface charm.
Tell me, Herald, I now want to learn
of Menelaos; is he safe and on his way
back here with you, the much-loved ruler of this land?
Herald: There's no way I can tell a fair false tale of which   620
my friends could reap the harvest for a good long time.

Agamemnon 53

1 Elder: If only you could tell a truth that sounded good.
    But still, when truth and good are torn apart, it cannot be concealed.
Herald: The man is missing from the fleet –
    he and his ship. I speak the truth.
1 Elder: Did he set out apart from others and then vanish, or
    did stormy weather hit the whole fleet, tearing him from you?
Herald: You've hit the mark just like a master of the bow –
    expressed a length of suffering in one short phrase.
1 Elder: What was the rumour spoken of his fate   630
    by other sailors – dead, or still alive?
Herald: No one knows enough to say with truth,
    except the Sun, who nurtures all the life on earth.
1 Elder: Then tell us how the storm came on the fleet –
    and how it ended – by the anger of the gods.
Herald: It is not right to mar a glorious day
    with words so bad. The honour due the gods stands far apart.
    But when a grim-faced herald brings the city news
    long prayed against, their army's loss,
    then it's a wound for the community –   640
    so many men, dragged out from many homes
    as sacrificial victims by the double whip the War-god loves,
    a two-pronged Ruin and a gory double harnessing.
    When one is loaded down with cares like that
    it's right to sing a paean to the Furies;
    but when one comes with messages that all is safe
    back to a city which rejoices in its fortune, how
    can I mix good things in with evil, telling you
    about the storm of anger from the gods against the Greeks?
    Two bitter, ancient enemies became allies –   650
    water and fire; they made a pledge
    between them to destroy the wretched Argive force.
    Evil, hostile waves rose in the night:
    the wind from Thrace made ship collide
    with ship; and they, ramming each other in the violence
    of storm and hurricane and driving rain, sank out
    of sight, rough-handled as by some vindictive shepherd.
    When bright daylight came,
    we saw the whole Aigeian sea blossom with shipwreck
    fragments and the corpses of the Greeks.   660
    Our ship escaped untouched –
    some god (it was no mortal man) stole us
    or begged us off, guiding our helm,
    and saving Fortune graciously sat on the ship;
    we did not have to anchor and risk being swamped
    nor were we run aground on rocky land.

54 Oresteia

So we escaped a watery grave, and in
the bright daylight, scarcely believing in our luck,
we thought about our recent sufferings –
the wreck and miserable pounding of the fleet.   670
And now, if any of them still remains alive,
they'll speak of us, of course, as dead;
we think the same fate's theirs.
May all turn out as best it can; you must
most certainly assume Menelaos is coming here;
and if some sunbeam's found that he
is still alive and well, by Zeus' will
who does not yet want to destroy our royal house,
there is some likelihood he'll get back home.
Know all you've heard is truth.   680

Exit Herald *left*.

Choros 3

Elders: (A1) Who can it be who once named you
                 so perfectly in every way –
                 was it not one we cannot see
                 guiding his voice successfully
                 who saw into her destiny,
                 and called the woman married by the spear
                 and fought for – Helen? Fittingly, for Helen means
                 destruction; she destroyed men, ships and cities
                 when she left her delicately curtained bed   690
                 to sail away upon the giant
                 West Wind breeze;
                 a hunting pack of many men with shields
                 chasing the vanished track of oars
                 beached on the leafy bank
                 of Simois,
                 drawn after her by bloody Strife.

          (A2) For Ilion the goddess Wrath
                 began the marriage-bond   700
                 which was a sorrow, and in later time
                 exacted vengeance for the outrage to
                 the guest-table and Zeus
                 god of the common hearth, from those
                 who loudly celebrated with a song
                 of honour to the bride,
                 the marriage-hymn which then

Agamemnon 55

the bridegroom's kinsmen had to sing.
In its place, the ancient citadel
of Priam had to learn a different song   710
of bitter lamentation, and it called
in agony on Paris of the fatal marriage,
who filled the Trojans' lives with tears
and utter devastation,
when they suffered pitiable bloodshed.

(B1)   Just so a man once reared
a lion's cub inside his house,
robbed of its mother's milk and longing for the breast;
and as its life began it was   720
so tame it loved to play
with children, and delighted all
the elders.
It got many treats, held in their arms
just like a nursling child,
glancing bright-eyed towards the hand,
fawning in hunger.

(B2)   But in time it showed
its parents' temper: it repaid
thanks to the fosterers
by slaughtering their flocks;   730
it made a feast unasked.
The house was fouled with blood,
an anguish that the household could not fight,
a murderous great wound;
the gods had reared inside their halls
a sacrificial priest of Ruin.

(C1)   And at that time I'd say there came
to Ilion the spirit of
a windless calm,
a delicate adornment to their wealth,   740
a soft dart from the eyes,
a flower of sex to pierce the heart.
She turned aside, and made
a bitter ending to the marriage-rites,
an evil and unbearable companion
whirling onto Priam's children,
sent by Zeus the lord of hosts and guests,
a Fury to bring bridal tears.

56   Oresteia

(C2) There is an aged saying,   750
      long established, that a man's
      prosperity full-grown
      gives birth – it does not die
      without a child; and from good fortune for a race
      is bred insatiable misery.
      I'm separate from others, isolated in
      my own belief; impiety
      gives birth in time to still more impious deeds
      in its own likeness, while the destiny   760
      of straight, just houses always is
      a handsome child.

(D1) Among the worst of men
      an ancient Violence always breeds
      a new, young Violence at some time
      or other, when the day comes round
      appointed for its birth –
      the goddess who cannot be fought,
      unholy daring of black Ruin on the halls,   770
      the very image of its parents.

(D2) Justice shines clear
      in smoky homes, and she respects
      a man who lives inside his destiny;
      she leaves the houses decked in gold
      where there is filth upon the hands
      with eyes averted, and she goes
      to pious ones – she cannot respect
      the power of wealth when falsely stamped
      with praise. And she steers everything   780
      right to its end.

Scene 4

Enter Agamemnon *and* Kassandra *in a carriage, right.*

1 Elder: My king, sacker of Troy,
             son of Atreus,
             how shall I greet you?
             How honour you,
             not shooting over or below the mark
             of favour due?
1 Elder: Many cross the boundaries
             of Justice, valuing appearances,
             and there are always people ready to lament

Agamemnon 57

	together with a victim, though the sting	790
	of grief misses their hearts.	
1 Elder:	They also force unsmiling faces into grins	
	which seem to share another's joy.	
	But if a man's a good judge of his flock,	
	he cannot be deceived by eyes	
	whose look seems to come from a loyal mind	
	but fawns with friendship weak as water.	
1 Elder:	Then, when you started with the army off to Troy	
	because of Helen, you (I won't deny the fact)	800
	were very ugly pictured, as	
	a man who'd lost his judgement,	
	giving courage by a sacrifice	
	to dying men.	
1 Elder:	But now in deep, true friendship I	
	am well disposed, since you have triumphed over suffering;	
	by inquiry you'll come to know in time	
	which of the citizens who stayed at home	
	has acted justly, and which has misused his time.	

Agamemnon: First it is just that I address   810
this city, Argos, and its gods, who are responsible with me
both for my homecoming and for the Justice I exacted from
King Priam's city: for the gods heard pleas
uttered by deaths, not tongues, and they unanimously cast their votes
into the urn for bloodshed and the sack of Troy; towards the urn
of mercy, Hope came near, but no hand filled the urn.
Still now the rising smoke marks captured Troy;
gusts of destruction thrive, and embers dying hard
send on their way rich breaths of wealth.   820
This favour of the gods must never be forgotten;
we must pay them thanks, because we have exacted price
for reckless theft, and for a woman's sake
the Argive beast has ground the city into dust –
the offspring of the Horse, the force of shield-bearers
which made its leap around the setting of the Pleiades;
springing across the battlements the ravening lion
licked up its fill of royal blood.

That was my prelude, drawn out to the gods;
as for your thought, I've heard, I will remember,   830
I agree – I'd say the same;
for there aren't many men who find it in their hearts
to reverence unjealously a friend's success;
the arrow of his discontent attacks the heart
redoubling the sufferer's pain;

58   Oresteia

he is himself weighed down by his own burden, and
weeps at the sight of all his neighbour's wealth.
I speak from knowledge – well I understand
the mirror of society – and loyalty
in friends is just the image of a shadow.
I know that many of the leaders of my army,
men who seemed to be my most devoted friends,   840
were hostile to me.[4]
Only Odysseus, one who sailed against his will,
when harnessed proved to be a ready trace-horse for me;
though I don't know if I speak of a man alive or dead.
For all the other matters that concern
the city and the gods, I shall have open meetings, and decide
in full assembly. Then we must determine how
to make the good things last,
and where there is a need for healing remedies,
we will use sensibly burning or surgery,
in an attempt to turn away disease's harm.   850
Now I will go into my house,

Doors open. Enter Klytaimestra *from the palace, followed by* Maidservants
with robes.

and make beside the hearth first greeting to the gods,
who sent me out so far and led me back again.
Since victory has followed me, let it stand firm.

Klytaimestra *(with a gesture, she prevents* Agamemnon *from leaving the
carriage):*   Men of the city, Elders of Argos, I
am not ashamed to speak of how I love
my husband. Time erodes
all reticence. I have not learnt from others –
I shall tell you of my wretched life
for all the time this man was camped before the
        walls of Troy.   860
First, for a woman to remain at home
alone, without a man – that is unbearable;
she has to hear so many fresh and wounding rumours –
one herald comes, and then another brings a tale of woe
worse than the last, crying sorrow for the house.
Indeed, if this man here had suffered from
as many wounds as rumours said
which reached us, he'd have more holes in him than a net.
And if he'd died as many deaths as stories claimed
he'd be a second Geryon with three bodies   870

and he could boast that he had got a triple cloak
of earth, a death for each of his three shapes.
Because of all these wounding tales
they often had to hold me forcibly,
and free my neck from nooses I had strung from up above.
That's why your child's not standing here
as he should be, the guardian of the pledges made
by me and you, Orestes; do not be amazed;
our faithful ally's looking after him,   880
Strophios the Phokian. He alerted me in cautious words
to dangers on two sides; first, your peril in the war
at Troy, and then the chance that popular
revolt might hatch a wicked plot,
since men often give a further kick when one is down.
So this excuse of mine bears no deceit.

But as for me, the gushing fountains of my tears
have now run dry, and not one drop is left.
With waiting late at night my eyes are sore
as I cried bitterly because the beacons for your victory   890
always refused to light; and in my dreams
I was awakened by the gentle rushing of a gnat
buzzing aloud, since I saw you suffering more
than could have happened in the time sleep shared with me.

Now I've endured all that, with joyful heart
I would proclaim this man the watchdog of a farm,
the saving forestay of a ship, a high-roofed house's
solid pillar, or a father's only son,
to thirsty travellers a flowing spring,
and land for sailors suddenly in sight beyond   900
their hopes, a fair day dawning after storm.   901[5]

Klytaimestra *prostrates herself full-length on the ground before* Agamemnon *in homage. After a few moments she rises to her feet again.*

These are the words in which I think it right to honour him: 903
may Jealousy stand far away; we have endured so much
before. And now, my dear beloved, step
out of this carriage – but do not permit your foot
to touch the ground, my king, the foot that conquered Troy.
Women, why do you wait? I have instructed you
to clothe the area with fabrics where he has to walk.

The Maidservants *strew robes between the palace doors and the carriage.*

60   Oresteia

Create at once a crimson path, where Justice may   910
lead him into a house he never sought to see.
All else a mind not overcome by sleep
will justly make, with gods' help, reach the fated end.

Agamemnon: Daughter of Leda, guardian of my home,
you matched your speech quite closely to my absence;
it was very long. And modest praise would be
a gift I should receive from other mouths than yours.
As for all this, you must not treat me softly
like a woman, nor as if you were from oriental lands
gape grovelling upon the ground to cry my praise.   920
Nor should you make my path into the house subject to jealousy
by strewing it with cloths: the gods alone deserve such honour;
I, a mortal man, can't walk upon such beautiful
and finely woven robes without evoking fear.
I tell you, pay me the reverence due a man, and not a god.
my fame shouts out aloud; it's obvious that finely woven robes
should not become foot-wiping cloths; and the gods' greatest gifts
are sense and judgement. Count only that man fortunate
who ends his life in peace and happiness.
If I can always act in such a way, I can be confident.   930

Klytaimestra: Now tell me this, and tell me what you judge to be the truth.
Agamemnon: Know that I never will destroy my judgement.
Klytaimestra: In a time of danger would you vow before the gods to do
                 this thing?
Agamemnon: Yes, if a prophet told me this is what I have to do.
Klytaimestra: If Priam had achieved all you have, what would he have done?
Agamemnon: I think he certainly would walk upon the robes.
Klytaimestra: In that case do not fear the censure of mere men.
Agamemnon: The people murmur, and their voice is full of strength.
Klytaimestra: But no one can be praised who is not envied too.
Agamemnon: All this desire for conflict is unwomanly.   940
Klytaimestra: Yet for the prosperous even defeat shows grace.
Agamemnon: So do you really value victory in this?
Klytaimestra: Give way; you win if you have yielded of your own free will
                 to me.
Agamemnon: Well, if it is your wish, let someone quickly take from me these
                 boots, the gear that's subject to my feet;

A Maidservant *removes his boots.*

and as I walk upon these sea-dyed crimson garments of the gods,
may Jealousy not strike me from a distant eye.
I feel great awe as I destroy part of my house; my feet
ruin the wealth of this rich, silver-purchased web.

Agamemnon 61

Agamemnon *steps from the carriage.*

> Enough of that; as for this stranger,   950
> welcome her into our house; the god looks kindly from afar
> on those who conquer, but do not abuse their power.
> No one wears the yoke of slavery with willingness;
> and she has come back here with me, the flower chosen
> by the army as my gift from all our wealth.
> But since I've been subdued into obeying you in this,
> I trample crimson as I go into my house.

Agamemnon *moves to the edge of the robes, but then hesitates.*

Klytaimestra: There is the sea, and who shall drain it dry?
> It breeds an ever-self-renewing stream
> of crimson dye for clothing, worth its weight in silver ore: 960
> thanks to the gods the house is rich in goods
> like these; my king, your house has never suffered poverty.
> I would have vowed the trampling down of many vestments,
> if we'd been told in oracles it was
> the only way to bring this man back here alive;
> for when the root is there, the leafage comes over a house
> extending shade above to shield us from the dog-star heat;
> now you have come back to your house and home,
> that signals warmth has come back in the winter-time;
> and when Zeus makes the wine from bitter, unripe grapes   970
> then there is coolness in the house
> when he, the man, fulfils his role and roams around his halls.

Exit Agamemnon *over the robes into the palace. The* Maidservants *remove the robes and exeunt into the palace.*

> Zeus, Zeus fulfiller; now fulfil my prayer;
> take care to fulfil all of this that you intend.

Exit Klytaimestra *into the palace. Doors close.*

Choros 4

Elders: (A1)   Tell me, why does this
> persistent fear
> hover in front of my prophetic heart?
> My song is full of prophecies,
> unbidden and unpaid,
> and my mind doesn't have the daring and the trust   980

62   Oresteia

to spit away their meaning like
a dream of doubtful outcome.
Time has grown old since mooring-ropes
were shipped and our fleet sailed for Ilion.

(A2) I have seen him return – I've witnessed it
with my own eyes;
but still my spirit sings
self-taught within a tuneless dirge,   990
fit for the Furies, since it is bereft of all
the welcome confidence of hope.
The innards of a man
do not tell idle tales;
my heart throbs ominously close
beside a mind which knows that Justice comes;
I pray that this may fall
out of my expectation, false
and unfulfilled.   1000

(B1) The moment where great health reaches its end
is all-destroying; for disease, its neighbour, shares
the party-wall and presses hard.
So too the destiny of one
who travels straight can strike a reef
that was invisible.
And caution can defend
his property, by casting out
goods bound with a large sling –   1010
the whole house will not founder, over-
burdened with excess;
he does not sink the ship.
A large gift from Zeus,
springing abundantly from ploughing every year,
wards off the plague of famine.

(B2) Once the black blood of death
has fallen in front of a man,   1020
who could recall it casting any spell?
The one who truly knew
to bring men back from death –
Zeus stopped him savagely.
And had the gods not set
each human fate so it prevents
the next from taking more,
my heart would overcome my tongue

Agamemnon 63

and pour out all it feels;
but as things are it murmurs in the dark, 1030
sick-spirited, and not expecting to bring anything
through to the end while my mind burns.

Scene 5

Doors open. Enter Klytaimestra *from the palace.*

Klytaimestra: You, go inside the house as well, Kassandra. Since
Zeus brought you in kindliness to share
this household's purifying rites, standing among
our many slaves beside his altar as the god of property,
get down from this carriage: don't be proud;
they say once even Herakles was sold 1040
and had to eat the bread of slavery.
And if Necessity bears down and brings one to this fate,
it is worth much to be the slave of masters who have long been rich.
Those who have reaped fine harvests suddenly,
beyond their expectations, they are cruel to slaves,
and treat them worse than proper rules require.
You've heard from me just what our customs are.
1 Elder: It's you she spoke to – very clearly, too;
since you are caught inside the net of fate
obey, if you are going to; perhaps you won't.
Klytaimestra: Unless she's like a swallow, speaking only 1050
unintelligible foreign sounds, I'm reaching
in her mind and am persuading her with words.
1 Elder: Follow; for as things stand she says what's best.
Obey, and leave your place here in the carriage.
Klytaimestra: I have no leisure now to waste time out of doors.
Beside the central hearth already stand
the sheep prepared for sacrifice –
a pleasure which we never hoped to see.
If you will do at all what I say, don't waste time;
but if you cannot fully understand my words 1060
then answer with the hand, as all barbarians do, instead of speech.
1 Elder: I think the stranger needs a clear interpreter;
she's like an animal just taken in a trap.
Klytaimestra: She must be mad, sent crazy signals by her mind,
to come here from a city newly sacked,
and not learn how to bear the bit, until
she's had her spirit broken in a foam of blood.
I will not waste more words on her and be disdained.

Exit Klytaimestra *into the palace. The doors remain open.*

64   Oresteia

Scene 6

1 Elder: Well, I will not be angry – for I pity her.
        Unhappy woman, leave the carriage, and willingly   1070
        yield to Necessity; accept this unaccustomed yoke.

Kassandra *leaps from the carriage, which is then removed by the left exit. She bursts into agonized, frenzied dance and song.*

Kassandra: (A1)   *(shrieks)* A-----h!
                 Oh Apollo, Apollo!
1 Elder: Why do you cry and name Apollo?
        He's not a god whom anyone lamenting should approach.
Kassandra: (A2)   *(shrieks)* Ah!
                 Oh Apollo, Apollo!
1 Elder: Now once again she cries out ominously to
        the god who cannot listen to a plaintive song.
Kassandra: (B1)   Oh Apollo, Apollo,
                 god of the ways, and my destroyer,   1080
                 once again you have destroyed me easily.
1 Elder: I think she's going to prophesy about her miseries;
        the god's gift stays with her, although she's a slave.
Kassandra: (B2)   Oh Apollo, Apollo,
                 god of the ways, and my destroyer.
                 Ah! Where have you led me? To what house?
1 Elder: The house of the Atreidai; if you don't know that
        I can inform you; then you will not speak it false.
Kassandra: (C1)   A house that hates the gods, and knows   1090
                 inside its heart murder of kindred, severed heads –
                 a slaughterhouse, a floor sprinkled with blood.
1 Elder: The foreign girl is like a hunting dog, keen on the scent.
        She searches for the track of murder; she will find it, too.
Kassandra: (C2)   Yes, I believe this evidence –
                 the baby children who lament
                 their slaughter, and their roasted flesh their father ate.
1 Elder: We certainly have heard of your prophetic gifts;
        but we want no predictions here today.
Kassandra: (D1)   Oh god, what's being plotted? What   1100
                 is this new grief? Great evil's
                 planned here in this house,
                 unbearable to all its friends, impossible to cure;
                 and help stands far away.
1 Elder: I cannot understand this prophecy; as for the others,
        I knew them; all of Argos cries them out.
Kassandra: (D2)   Oh wretched woman, is this your design?
                 To wash your husband in a ritual bath,

Agamemnon 65

                        then – how shall I speak the end?
                        It will come quickly – look, she reaches out,   1110
                        stretches each hand in turn.
1 Elder: I don't yet understand; for now after her riddles
          I am bewildered by these obscure oracles.
Kassandra: (E1)   Oh God, Oh God, what's this?
                        A net of death?
                        But no, the snare's the partner in his bed
                        and in his murder; in this family insatiable strife
                        must cry a victory-song for sacrifice to be avenged.
1 Elder: What kind of Fury do you ask to raise her cry
          over this house? Your words bring me no joy.   1120
Elders: But to the heart the saffron drop
                        runs fast, the blood which for men speared
                        reaches its end as life's sun sets.
                        Destruction quickly comes.
Kassandra: (E2)   Ah! Ah! Keep the bull
                        from the cow. She's tangled him
                        in robes, a black-horned thing.
                        She strikes; he falls into the water.
                        I tell you the treachery that happens in the bath.
1 Elder: I would not boast that I am really good   1130
          at understanding prophecies; but I do not like this.
Elders: What happy word for mankind
                        ever comes from oracles? Only through misfortune
                        do the wordy crafts of prophets bring
                        their tales of terror for us all to learn.
Kassandra: (F1)   Oh! What about my miserable, evil fate?
                        I cry aloud, pouring out my own sufferings as well.
                        Why did you bring me here in all my misery,
                        except to die with him? What else?
Elders: You're frenzied, carried from us by the gods,   1140
                        as you cry your own tuneless elegy,
                        just like the tawny nightingale whose miserable heart
                        laments unendingly for her dead son
                        slaughtered by both his parents.
Kassandra: (F2)   I wish my fate were like
                        the tuneful nightingale's; the gods gave her
                        a feathered shape and sweet life free from pain;
                        I will be cloven by a double-sided blade.
Elders: Which god impels these rushing stabs   1150
                        of useless inspiration? Why do you
                        mould to a melody of dissonant and piercing strain
                        such fearful things?
                        Who marked for you the limits of this path
                        of evil-omened prophecy?

66   Oresteia

Kassandra: (G1)   Oh Paris, when you married you destroyed your family!
Skamander, river of my native land,
beside your banks I once was nursed and grew unhappy;
now it seems I soon will prophesy   1160
around the rivers Acheron and Kokytos.

Elders: This is all too clear! Why do you say
such things a baby child could understand?
A deadly sting attacks me as you cry
so pitiably for your dreadful fate,   1165
It breaks my heart to hear.

Kassandra: (G2)   Oh pain, pain of my city utterly destroyed,
and sacrifice my father made before the walls
so rich in slaughter of the grazing flocks.
There was no cure to save   1170
my city from its fate;
and I will swiftly fall warm-blooded to the ground.

Kassandra *collapses.*

Elders: This follows what you said before;
and some malignant daemon weighs so heavily
he forces you to sing of miserable suffering and death;
I cannot see how this will end.

Kassandra (slowly rises to her feet):   Now my oracle will no more peek
from under veils like some new-married bride –
no, it will come in radiance, as does the wind   1180
at sunrise, so that miseries far greater than
our present woes will surge like waves towards
the light. I will teach you now in no
more riddles; witness how I run close and scent out
the trail of all the crimes that happened here.
A chorus lives inside this house, and sings
in unison a tuneless melody that does not tell of good.
To gain more courage they have drunk their fill
of human blood, and stay to celebrate an orgy in the house,
impossible to send away – the Furies of this family.   1190
The song they sing as they besiege this house
tells of the first-beginning crime, and turn by turn they spit upon
the brother's marriage-bed in hatred of the man who trampled it.
Well, have I missed – or do I shoot and hit my prey?
Or am I just a phoney prophet peddling nonsense door to door?
You be my witnesses, and swear on oath that I know all
the ancient crimes committed in this house.

Agamemnon 67

1 Elder: But how could any oath, though truly taken, heal	
this wound? I am amazed that you,	
grown up across the sea, can speak about a foreign city with	1200
as much authority as if you had been here yourself.	
Kassandra: The prophet-god Apollo gave this power to me.	1202
1 Elder: Was he, although a god, struck by desire for you?	1204
Kassandra: Before now I was too ashamed to speak of it.	1203
1 Elder: Yes, anyone can have that luxury when prosperous.	1205
Kassandra: He was a wrestler who breathed favour strongly onto me.	
1 Elder: And did you come together to the work of making children?	
Kassandra: No, I consented and then broke my word. [6]	
1 Elder: After you'd been possessed by the god's skill of prophecy?	
Kassandra: I had already told the Trojans of their future sufferings.	1210
1 Elder: How were you not harmed by the anger of the god?	
Kassandra: Since this offence, no one believes a word I say.	
1 Elder: To us, at least, all that you prophesy seems true.	
Kassandra: Ah, Ah! Agony!	

Once more the fearful pain of true prophetic sight
whirls me around inside and vexes me – the prelude to a trance.
Look, can you see these young ones sitting close
beside the house, like in their shape to dreams?
Children, it seems, whom their own relatives have killed,
their hands are full of meat – their own flesh served as food,   1220
a pitiable burden! I can see them holding up
the vitals and the entrails, which their father tasted.
I tell you someone plans to be avenged for this,
a wolf-coward[7] who wallows in the marriage bed,
a stay-at-home takes vengeance on the man who has returned.   1225[8]
Commander of the fleet, sacker of Ilion,   1227
he does not see that soon the hated bitch's tongue
which spoke at length to welcome him with joy
will strike by evil fortune at its target – hidden death.   1230
Such is her daring – she, the woman, is the slayer of
her man; what fearful monster can I call her
and be right? An amphisbaina, or a Skylla lurking
in the rocks, to bring destruction down on sailors;
raging, hellish mother who breathes out relentless War
against her kindred! How she trumpeted her victory,
all-daring, just as if she'd turned the tide in battle –
while she seemed to be rejoicing at his safe return.
And if you don't believe me – well, so what?
        It's all the same.
The future comes, and very soon, if you stay here, you'll see,   1240
and pity me, and call me all too true a prophetess.

68 Oresteia

1 Elder: The feasting of Thyestes on his children's flesh
 I understand, and shudder at it – fear grips me
 to hear these things told truly, not in flights of fantasy.
 As to the rest, I've fallen far outside the track.
Kassandra: I tell you that you'll witness Agamemnon's death.
1 Elder: Silence, unhappy woman; do not speak ill-omened words.
Kassandra: No god of healing governs what I say.
1 Elder: No, not if that's to happen; but I beg it won't.
Kassandra: While you say prayers, they're planning how to kill.   1250
1 Elder: Who is the man preparing for this crime?
Kassandra: You've really lost the path of all my prophecies.
1 Elder: Yes, for I cannot see what means the murderer could use.
Kassandra: And yet I can speak Greek – perhaps too well.
1 Elder: The oracles at Delphi, though they're Greek, are hard to
   understand.
Kassandra: Ah! The fire again! It's coming at me!
 Oh Apollo, wolf-god, let me go!
 A double-footed lioness beds down beside
 the wolf, during the absence of the noble lion.
 She's the one who'll kill him! Like someone preparing drugs   1260
 she'll add my quittance to her brew of hate;
 and as she sharpens up her sword to kill the man
 she'll boast that she is paying him for bringing me back here.
 Why do I still wear all these things that mock at me –
 this sceptre, and a prophetess's woollen bands around my neck?
 I will destroy you now, before I die myself!

Kassandra *throws off the emblems of prophecy.*

 Just go to hell. There, drop; that's how I pay you back.
 Enrich some other girl with misery instead of me.
 Look now, Apollo, no-one else, is stripping me
 of my prophetic garments. He has seen me mocked   1270
 most terribly by 'friends' who were my enemies.
 As if I were a wanderer in search of alms from door to door
 I was called beggar, wretch, and starveling –
 that is what I had to suffer. Now the prophet-god has finished with
 his prophetess, and brought me here to meet my death.
 Instead of our ancestral shrine, a butcher's block waits here for me,
 still warm from the man's bloody sacrifice.

 But yet we will not die dishonoured by the gods;
 for there will come another, one who will requite our fates –   1280
 an offspring who will kill his mother, to avenge his father's death.
 An exile, wanderer, a stranger to this land

Agamemnon 69

he will return to put the coping-stone on all these
      kindred deeds of hate.   1283
For there has been a mighty oath sworn by the gods   1290
that his dead father's corpse will bring him back.   1284
Why do I still lament so piteously?
Since I have seen my native city, Ilion,
suffer the way it did, and those who captured Troy
ending like this under the verdict of the gods,
I'll go; I will begin the rite; I can endure my death.   1289
Now I address these doors as those that lead to Hades;   1291
may I meet one lethal stroke
so I may close my eyes without a struggle,
as my blood streams from me, an easy death.

1 Elder: You are a lady greatly to be pitied; wise as well
in your long speech. But if you truly know
that you yourself will die, how can you tread the path
towards the altar with the courage of an ox driven by gods?

Kassandra: Strangers, there's no escape for any further time.

1 Elder: Last moments are the highest valued.   1300

Kassandra: This day has come. I gain nothing by flight.

1 Elder: Your constancy's the mark of a courageous soul.

Kassandra: Fortunate people never have to hear such words.

1 Elder: Still, a glorious death brings fame.

Kassandra: Oh, my father, and your noble children!

1 Elder: What is it? What fear turns you back again?

Kassandra: Oh! Oh!

1 Elder: Why d'you cry out? Some horror in your mind?

Kassandra: This house breathes out a bloody stench of murder.

1 Elder: That's the smell of sacrifices at the hearth.   1310

Kassandra: The reek is putrid like that from a grave.

1 Elder: You certainly aren't speaking of a Syrian incense
      in the house.

Kassandra: Well, I will go and in the house I will lament
my own and Agamemnon's fate; I've had enough of life.

Oh strangers,
do not think I'm trembling, like a bird scared of the trap;
I simply beg you be my witnesses after my death,
when one more woman dies in recompense for me,
and for the man so badly married yet another falls in turn.
I ask this of you as a stranger who's about to die.   1320

1 Elder: Unhappy one, I pity you the fate you have foreseen.

Kassandra: I want to utter one more speech – or dirge –
my very own; I pray to this, the last
sunlight that I will ever see, that those who come

70 Oresteia

to kill in vengeance for my master take revenge as well
for me, a slave who died, an easy thing to kill.

Oh, the fate of human beings! When prosperous
they're like a shadow; if misfortune strikes
one stroke of a wet sponge destroys the picture.
I pity this more even than our pitiable fate.   1330

Exit Kassandra *into the palace. Doors close.*

Choros 5

Elders: Success is an insatiable danger for
mankind; but no one bars it from the halls
that all men point at, saying:
'Do not come here any more.'
The blessed ones gave this man the great gift
of sacking Troy, and he returned
home honoured by the gods;
so if he now must pay for blood
shed long ago, and by his death causes the dead
to exact further deaths as penalty,   1340
what mortal man could boast that he
was born under a daemon who protects from harm?

Scene 7

Agamemnon (inside the palace):   Oh god, I'm struck a deep and
         mortal wound.
1 Elder: Silence! Who cries that he is struck a deadly blow?
Agamemnon: Oh god, I'm struck again.
1 Elder: From the king's cries I think the deed is done;
let us take common counsel; is there some safe plan?
1 Elder: I'll tell you what I think; let's have a herald tell
the citizens to come and bring help to the royal house.
1 Elder: No; I think we had better break in there at once   1350
and prove the deed while the sword flows fresh blood.
1 Elder: I share his views completely, and I vote
that we do something; it's a time for no delay.
1 Elder: It is quite clear; this is the work of people who
intend imposing tyranny upon the city-state.
1 Elder: Yes, we are wasting time, while they tread underfoot
gracious Delay; their hands are not asleep.
1 Elder: I haven't got a plan to offer; and
no one should act unless he has already planned.

Agamemnon 71

1 Elder: I agree; I do not know how any words   1360
      could bring the dead man back to life again.
1 Elder: Shall we then yield, and just drag out our lives
      subjected to these people who've defiled the house?
1 Elder: It is insufferable; I'd rather be dead.
      That's a less bitter fate than tyranny.
1 Elder: But are we just presuming he is dead
      upon the evidence of those two cries?
1 Elder: We really shouldn't talk about this till we know,
      for guessing is a very different thing from certainty.
1 Elder: I'm filled from every side with votes for this;   1370
      that we must know exactly what has happened to the king.

Doors open. Enter Klytaimestra, *with bloodstained sword, on the* ekkuklēma *over the bodies of* Agamemnon, *covered by a net-like robe and still in the 'silver-sided bath', and* Kassandra.

Klytaimestra: Much I have said before to suit the moment, and
      I'm not ashamed to contradict it all;
      how else could anyone contrive hostilities against an enemy
      who seemed to be a friend, and fence the hunting-nets
      of pain up to a height beyond escape?
      This conflict is the climax of an ancient feud –
      it's been a long time in my mind, but still at last it came.
      I stand just where I struck; the deed's been done.
      And I will not deny that I made sure   1380
      he had no chance to escape or ward off his fate.
      I cast an endless mesh around him, like
      a net for fish – a rich and evil robe.
      I strike him twice, and with two cries
      his limbs went slack, and when he'd fallen
      I give him a third, a votive offering
      of thanks to Pluto, saviour of the dead.
      And as he lies he breathes his life away,
      and blowing out a rapid spurt of blood
      he strikes me with black showers of murderous dew,   1390
      and I rejoice no less than does the growing corn
      in Zeus' rain during the birth-pangs of the bud.

      Elders of Argos, this is how things are;
      be glad, if that's your will, and I will glory openly.
      If it were right to pour libations now
      upon this corpse, this would be just, it would be more than just;
      such was the bowl of cursed evils this man filled
      inside our house, and drains it now on his return.

72   Oresteia

1 Elder: We marvel at your tongue, the boldness of your speech,
 for you to make a boast like this over your husband's corpse. 1400
Klytaimestra: You try me like a woman of no sense,
 but I speak out to you, who know it well,
 with fearless heart; whether you wish to praise me or to blame,
 it's all the same. This is Agamemnon, my husband,
 now a corpse, the work of this right hand,
 a just executant. And that is all.
Elders: (A1) Woman, what evil drug
  grown in the earth, or drink
  sprung from the sea did you consume
  to give the daring for this act of murder? You
  reject and cut away the people's curses; you will be 1410
  cast out, loathed by the citizens.
Klytaimestra: So now you judge it right that I be exiled from this land
 and have the hatred of the citizens and people's curses,
 when he, not caring much about it, just as if an animal was dead
 out of abundant flocks of fleecy sheep,
 killed his own daughter, dearest fruit sprung from
 my labour-pangs, to charm away the winds from Thrace.
 Should you not rather then have driven him out of this land
 to expiate this crime? But when you come to look 1420
 into my deeds, you are a savage judge. I tell you this:
 if you make threats, know I'm prepared
 on equal terms; if someone conquers me by force
 then he may rule; but if the god ordains my victory,
 you'll learn discretion, late although the lesson comes.
Elders: (A2) You aim too high,
  your words are over-proud; your mind
  is maddened by your murderous deed,
  your eyes are flecked with blood.
  Bereft of friends, you will one day pay for this crime
  with blow in turn for blow. 1430
Klytaimestra: Now hear my solemn, righteous oath:
 by the fulfilled Justice of my child, and by
 Destruction and her Fury, goddesses to whom I sacrificed this man,
 fear does not stalk my house
 so long as fire is kindled at my hearth
 by Aigisthos, who now, as always, cares for me;
 he is my mighty shield of confidence.

 Here lies the man who has defiled my womanhood,
 the one who charmed each golden girl he saw outside the walls of Troy,
 and here's the captive, portent-reading 1440
 concubine who gave him oracles,

Agamemnon 73

his faithful mistress, she who rubbed his mast as she lay with him on
the benches of the ship. They have both received what they deserve;
he died as I have told, while she sang her last song,
her funeral lament, just like a swan, and lies
beside him as his lover; she has given me
a dainty side-dish for my feast of sexual ecstasy.

Elders: (B1)   Oh, if only sudden death – not fraught
        with agony or lengthy pain – could come, and bring to us   1450
        eternal, everlasting sleep, now that
        our kind protector's been struck down;
        after enduring much for one woman,
        another woman took his life.

        Demented Helen,
        you alone destroyed those many,
        many lives at Troy; and now
        you've crowned yourself with this last, perfect
        ornament through ineradicable blood. Surely there then   1460
        was in this house a Strife, the sorrow that destroyed this man.

Klytaimestra: Do not pray for death
        weighed down by this,
        and do not turn your anger onto Helen,
        calling her a man-destroyer, claiming she
        alone destroyed the lives of many Greeks,
        creating pain beyond our power to heal.

Elders: (B2)   Oh daemon, as you fall upon this house
        and on Tantalos' two so different descendants,
        you show your power that bites my heart   1470
        through women who are kindred souls; look,
        like a hostile crow she stands
        over the body, and she glories
        in her tuneless song of joy.

Klytaimestra: Now you have mended what you say, invoking him,
        the thrice-gorged daemon of this race;
        through him the thirst for lapping blood
        is nurtured in the belly; before an ancient sore
        is healed, new pus breaks out.   1480

Elders: (C1)   The daemon whom you speak about
        is truly great, and heavy in his wrath
        against this house; an evil song of praise,
        full of insatiable disaster,
        all through Zeus,
        the cause and the contriver of it all;
        for what's fulfilled for mankind without Zeus?
        Is any of this not ordained by gods?

74   Oresteia

Oh my king, my king,
how shall I weep for you?   1490
What can my loving heart tell you?
You lie here in this woven spider's web
breathing your life away, murdered outrageously,
trapped like a slave,
tamed to a treacherous death,
struck by her double-sided sword.

Klytaimestra: You claim the deed was mine?
You're wrong; do not suppose
that I am Agamemnon's wife.
The sharp avenging spirit born   1500
from Atreus' cruel feast
took the shape of this man's wife,
giving him, full-grown,
as crowning sacrificial payment to the young.

Elders: (C2)   Who will say that you
are not at fault in this man's death?
How? How? But still, the spirit sprung
for vengeance from his father might have taken part.
The black War-god forces his way
with streams of kindred blood,   1510
until his path brings payment for
the eaten children's clotted gore.

Oh my king, my king,
how shall I weep for you?
What can my loving heart tell you?
You lie here in this woven spider's web
breathing your life away, murdered outrageously,
trapped like a slave,
tamed to a treacherous death,
struck by her double-sided sword.   1520

Klytaimestra: I do not think his death was slavish:
no – he justly died by treachery
for did not he too lay deceit
and ruin on our house?
He sacrificed my own child whom he had conceived,
my much-lamented Iphigenia, and for what
he did unjustly to her he now suffers
justice; let him not
talk big in Hades, since death by the sword
took payment from him for what he began.

Elders: (D1)   I am bereft of thought's   1530
resourceful care; the house

Agamemnon 75

is falling, and I do not know
which way to turn.
I fear the drumming of this stream of blood
that shakes the house; it is no drizzle now.
Justice is being sharpened for another deed
of harm, at other sharpening-stones of Destiny.

Oh Earth, Earth, if only you
had taken me before I saw him in
this wretched resting-place, the silver-sided bath.   1540
Who will lament him? Who will bury him?
Will you dare to kill
your husband and bewail him too,
unjustly pay his shade a tribute that is no
true tribute for his mighty deeds?
Who will speak the funeral praise
over this godlike man,
and do the task sincerely, tearfully?   1550

Klytaimestra: It's not your business to concern yourself
with this; he fell and died
at my hands, and I'll bury him –
not with laments by people from his home;
no. At the swiftly flowing crossing
of the stream of tears
his daughter, as is right,
Iphigenia, will
embrace and kiss her father lovingly.

Elders: (D2)   Now taunt meets counter-taunt   1560
and it is hard to judge.
The robber's robbed, the killer pays,
and this remains as long as Zeus sits on his throne;
he who does, shall suffer; that is law.
Who could cast the seed of curses from the house?
This family is glued fast to destruction.

Klytaimestra: Your words of prophecy are filled
with truth: but I for my part want
to swear a bargain with the daemon
of this house, to tolerate what's happened   1570
(though it's hard to bear); and for the future
he must leave this house, to wear away
another family with kindred murders.
Keeping just a small amount of all
my wealth's enough, and would content me, if
I've rid these halls of mania for murder.

76 Oresteia

Scene 8

Enter Aigisthos *with armed* Bodyguards, *left.*

Aigisthos: Oh welcome light! This is the day of justice!
        I would say at last the gods avenge mankind
        as they look down from on high upon the sorrows of this earth,
        now I can see this man lie here in woven robes devised   1580
        by Furies, a delight to me, as he pays us in turn
        for all the fearful guile his father's hand contrived.
        For Atreus, when ruler of this land, the father of this man,
        expelled Thyestes from the city and his house
        (Thyestes was my father, let me tell the story
        lucidly) – when there was a dispute about his right to power.
        Later, unfortunate Thyestes came back here as suppliant,
        took refuge at the hearth, and so obtained a safe retreat:
        he did not die and pour blood on his native soil –
        at least not his; to welcome him the godless father of this man   1590
        Atreus, more in eagerness than friendship, entertained
        my father under pretext of a splendid feast,
        and served a meal made of his children's flesh.
        The feet and hands he cut up small,
        concealed them under flesh so they could not be seen, then gave
        this dish to Thyestes, who sat alone; he took and ate
        in ignorance the meal that's brought destruction, as you see,
                upon this race.
        And when he realized the ghastly thing he'd done,
        he cried aloud and fell back spewing out the bitter meat,
        and vowed intolerable death for all the sons of Pelops,   1600
        kicking the banquet-table over as he laid his curse,
        'So perish the whole race of the Pleisthenidai'.
        That is the reason you can see this man lie here;
        and it is just that I contrived this act of murder.
        He drove me, the third child, together with my wretched father
        into exile, still a babe in swaddling clothes;
        but when I had grown up Justice led me back home,
        and I laid hold of this man – though I was not actually here –
        when I devised the many details of this plan of treachery.
        Indeed, even my death would be a joy to me,   1610
        now I have seen him in the net that Justice wove.
1 Elder: Aigisthos, I have no respect for one who gloats among
        misfortunes. You say you killed this man
        of your free will, and you alone contrived his pitiable death;
        then I say in the hour of justice you will not escape
        curses that threaten death by stoning at the people's hands.

Agamemnon 77

Aigisthos: So this is how you talk, as you sit down below
  upon the lower deck, while we, the masters of the ship, are on
      the bridge?
  In your old age you'll see how hard it is
  to learn at such a time of life, when calm discretion is imperative; 1620
  imprisonment and hunger-pangs are two must excellent
  prophets and healers for the mind, even of senile men.
  Have you got eyes, and yet cannot see this?
  Don't kick against sharp spikes, or you will suffer pain.
1 Elder: You woman, did you wait for them to come back from the war,
  and while you stayed at home defiled a husband's bed,
  as well as plotting death against our army's general?
Aigisthos: Here are yet more words bound to end in tears!
  Your tongue is just the opposite of Orpheus';
  for he seduced all creatures by the pleasure that his singing gave, 1630
  while you stir up my anger by your childish barking. You'll
  be led away, and when you're mastered we will see you
      much more tame.
1 Elder: So you will really be our tyrant here in Argos,
  you who planned the murder of the king,
  but did not dare to do the deed yourself?
Aigisthos: Well, the deceit was clearly woman's work,
  while I was suspect as an enemy from long ago.
  I shall attempt to use the wealth of this man's house
  to rule the citizens; if anyone does not obey,
  I'll place a heavy yoke on him – he won't be   1640
  a barley-fattened trace-horse! Darkness has
  a fearful housemate, Hunger, and she'll make him powerless.
1 Elder: Given your evil purpose, why did you
  not slaughter him yourself? Why allow the woman
  to pollute this country and its gods, in killing him
  with you? Oh, if Orestes somewhere sees the light,
  that he may come back here, and with good fortune win
  the victory by killing both of them.
Aigisthos: If that's the way you talk and act, you'll soon know better.
1 Elder: Hey! On guard, my friends; action is coming now.   1650
Aigisthos: Hey! Everyone, sword ready, hilt forward!
1 Elder: I too am hilt-forward, and I do not refuse to die.
Aigisthos: We accept your talk of death, and welcome it.
Klytaimestra: No, dearest man; let us do no more harm.
  So many grievous things have now been done that they will be
      a bitter harvest.
  There has been enough torment already; let us not be stained
      with blood.
  Elders, please go back to your homes; it's better to take thought

78   Oresteia

before you act and suffer; we must all accept what has been done. [9]
If only we could say: 'Here is the end of all our troubles';
we have been mangled terribly by the god's heavy claw.   1660
These are a woman's words, if anyone thinks them worth learning from.
Aigisthos: No. They are aiming empty threats at me,
and chance their luck by throwing out such words.
You lack all self-restraint and sense, to heap abuse upon your master.

The Elders *begin to exit left, some individually and some in small groups.*

1 Elder: It would not be the Argive way to fawn upon so base a man.
Aigisthos: I'll persecute you later on, and be revenged for this.
1 Elder: Not if the god decides to bring Orestes back.
Aigisthos: I know it well; all exiles feed on hope.
1 Elder: Go on, grow fat, soil Justice, while you can.
Aigisthos: You will pay me amends, be sure, for all this foolishness.   1670
1 Elder: Boast and be confident, just like a cock beside his hen.

The last Elders *exeunt.*

Klytaimestra: Take no account of all this idle barking; you and I
will rule this house and order all things well.

Exeunt Klytaimestra *and* Aigisthos *into the palace. Exeunt* Bodyguards *left.
Withdraw* ekkuklēma. *Doors close.*

Notes

1 A subject is needed for the 'utter and insensate rage', and editors have supplied *sph'* ('he', 'she' or 'they'), translating it as 'they' (i.e. the chieftains). But the chieftains have been described in stanza D1 as viewing the sacrifice of Iphigenia as 'a cure more heavy…than the cause itself', so this makes no sense. In Ewans 1975, I argued that *sph'* should be translated as 'she', referring to Artemis; this interpretation was approved by Winnington-Ingram (1983: 85). But it has mostly been ignored, although Artemis is the only person in the narrative who is angry and demanding the sacrifice (see 138, 143).
2 The distance between Mount Athos and Makistos is implausibly long for visibility, and it is possible that a line containing a relay-point between them has dropped out of the text here.
3 Text uncertain.
4 839–41. Some words lost.
5 902. A spurious line has been deleted.
6 There may be a line or two missing here; see Kovacs 1987.
7 I accept Sommerstein's proposal of 'wolf' instead of 'lion' in this corrupt line.
8 A spurious line has been deleted.
9 This whole sentence is corrupt in the manuscripts; I print a possible reconstruction.

Libation Bearers

CAST (IN ORDER OF APPEARANCE)

Orestes, son of Agamemnon and Klytaimestra
Pylades, son of Strophios, Orestes' companion
Elektra, Orestes' sister
The libation bearers
Servant (male)
Klytaimestra
Kilissa, Orestes' old nurse
Aigisthos

80   Oresteia

Open countryside. Pre-set Agamemnon's grave at the centre of the playing space.

Scene 1

Enter Orestes *and* Pylades *right, in travelling clothes and carrying baggage.*

Orestes: Hermes! God below the earth, protector of my father's power,	
become my saviour, fight beside me as I ask you now.	
For I have come back to this land: I'm home once more,	
determined to avenge my father;	3a
he was slaughtered by a woman's hands	3b
with force and secret treachery.	3c
Now here upon his burial mound I call out to my father;	
Hear me! Listen!	

Orestes cuts two locks of hair and places them on the grave.

This is a lock of hair for Inachos, where I grew up;
and this a second lock, a token of my grief.
For I was not here, father, to lament your death,
nor could I raise my hands in tribute when they carried out your
            corpse.[1]

What do I see? Who are those women, all together, clothed in black	10
and coming here? What misfortune could this be?	
Has some new torment fallen on our house,	
or would I be right if I guess that they have brought	
libations for my father, offerings to soothe the dead?	
It's that and nothing else! I'm sure one of them is	
my sister, Elektra, marked out by her special grief.	
Zeus, grant that I avenge my father's death;	
become my ally of your own free will.	

Pylades, let's stand out of the way, so I may clearly learn	20
just why this group of women has come here.	

Orestes *and* Pylades *withdraw out of the playing space into the mouth of the right entrance.*

Enter Elektra *and the* Libation Bearers, *left. The* Libation Bearers *carry jugs containing wine and honey, and a bowl for mixing them.* Elektra *carries garlands.*

Libation Bearers 81

Choros 1

Libation Bearers: (A1)   We have come from the house, sent here
        to bring libations. Sharp blows rained on us.
        Look at these gashes on my cheek –
        they're new, cut by my nails; but for a long time now
        my heart has fed itself on misery.
        We've rent the linen of our clothes in grief,
        we've torn and crushed the fabric round our breasts.   30
        These are disasters which bring no one joy.

     (A2)   A piercing cry rang out,
        it made my hair stand up!
        At dead of night shrill fear, the dream-interpreter,
        roared out its anger in her sleep
        deep in the house,
        and fell in fury on the women's rooms.
        The those who judge the meaning of such dreams
        swore oaths before the gods to tell the truth
        and said it meant that those below the earth
        were furiously angry,   40
        raged against their murderers.

     (B1)   Oh Mother Earth! This is no real favour to the dead!
        That godless woman sent me here
        to ward off torment from herself,
        and I'm afraid to speak the words she wants.
        How can the house be purified, once blood's been shed?
        Oh hearth of utter misery!
        Oh ruined house!   50
        Sunless, hateful mists of darkness shroud these halls
        where the true kings are dead.

     (B2)   Their glory once could not be fought or tamed.
        It found its place in every Argive heart;
        and now it's gone. We're all afraid. Success –
        for everyone that is a god, more than a god.   60
        But Justice holds her scales,
        and swiftly strikes down those in the light,
        while suffering blossoms in twilight.
        Unfathomable darkness holds yet more.

     (C1)   The earth our mother's soaked up too much blood;
        the gore of vengeance clots, and cannot be dissolved.
        A painful Ruin keeps the murderer alive, and sickness
        lasts and lasts.   70

82   Oresteia

(C2) There is no going back for anyone who rapes
      a virgin girl, and just the same
      if every river in the world ran through a single stream,
      even they could never purify
      the man whose hands the blood of murder has defiled.

(C3) The gods imposed their yoke upon my city.
      I was led out from my father's house
      to suffer, fated evermore to be a slave.
      I must approve of everything they do,
      just and unjust; I am compelled   80
      to overcome my bitter hatred.
      I weep beneath my cloak for the
      senseless misfortunes of the rightful kings,
      chilled by hidden grief.

Scene 2

Elektra: Slave-women, keepers of the house,
      since you are here as my attendants
      for this ceremony, please advise me now;
      what shall I say, as I pour these libations at his grave?
      How can I please him? What should I ask of my father?
      Am I to tell him that I bring these offerings from a loving wife
      to her beloved husband – when the gift is from my mother?   90
      I dare not do that; I don't know what I should say
      as I present this offering at my father's tomb.
      Should I use the old form of words that starts:
      'To those who've sent these garlands, grant their just rewards' –
      in this case, that would mean a payment worthy of their evil deeds.
      Or should I just pour out this stream of liquid for the earth to drink
      in silence just as deep as when my father died,
      pay him no honour, then creep off
      like one disposing of the residue from sacrifice,
      and throw away the pot with eyes averted?
      Friends, help me in this quandary,   100
      for we all share a common hatred in our home.
      Don't hide your thoughts inside your hearts through fear.
      If something's fated no one can escape it, whether he
      be free as he was born, or someone else's slave.
      Please tell me; have you thought of anything?
1 Libation Bearer: I reverence your father's tomb as if it were
      a sacred altar; here, as you ask, I'll tell you what I really feel.
Elektra: Please tell me, since you reverence my father's grave.
1 L.B.:   You must say words which show you care for all your friends.

Libation Bearers 83

Elektra:	Who are the people I should call my friends?	110
1 L.B.:	First yourself, and all who hate Aigisthos.	
Elektra:	So this should be a prayer for you and me.	
1 L.B.:	You've realized what you should do; go on.	
Elektra:	Should I add anybody else?	
1 L.B.:	Do not forget Orestes, even though he is no longer in the house.	
Elektra:	That is good; you are right to remind me.	
1 L.B.:	Now, when you get to Agamemnon's murderers –	
Elektra:	What shall I say? Teach me, lead me; I must know.	
1 L.B.:	– pray that some god or mortal man may come –	
Elektra:	To judge them, or to be the instrument of Justice?	120
1 L.B.:	Simply say; to kill them in their turn.	
Elektra:	Would the gods see this as a pious prayer?	
1 L.B.:	How could they not? It's right to pay your enemies	

for what they've done to you.   123

Elektra *kneels, places the garlands on the grave, and takes the mixing bowl.*

Elektra:	Hermes, great herald of the gods above us and below,	165
	help me! Lord of the earth, I beg you be my messenger	124
	and take my prayers to the gods beneath the earth,	
	the guardians of my father's house,	
	and Earth herself, she who gives birth to every living thing	
	and nurtures it, and takes them back again.	

Some of the Libation Bearers *mix wine with milk and honey in* Elektra's *bowl.*

Now, as I pour out this libation to the dead,
I say this, calling on my father: 'Pity me   130
and bring the light back to this house, your dear son Orestes.
For as it is we wander, just as if we had been sold,
and in exchange for us our mother took a man,
Aigisthos, who was with her when she murdered you.
I live like a slave; Orestes is in exile, and bereft
of all his property, while they rejoice
exultantly in all the wealth you laboured for.
Father, I pray to you that by some turn of fate
Orestes may come here – I charge you, hear me!
For myself, make me a better woman than my mother,   140
more chaste, and reverent in everything I do.
These are my prayers for us: but for our enemies
I say that you must be avenged;
the murderers must die, in just reprisal for their deeds.
This I place among my prayers for good;
I have pronounced a curse on them alone.

84   Oresteia

For us, send up your blessings; with the aid
of all the gods, and Mother Earth, may Justice bring us victory!'

These are my prayers; to follow them, I will pour out these offerings;

Elektra *pours the libations.*

custom demands that you must help their power to bloom   150
by crying out in lamentation; sing a song of victory for the dead!

(Choros 2)

L.B.:   Let out a tear! It drops, it dies
         just like the king it's shed for
         as it falls upon this mound,
         defender of good, and enemy of evil.
         Now that these offerings have been poured
         may all pollution be removed.
         Hear me great majesty! Hear me, great king
         although your senses are now dimmed.
         Oh...!

Elektra *sees, and moves to, the lock of hair.*

A man must liberate this house,   160
a strong man with a spear,[2]
a War-god brandishing his bow
in combat, ready for the work,
or fighting hand to hand and sword with sword.

Elektra: My father has his offerings; they've soaked into the earth.   164[3]
            But now, share something new with me.   166
1 L.B.:   What is it? My heart leaps with fear.
Elektra: I see a lock of hair that someone's cut and laid upon the grave.
1 L.B.:   Who could it be? What man or slim girl would do that?
Elektra: Easy. Anyone could guess.   170
1 L.B.:   You must teach me, even though I'm older and you're young.
Elektra: No one but me could have cut off this lock.
1 L.B.:   Yes; those who should be mourning for him are all enemies.
Elektra: Still, it's here, and if you look it's very like –
1 L.B.:   What kind of hair? That's what I want to know.
Elektra: It has a close resemblance to my own.
1 L.B.:   Could it be a secret gift from Orestes?
Elektra: It does look very like his hair.
1 L.B.:   But how would he dare to come here?

Libation Bearers 85

Elektra: He hasn't; he's just sent a cut-off lock, in homage to his father. 180
1 L.B.: We have then no less cause to weep,
  if this means he will never set foot in this land again.
Elektra: Now a wave of bitter bile has surged up to my heart,
  and it's as if a dart had pierced right through me.
  From my eyes thirsty tears pour down
  like winter floods against my will, when I
  look at this lock of hair. How could I think
  that any ordinary citizen could be the owner of such tresses?
  Nor would she, the murderess, have ever dared to offer it,
  my so-called mother, who does not deserve the name   190
  because she's filled her heart with godless hatred for her children.
  But then, how can I simply welcome it, and be sure
  this is adornment from the dearest of all men to me,
  Orestes? I am fawned upon by hope.
  Oh!
  If only it had sense and voice, just like a messenger,
  then I would not be so distracted and confused;
  it could tell me plainly whether I should spit away the hair –
  if it has come from enemies of ours –
  or if it is a kindred lock, and so could grieve with me,
  a true adornment for this grave, an honour given to my father.   200
  We call upon the gods, who know
  that great waves toss us all around
  like men at sea; but when we're fated to survive,
  a small seed often grows into a great tree-trunk.[4]   204

  Oh, this is anguish, and my senses are destroyed.   211

Orestes *and* Pylades *advance into the playing space.*

Orestes: Tell the gods your prayers have been fulfilled;
  now you can pray your future will be prosperous as well.
Elektra: What is it that I've now been given by the gods?
Orestes: You see at last the sight you've long desired.
Elektra: Whom do you think I've prayed for?
Orestes: I know that you have often missed Orestes.
Elektra: But how have I an answer to my prayer?
Orestes: I'm he; do not seek anyone more dear to you than me.
Elektra: Stranger, is this some trap that you are casting round me?   220
Orestes: If I did that, I would be weaving snares to catch myself.
Elektra: Do you just want to mock me in my misery?
Orestes: I would be mocking my own misery, if I mocked yours.
Elektra: So I must really call you by his name?
Orestes: You are so slow to realize now you see me in the flesh;

86   Oresteia

but when you saw this offering of kindred hair,   226
your heart flew like a bird, as if Orestes was before your eyes,   227[5]
Look! Place that lock of hair where it was cut –   230
it is your brother's hair, and much resembles yours –   229
now see this piece of weaving, done by your own hands;   231
here are the strokes of your own needle, this is your design –
       wild animals.
No, no – do not go mad with joy;
for I am well aware our so-called family
are bitter enemies to us.

Elektra: My dearest, darling of your father's house,
beloved hope, seed of salvation,
trust in your strength; you will regain your father's house.
Oh glorious sight! You have four parts to play for me;
I must now turn to you in place of my dead father,
all my mother-love is turned to you   240
because I hate her utterly; and then, my sister-love for her
who was so mercilessly slaughtered – all is yours.
You were a faithful brother, bringing respect back into my life;
may Strength be with you now, and Justice, with the third,
the greatest god of all – lord Zeus!

Orestes: Zeus! Zeus! Look down and witness this!
You see the orphaned offspring of the eagle who has died –
a fearful serpent's trapped him in its coils. They are bereft
of father-love, and suffer pangs of hunger; they're not
       strong enough   250
to hunt food like their father, bring it to the nest.
That's how we are. Here you can see Orestes and Elektra,
children who no longer have a father,
both of us in exile from our home.
And yet our father sacrificed, and paid great services to you;
if you let his young children be destroyed, where will you find
such rich and splendid gifts from other hands?
If you were to annihilate the eagle's brood, you could not send
back any sign of hope to mortal men;
and if this tree of kinship shrivels up and dies   260
we will not be your ministers upon the festive days of sacrifice.
So keep it safe! From such a little start you can raise up once more
a great house, which men now believe
has fallen utterly.

1 L.B.:   Dear children! Saviours of your father's house!
Do not say more; let no one overhear, and
just because he wants to talk, tell all you've said
to those who now command us. How I want to see
them dying, plunged in oozing, boiling pitch!

Libation Bearers 87

Orestes: Apollo's great and mighty oracle will not forsake me.
He ordered me to pass through all these dangers, 270
shrieking out his prophecies; he told
of vile and frosty torments that would chill my headstrong heart
if I did not pursue those who contrived my father's death
in just the same way – meaning I must kill them by deceit. 274
He said that I would pay with my dear life – but first 276
would suffer ghastly tortures; I would lose my heritage 277
and this would drive me mad and violent as a bull. 275
There are – he told me – hostile powers below the earth 278
and there are also terrible diseases,
creatures which invade the flesh with vicious teeth, 280
cankers which eat at healthy skin,
and leprosy, whose ulcers blossom with white hair!
Then Apollo spoke of other enemies; it would not matter
whether I was still alive, or in the underworld,
the Furies would pursue me, springing from my father's blood.
The long dark arrows of the dead below
are sent by suppliants – fathers and grandfathers who died
an unjust death, and cry for vengeance; madness, empty terrors in
            the night
attack, harass, and drive him out
of his own city, shamed with a metal collar round his neck. 290
A man like that is not allowed to share the common bowl
of wine, nor in the pouring of libations among friends.
His father's anger comes unseen to drive him back
from altars; he cannot be welcomed in
to take his rest under another's roof. He'll die at last
unloved, uncared for; he will shrivel up
and end his life in fearful pain.

Should I not trust such oracles as these?
And even if I don't, this still remains a deed that must be done.
Here many different needs fall into one;
the god's command, my father's suffering, 300
and also I am weighed down by the lack of my inheritance –
it is not right that citizens of Argos, noble-hearted men
who gained eternal glory from the sack of Troy
should be the subjects of this pair of women.
For his heart is a woman's; whether I am right or not, he will soon see.

(Kommos)

1 L.B.: You mighty Powers of Destiny,
            may Zeus grant us the outcome we desire,

88 Oresteia

and may Justice prevail.
They speak in words of hatred;
let our words of hatred answer them.
Justice cries out aloud as she exacts her debt: 310
'For bloody blows let bloody blows
take vengeance'. 'He who does, must suffer';
that is the wisdom of the ages.

Orestes: (A1) Oh my father, my suffering, dead father,
What can I say or do to reach
you in the far place where you lie?
The light is very different from the dark;
but just the same a noble act of lamentation   320
will bring some joy to you, great son of Atreus.[6]

L.B.: (B1) Dear son, the ravening jaws of flame
cannot subdue a dead man's powers of thought.
He shows his anger even after death.
We sing his dirge,
he comes for his revenge.
And lamentation for a father,
if stirred up abundantly,   330
will hunt down his murderers.

Elektra: (A2) Now, father, hear in turn
the sorrows which have made me weep.
Here are your two children standing at your grave
to chant the song of lamentation.
Exile and suppliant, this tomb has welcomed us.
Is my life nothing but suffering?
Can we never conquer misfortune?

1 L.B.: The god may still lead us to sing a sweeter song   340
if that is his desire.
Now we are chanting dirges at a tomb –
but may a song of victory soon sound
inside the royal house
and welcome back the new-mixed bowl of wine.

Orestes: (C1) If only you had died at Troy,
my father, cut down by a Lykian warrior's spear;
you would have been revered throughout your halls,
held in high regard
because your children were admired.
Your grave would be a noble mound   350
beyond the sea,
no burden for your house to bear.

L.B.: (B2) His fellow warriors would have welcomed him,
all those who died with glory in the Trojan War;
he is an honoured leader of the dead,

Libation Bearers 89

the servant only of the highest kings,
the gods who rule the underworld.
For while he lived he was a king   360
and in his mighty hands
the sceptre held the power of life and death.

Elektra: (C2) No! My father, you should not even have died
under the walls of Troy!
And not be buried there, beside the waters of
Skamander, with the other warriors.
His killers should have met
their share of death
in just the way he did;
a kind of death so terrible
that far away
men who know nothing of our suffering   370
would hear about it.

1 L.B.: What you are asking is better
than gold, or great good luck.
And you can ask.
But look! Your ceremony is a double lash,
its blows strike home;
our allies are here, below the earth.
The rulers' hands are stained, and they,
the cause of all these sufferings,[7]
pour shame upon your father, even more on you.

Orestes: (D1) This goes straight to my ear   380
like a javelin.
Zeus, send up vengeance, all too long delayed,
for the reckless heart and the daring hand;
the debt I owe my parents
will be paid!

L.B.: (E1) May it only be my right
to sing the blazing song of victory
when he is dead and she has been destroyed;
why should I hide the thought
which always flutters in my heart?
Ahead of my heart's prow   390
blows a harsh wind
of anger, bitter hatred.

Elektra: (D2) When will Zeus in his abundant power
bring down his hand upon them,
smash their heads?
Make pledges to this land!
I ask for Justice to reverse injustice.
Hear me, Earth, and hear me, powers below.

90 Oresteia

1 L.B.:   When drops of murdered blood   400
fall to the earth, they call for yet more blood;
that is the law. Slaughter calls out a Fury
from the bodies of the dead
to pile disaster on disaster.

Orestes: (F1)   Hear me, lords of the underworld;
See us, mighty Curses of the dead,
see the last survivors of the house of Atreus
helpless, cast out from our halls.
Oh Zeus, where can we turn?

L.B.: (E2)   My heart is shaken   410
as I hear this bitter lament.
Sometimes my hope is dim
and I go black inside
listening to your words;
but when I see you strong again
hope easily drives out my anguish;
all will turn out well.

Elektra: (F2)   What should we say to get through to him?
Just tell of the anguish we have suffered?
She can fawn on us, but it will not be soothed.
We are savage, just like wolves;   420
we have an angry spirit stirred up by my mother;
it cannot be tamed.

L.B.:   I beat my breast and sing the dirge
of Asiatic wailing women.
You can see my hands –
they strike, they clutch, they press
spattered with blood,
stretched out from high, from high above
until my head is tortured by the blows.

Elektra: (H1)   Oh my cruel, all-daring mother,
how did you dare   430
to take him out and bury him?
No citizen went with the king,
no one was there to sorrow for him
or cry lament for him. A cruel funeral!   433

L.B.: (I1)   Know this; he was mutilated,   439[8]
She did it when she buried him   440
to make his fate unbearable for you.
Now you have heard the outrages they did your father.   443

Orestes: (I2)   All that you've said humiliated him!   434
Will she not pay for my father's shame?
The gods will help

Libation Bearers 91

       my hands will help
       when I have killed her let me suffer pain.   438
Elektra: (G2)   You tell of how my father died.   444
       I stood apart, humiliated, worthless,
       shut off in my bedroom like some savage dog.
       I needed to conceal my grief; I could not laugh;
       instead I swamped it in a flood of tears.
       Listen to this and carve it on your heart.   450
L.B.: (H2)   Yes, carve it! Let this story pierce
       your ears and come to the quiet depths
       of your mind. This is how things are;
       now burn to know how they will be!
       If you would win, you must not lose your strength.
Orestes: (J1)   Father, I beg you. Help your children.
Elektra: Through my tears I ask this too.
L.B.:   We all echo them;
       listen, come into the light,
       help us against your enemies.   460
Orestes: (J2)   War-god will clash with War-god, right with right.
Elektra: Oh gods, fulfil our prayers; bring justice.
L.B.:   I shiver as I hear them pray.
       The hour of destiny has waited long;
       it may come now they plead for it!
   (K1) Oh suffering innate within the race
       and bloody, hideous discordant stroke
       of utter ruin,
       lamentable weight of grief,
       unbearable disease.   470
   (K2) The house must find
       the dressing for this wound,
       and not from others from outside
       but only from its own,
       through savage, bloody strife.
       This hymn is for the gods below the earth.
1 L.B.:   But hear us, blessed powers of the underworld;
       answer this prayer by sending help.
       Be eager for the children's victory; let them prevail.

Orestes: Father, you did not die a kingly death;
      give me the power I ask for in your house.   480
Elektra: Father, I have this need of you;
      let me contrive Aigisthos' death, and find a man.
Orestes: If you do this you will receive from us the banquets
      you deserve; but if you don't, when other dead feast joyfully
      on rich burnt offerings, you won't receive your share.

92   Oresteia

Elektra: And I will give you offerings, when I inherit all that is my due,
  libations on my wedding-day from our ancestral store.
  This is the tomb which I will honour more than any other one.
Orestes: Oh Earth, release my father, let him watch me fight.
Elektra: Oh goddess of the underworld, grant us the beauty
              of victory.   490
Orestes: Think of the bath in which she murdered you.
Elektra: Think of the net, a foul device.
Orestes: They hunted you with fetters that no blacksmith made.
Elektra: They trapped you in a cloak of shame.
Orestes: Are you not moved by these reproaches?
Elektra: Do you raise up your dearest head, my father?
Orestes: Send Justice up to be an ally for your children
  or else help us to bind them fast, the same as they did you.
  They beat you; don't you want to throw them down in turn?
Elektra: Father, hear one more cry from me.   500[9]
  Look at your offspring as they nestle on this grave.
  Pity us both, the man and woman joined together by their grief.
  Do not destroy us, offspring of the house
  of Pelops; while we live, you live.
  Children preserve a hero's glory past his death,
  just like the corks that hold a net afloat
  and stop the meshes sinking out of reach.
  So hear us. All of this lament has been for you,
  and you'll be saved forever if you honour what we've said.
1 L.B.:   No one could blame you for these many words;   510
  you've given honour to a grave – and to a fate – no one has ever
              mourned.
  But now, since you're resolved, you can proceed;
  test if the daemon's still with you.
Orestes: I shall. But it will not deflect me from my course to ask
  why she sent these libations, what persuaded her to try
  too late to make up for irreparable suffering.
  This was a paltry act of honour for a king
  who's dead. I cannot understand.
  Her gifts are so much smaller than her crime.
  You could pour out all you have in recompense for just   520
  one act of bloodshed, and your labour would be wasted; so the
              saying goes.
  Please tell me why she did it, if you know.
1 L.B.:   I do know – I was there. She was terrified
  by dreams and roving horrors which attacked her in the night.
  That's why the godless woman sent these offerings.
Orestes: Do you know her dream enough to tell it right?

Libation Bearers 93

1 L.B.:   She told us herself; she dreamt she gave birth to a snake.
Orestes: Go on. What was the end of the story?
1 L.B.:   It nestled in its swaddling-clothes just like a human child.
Orestes: This new-born viper, did it want to eat?   530
1 L.B.:   She dreamt that she herself gave it her breast to suck.
Orestes: How could a deadly thing like that not wound her breast?
1 L.B.:   It did – a clot of blood poured out into the milk.
Orestes: This is no empty vision.
1 L.B.:   Screaming in terror, she woke up.
            The braziers were blazing up around the house
            to soothe our mistress – but the darkness blinded them.
            Then she sent these offerings,
            hoping to find a cure that would cut through her torments.
Orestes: But I pray now to Earth and to my father's grave   540
            that this dream may be fulfilled for me, and this interpretation sticks
                  like glue.
            For if this snake emerged from that same place as I
            and then was wrapped in swaddling-clothes
            and put its fangs around the breast that nurtured me
            and made a clot of blood mix with her loving milk
            so that she cried aloud in fright and pain,
            then she, because she nurtured such a terrifying portent,
            must die by violence; I become the snake
            and kill her. That's what this dream says.   550
1 L.B.:   I choose you as my dream-interpreter;
            may you be right! Now tell your friends
            what they must do; for some, this means what not to do.
Orestes: My plan is simple. Elektra is to go inside the house.
            I charge *you* to keep secret all our plans,
            so they, who killed a noble man by treachery,
            shall die by treachery in turn, and die
            in that same net – for so has Loxias ordained,
            the lord Apollo, prophet who has never lied.
            I shall take baggage and disguise myself in travelling clothes   560
            and go with this man, Pylades, right to the outer door –
            he is a friend and ally of the house.
            We'll both assume a dialect – Parnassian –
            and talk the way they do in Phokis.
            It's possible the doorkeepers won't welcome us
            with open hearts, because the gods have filled the house
            with evil fortune. Then we'll stay, so anyone who walks along
            beside the palace will be quite amazed, and say:
            'Why does Aigisthos not received the suppliant at once,
            if he is somewhere in the city and has been informed?'   570

94 Oresteia

But should I cross the threshold of the outer gates
and find him sitting on my father's throne,
or if he comes back home to speak to me –
you may be sure he'll meet me man to man –
before he says: 'Where is the stranger from?', he'll be a corpse,
impaled upon my sword so fast you'll hardly see.
And so the Fury who's not starved of deaths
will drain the third and final cup of kindred blood.

Elektra, you must supervise with care all that goes on inside
       the house,
so that this plan of ours may hold together,   580
while *you* must watch your words almost religiously;
be silent when need be, speak only what will help our cause.
All else, I call on Hermes now to oversee;
guide me, let my sword win the contest!

Exeunt Orestes, Pylades, Elektra *and the* Libation Bearers, *left.*
   Strike Agamemnon's *grave. The façade now represents the palace, as in*
Agamemnon.
   Enter Elektra, *right; she knocks and is admitted at the doors.*
   Enter the Libation Bearers, *right.*

Choros 3

Libation Bearers: (A1)   The earth breeds beasts
           that cause terrible suffering;
           In her embrace the sea
           encompasses a multitude
           of monsters that can kill.
           Up in the sky are comets, meteors –
           like flying torches which harm birds and beasts.   590
           Then think of the hurricane,
           the anger of the storm-wind.

(A2)   But who can find words to speak
           of the ever-daring mind of man
           or woman's love that dares all,
           ruthless passion wedded to disaster?
           When perverted love conquers
           the female, it destroys
           the unions of animals,   600
           the marriages of men and women.

(B1)   So listen! If your thoughts do not fly too high
           learn from the cruel one, Althaia who destroyed her child.

Libation Bearers 95

She lit a blood-red torch
the day he came out, crying,
from his mother's womb.
It followed him throughout his life;   610
when it blew out, his fate was death.

(B2) There is another one to hate in the old tales,
a murderous girl.
She killed her father for her city's enemies,
persuaded by a necklace wrought of gold,
the gift of Minos, king of Crete.
Her father Nisos did not know;
the bitch cut off the lock of hair
that gave him everlasting life   620
as he lay unsuspecting in his sleep.
Death has him now.

(C1)[10] Since I've remembered cruelties
which cannot be assuaged, should I not speak
about the bitter marriage here
that's hateful to the house,
the evil plans which took shape in this woman's heart
against a warrior, a man of glory who
enjoyed respect from all his people?
May my hearth not be warmed by civil strife,
may woman's strength not turn to outrage.   630

(C2) Of all the crimes in legend
the Lemnian is the worst;
people lament and spit it out.
The name of Lemnos is a proverb for
the ultimate in horror.
Polluted, hated by the gods
their race has been dishonoured, cast out by mankind.
No one respects those whom the gods reject.
Am I not right to tell these stories?

Enter Orestes *(with luggage) and* Pylades, *right.*

(D1) The sword strikes to the lungs;
it's sharp, it goes straight through;
Right's driving it!   640
They trampled Justice to the ground;
they broke with everything that's good
and went against the majesty of Zeus.

96   Oresteia

(D2)   The anvil of Justice is planted in the ground.
Destiny's the blacksmith, she forges the sword.
The glorious Fury's planned both long and well,
and now she brings back to this house
a child to make return in time   650
for all the bloodstains of the past.

Scene 3

Orestes: (knocks)

Hey, slave, do you not hear me knocking on the courtyard door?
(knocks)
Is anyone at home? Slave, I'm calling you a second time!
(Pause. Knocks again)
This is my third demand for someone to come out
if Aigisthos allows this house to welcome travellers.
Servant: (inside the palace) All right, I can hear you. *(enters)* Who's the
stranger? Where's he from?
Orestes: Announce me to the masters of this household; say
I've come to see them, and I bring some news.
Be quick, though, since the night's dark chariot   660
is speeding on, *(exit Servant into the palace)* and it's the time
when travellers need to find
a friendly house, where they can drop anchor and feel safe.
Someone should come who has authority –
the woman who is mistress? Better still, perhaps, a man.

Doors open. Enter Klytaimestra *from the palace, attended by* Elektra.

For reticence in conversation makes one's words
obscure. A man can speak with confidence
before another man, and will convey quite clearly what
he means.
Klytaimestra: Strangers, you can tell me what you need; for here we have
all that you would expect in such a house as this –
warm baths, soft beds to charm away   670
your aches and pains, and people round you who are properly
behaved.
But if you want to transact business of importance, then
that is the work of men, and I must share it with them.
Orestes: I am a Daulian; I've come from Phokis.
I've carried all the luggage that I own, and I was on my way
to this place, Argos, where I've now arrived.

Libation Bearers 97

I met a man I did not know, and he did not know me;
but when he'd asked my destination and had told me his,
I learnt his name – Strophios the Phokian; here is what he said.
'My friend, since you are bound for Argos anyway,   680
whatever else you do, remember this; tell his parents that
Orestes is dead – please don't forget!
I don't know if his relatives will want to bring him home,
or if they would prefer to have him buried here, an immigrant, our guest
for all eternity. We mourned him well, and now
his ashes wait, surrounded by the bronze sides of an urn.
Bring their instructions back to me.'
I've said all that I've heard. But I don't know
if you're the people I should really say this to;
I think his father should be told.   690
Klytaimestra: How utterly we are besieged!
Oh Curse upon this house, so hard to wrestle with,
so many things attract your eye – even those we tried to place
out of your way. You bring us down with deadly arrow-shots,
you strip me of my relatives, and I have nothing left.
Orestes now! He was no fool; he kept his feet
far distant from this deadly swamp.
But now the Hope has gone, which was the cure
for those foul Furies' orgy in this house.
Mark down that it's betrayed us.
Orestes: When a host is prosperous like you,   700
I would have liked to introduce myself by giving joyful news
and earn your hospitality. For no relationship is closer than
that between guest and host.
But I felt it would be almost impious
if I had not informed Orestes' relatives
when I had pledged to do so and was welcome here.
Klytaimestra: You will not be received less worthily than you deserve,
nor are you any less this house's friend.
This news would have come anyway; it's all the same.
But now it is the time when those who've spent all day   710
upon the road should be supplied with what they need.
Take him to the apartment for male visitors,
together with his fellow-traveller here,
and let them receive all that they deserve.
I tell you, do this well; you are responsible to me.
I shall report this news to those in power.
We do not lack for friends; we will take their advice about
      this new disaster.

Exeunt Klytaimestra, Orestes, Pylades *and* Elektra *into the palace. Doors close.*

98   Oresteia

Choros 4

1 L.B.:   Now, dear friends, servants of this house
                 when will we show that our lips have the power   720
                 to help Orestes' cause?
L.B.:   Oh mighty Earth, oh mighty mound
                 that now lies piled
                 upon the body of our king, the lord of ships,
                 hear us now! Help us now!
                 This is the time; now sly
                 Persuasion must come down
                 to help us; and Hermes, the ruler of the dark
                 must guide them as
                 they draw their swords and fight.

Scene 4

Enter Kilissa *from the palace.*

1 L.B.:   I think the stranger's up to something.   730
            Look – here's Orestes' nurse, in tears.
            Kilissa, why are you leaving the house?
            Where are you going? Grief goes with you, like
            a fellow-traveller you do not want.
Kilissa: That woman – our mistress – has ordered me to fetch Aigisthos
            as fast as possible to see the strangers, so he may learn this news
            more clearly, man from man. In front of us
            her eyes were sad and full of grief; but it was all a sham
            to hide her joy at news which is so good
            for her, but utterly disastrous for this house,   740
            because of what the strangers clearly said.
            Aigisthos will be overjoyed the moment he is told.
            But as for me – all the old miseries mixed in together
            here in the house of Atreus – they're so hard to bear
            my heart is nearly broken.

            Never have I suffered a grief like this.
            I bore the others and made no complaint,
            but – dear Orestes! I wore myself out for him.
            His mother gave him to me and I brought him up.   750
            He used to cry out in the night and get me out of bed,
            and I did so much work for him – now gone for nothing.
            Babies are just like animals; they never think, and you have got
            to bring them up the way you want.
            When he is still in swaddling-clothes, a baby doesn't tell you

Libation Bearers 99

if he needs food, or drink, or wants to pee –
boys' young bladders have a will of their own.
I had to guess when that was, and I know
I often got it wrong – which meant I had to wash his clothes,
since I was nurse and laundrywoman too.   760
I was skilled at both these jobs,
that's why Orestes' master gave me him to mind.
Now I'm sad. I have been told that he is dead,
and I must go to see a man who has defiled
this house, and will be glad to learn the news.

1 L.B.:   How did she say he should equip himself?
Kilissa: What do you mean? Say that again, so I may understand.
1 L.B.:   Is he to bring his bodyguard, or come alone?
Kilissa: She says he should bring armed men to attend him.
1 L.B.:   Don't tell our hated master that!   770
    Tell him to come alone, as fast as possible – and say it cheerfully,
    so he will listen to you without taking fright.
    The messenger can make a bent word straight.
Kilissa: Are you pleased with what I've told you?
1 L.B.:   Just suppose that Zeus might free us from our misery.
Kilissa: But how? Our only hope, Orestes, is now dead.
1 L.B.:   Not yet. He would be a poor prophet who said that.
Kilissa: What do you mean? Do you know something different?
1 L.B.:   Take your message, do what you've been told.
    This is the gods' concern, and they will handle it.
Kilissa: Well, I will go, and do what you have asked.   780
    May the gods grant it turn out for the best.

Exit Kilissa, *left*.

Choros 5[11]

L.B.: (A1)   Now I ask you, Zeus,
          father of the gods,
          grant success to those who strive for it,
          the rightful owners of this house.
          All I have said is just;
          Zeus, fulfil my words.

    (A1a) Ah! Ah! Now he is in the house
          let him conquer his enemies;
          he will repay you willingly   790
          twice over, three times over,
          if he is raised to greatness.

100   Oresteia

(A2)   Know this! The orphaned colt
       of one who was once dear to you
       is harnessed to a chariot;
       impose a rhythm on his strides,
       grant he not lose his pace;
       let him finish the course.

(B1)   You gods who live inside the house   800
       and tend our glorious store of wealth
       listen, since you are on our side!
       Reach a new verdict, and dispel
       the bloodshed of the past
       with new acts of justice.
       May the old massacres no more
       give birth within this house.

(B1a) Apollo, you who live at the great entrance-way,
       grant that Orestes' house may raise its head in joy,
       and let it see in him with friendly eyes
       the brilliant light of freedom,   810
       freed from veils of darkness.

(B2)   Hermes may justly lend his hand,
       the god who is most apt
       to waft a favourable outcome.
       He makes what's obscure plain,
       he speaks deceptive words,
       he can cast darkness on our sight
       and he is never seen, even by day.

(C1)   Then we shall sing at last! –
       a female song with the wind set fair   820
       for a house set free:
       'All is sailing well!
       That is my glory, mine alone;
       disasters are now far from those I love.'

(C1a) But you! When the moment comes
       take courage.
       If she cries 'Child!', shout back:
       'Truly I am my father's child.'
       Go through with it; you may kill her
       and never suffer blame.   830

(C2)   Your deed is the desire
       both of your loved ones now below the earth

Libation Bearers 101

and of the gods above;
be brave as Perseus;
give bloody murder to the dreaded Gorgon in this house,
and destroy the one to blame!

Scene 5

Enter Aigisthos, *left.*

Aigisthos: I come not of my own accord, but summoned by a messenger.
I understand that certain strangers have arrived
and bring some news that gives me no delight –   840
Orestes' death. This would be a bloodstained burden
for the house to bear, already wounded as it is,
poisoned by bitter murders long ago.
How can I think it is a living truth?
Are these perhaps just fearful, women's words
which leap high in the air, then die in vain?
What can you tell of this to clear my mind?
1 L.B.:   We've heard. But you must go inside
and find out from the strangers. It's nowhere near as good
to let a messenger tell you as if you hear yourself, from
        man to man.   850
Aigisthos: I want to see this messenger and question him carefully.
to learn if he was there and saw Orestes die,
or just reports a rumour he has heard.
My mind has eyes; it cannot be deceived.

Exit Aigisthos *into the palace.*

Choros 6

L.B.:   Zeus, Zeus, what shall I say?
How should I call on you?
I wish him well, but how
can my words be enough
to achieve what is right?
Now bloody chopping-knives will kill   860
and either utterly destroy
the house of Agamemnon for eternity
or else the son will kindle fire and light
for freedom, rule his city and
inherit all the riches of his ancestors.
Such is the contest that godlike Orestes joins.
one against two.
May victory be his!

102   Oresteia

Scene 6

Aigisthos' *prolonged death-cry is heard from inside the palace.*

1 L.B.:   That's it!   870
   (pause)
         What's happened? What's the fate of the house?

1 L.B.:   The end is near; let us stand back,
      so we may seem not to have played a part
      in causing evil things. The battle's finished now.

Enter Servant *from the palace. Doors stay open.*

Servant: Cry out in sorrow for our stricken lord,
      cry sorrow yet again,
      Aigisthos is no more. But open up
      as fast as you can, undo the bolts
      upon the women's doors. It needs a younger man,
      and not to help Aigisthos; he is dead. What can I do?   880
      Hey! Hey!
      I'm calling to the deaf; I'm babbling while they
      waste time asleep. Where's Klytaimestra? What's she doing?
      Her neck is right beside the chopping-block
      with Justice poised to strike.

Enter Klytaimestra *from the palace.*

Klytaimestra: What is it? Why this cry of help to the house?
Servant: I tell you that the living die, killed by the dead.
Klytaimestra: Oh god, I understand the riddle. Now
      we die by treachery, just as we killed.
      Get me an axe at once; *(exit Servant into the palace)*
      Let's see if we are finished, or still have a chance;   890
      this terrible affair has gone that far.

Enter Orestes *and* Pylades *from the palace,* Orestes *with drawn, blood-stained sword.*

Orestes: It's you I'm looking for; *he's* had enough.
Klytaimestra: Oh god, you're dead, my darling, strong Aigisthos.
Orestes: You love the man? Then you shall lie
      together in the grave; he is dead, and you
      will never be unfaithful to him.

Libation Bearers 103

Klytaimestra: Stop, my son; show awe
   before this breast, at which you often drowsily
   sucked with your gums the milk that gave you life.
Orestes: Pylades, what shall I do? Should I not fear to kill my mother?
Pylades: Would you destroy the standing of Apollo's oracles   900
   for all the rest of time, and of his solemn oaths?
   Count all men as your enemies rather than gods.
Orestes: I judge that you have won, and your advice is good.
   Follow me; I mean to kill you at Aigisthos' side.
   In life you thought him greater than my father.
   Now sleep with him in death;
   you loved this man, and hated him you ought to love.
Klytaimestra: I brought you up; let me grow old with you.
Orestes: You killed my father, and you want to share my house?
Klytaimestra: Fate had a certain share in that, my son.   910
Orestes: Well then, it's Fate that brings death to you now.
Klytaimestra: Do you not fear the curses of a mother?
Orestes: No. You gave me birth, but threw me out to suffer pain.
Klytaimestra: Not so, I sent you out to live with friends.
Orestes: I was a free man's son, sold like a slave.
Klytaimestra: Then where's the price I got for you?
Orestes: I am ashamed to name it clearly – you would be disgraced.
Klytaimestra: Your father strayed as well – why don't you mention that?
Orestes: Don't blame the man. He laboured while you sat at home.
Klytaimestra: It hurts a woman not to have a man, my child.   920
Orestes: The man's hard work supports the women who remain at home.
Klytaimestra: I see, my son, you mean to kill your mother.
Orestes: It's you who'll kill yourself, not I.
Klytaimestra: Watch out! Beware your mother's angry, hounding Furies.
Orestes: But how should I escape my father's Furies, if I do not do this deed?
Klytaimestra: It seems as if I'm weeping uselessly, while still alive,
                 before my tomb.
Orestes: Yes, now my father's fate wafts death towards you.
Klytaimestra: Oh god, this is the snake I bore, and nurtured at my breast.
Orestes: How true a prophet was that fearful dream.
   You killed, and it was wrong; now suffer wrong.   930

Exeunt Klytaimestra*,* Orestes *and* Pylades *into the palace. Doors close.*

1 L.B.:   I even mourn for these two, and their fate;
   but now, now that our poor Orestes sets
   the coping-stone upon these many streams of blood,
   we just want this; may he, the eye of the house,
   not fall and be destroyed.

104   Oresteia

Choros 7[12]

L.B.: (A1)   Justice came!
In time the Trojans suffered
heavy punishment.
They came
to the house of Agamemnon
like two lions or two gods of war.
The exile guided by the god of Delphi,   940
sped on his way by wisdom of the gods
has won!

(A1a) Cry out in joy!
Our masters' house
is freed from all its suffering, and from
the wasting of its riches by those two defilers,
lamentable fate.

(A2) She came!
Revenge, whose work is secret war
and stealthy punishment.
And the daughter of Zeus, the faithful one,
guided his hand –
we call her Justice   950
when we name her right –
breathing destructive anger on her enemies.

(B1) She whom our lord Apollo, the Parnassian,
proclaimed without deceit to have
been injured by deceit.
Justice delayed long, but has now attacked
the ingrained wickedness inside this house.
The will of the gods prevails;
they cut away all evil.
It is right to worship the lords of heaven.   960

(B1a) The light is here to see, and the vast yoke
is lifted from these halls.
Oh house, rise up! For too much time
you have lain tumbled on the ground.

(B2) And now great Time, fulfiller of all things,
will pass between our entrance doors,
when all the stain has vanished from the hearth,
and we have purified it, driven all disaster out.

Libation Bearers 105

Fortune has turned; it will be fair of face
and will live happily   970
inside this house.

Scene 7

Enter from the palace on the ekkuklēma Orestes, *sword in hand,* Pylades, *holding an olive branch decorated with wool, and* Elektra, *with the corpses of* Aigisthos *and* Klytaimestra *covered by Agamemnon's net-like death-robe.*

Orestes: Look! Here are the tyrants of our land;
          they killed my father and they sacked this house.
          Then they seemed very grand, both seated on their thrones,
          and I would guess that they are lovers even now.
          They've died together, faithful to their vows –
          for they once took an oath to kill my wretched father
          and die together. That's turned out all right; they've kept
                   their pledge.
          Now, as you listen to these evil things, just look at this,   980
          the horrible device with which they bound my wretched father,
          shackled him both hand and foot.
          Stand round in a circle, stretch it out,
          the inescapable device that made him helpless;   983a[13]
          show this thing with which they overcame a man
          so that the father, Zeus who looks down on us all,   985[14]
          may come, when I am brought to trial,   987
          and be my witness that it was with justice I pursued
          this murder of my mother. I don't count Aigisthos' death –
          he met the lawful fate of all adulterers.   990

          What shall I call this, and be right?   997[15]
          A huntsman's net, or else a shroud-like
          bather's wrap? You surely could well say
          a trap, a net, a robe that hems men in.   1000
          It is the sort of lure a thief might use
          to snare a traveller and rob him of his silver,
          That's a way to make a living! He would warm his heart
          by killing many victims with a trap like this.   1004

          But she – who plotted this foul deed against the very man   991
          whose children she had carried once inside her womb.
          Then she was glad to bear us as her burden, now we are
          her deadly enemies, as you can see...what do you think?
          It she had been a sea-snake or a viper, she could make men's flesh
                   dissolve

106   Oresteia

without a bite, so great her daring
and the power of her evil mind.   996
May such a woman never come to share my house;   1005
I'd be far better dead, struck childless by the gods.

L.B.:   Ah! Miserable deed!
It is a hateful death that you have given them.
Pain blossoms for the living too.

Orestes: Did she do it or not? This robe bears witness for me   1010
how she stained Aigisthos' sword with gore.
The spurt of blood conspires with Time
and they've defeated every dye put on the finely woven cloth.
Now I can praise him, now I am here to mourn him properly,
as I address this web in which my father died.
I grieve for what she did, this suffering, and all our family.
I've won; but my victory is tainted, and no one would envy me.

L.B.:   Ah!
No mortal ever lives his life right through
free both from punishment and harm.
There is pain now, and more will come.   1020

Orestes: You must know now, I do not know how this will end.
I'm like a charioteer who's forced to drive
outside the course; I'm beaten, and cannot control
my senses. Terror comes prepared to sing its song of hate
beside my heart, and join the dance.
While I still have my sanity, I want to tell my friends
I killed my mother not without some justice;
she was polluted by my father's death and hated by the gods.
And for the drug which gave me courage for this deed
I name in chief Apollo, seer of Delphi; for he prophesied   1030
that if I did this I would be beyond the charge
of wickedness; but if I let it go...I will not speak the penalty,
for no one's bow could hit the mark of such an agony.

Pylades *hands him the wreathed olive branch.*

That's why you see me now, prepared.
With this young olive branch and wreath of wool
I shall approach the navel of the earth,
the shrine, Apollo's sacred place
and the bright blaze of fire that we are told
is everlasting. There I will escape this stain

Libation Bearers 107

of kindred blood. For Loxias instructed me
that I should not turn to another hearth than his.
And now I bid all Argives, in the time to come, 1040
remember how these evil things were done,
and testify for me to Menelaos if he should return.[16]
I am a wanderer, an exile banished from my native land;
living or dead, I leave behind me nothing but my fame
as an avenger and a matricide.[17]

1 L.B.: No. You have done well; do not let your mouth be forced
to speak ill-omened words; do not let evil touch your lips.
You liberated our whole city-state of Argos when
you cut with ease the heads off those two snakes!

Orestes: Ah! Ah!
These frightful women! Gorgons
robed in grey, and intertwined with myriads
of snakes. I can no longer stay. 1050

1 L.B.: What are these visions spinning you around,
Orestes, dearest to his father of all men?
Be strong; do not give way to fear; you've won so much.

Orestes: These are no fantasies of evil; I can see
they are my mother's enraged hunting dogs.

1 L.B.: The blood is fresh still on your hands;
that's why your senses are confused.

Orestes: Oh lord Apollo! There are more and more of them,
and loathsome pus is dripping from their eyes.

1 L.B.: There is one cure; Loxias can touch you with his hands;
he will release you from these sufferings. 1060

Orestes: You do not see these creatures; I see them.
They drive me from this place; I cannot stay.

Exit Orestes, *right.*

1 L.B.: May you find good fortune! May the god
look kindly on you, and protect you with his timely help.

Choros 8

L.B.: This is the third storm
to vent its rage
in the royal house.
First was the pitiable torment of
the eating of the children;
then, the death of a king, 1070
when Agamemnon, leader of the Greeks in war,
was slaughtered in his bath.

108   Oresteia

> Now he has come, the third, the saviour –
> or should I call this death?
> Where will it end? When will it be sated,
> lulled to sleep, the force of destruction?

Withdraw ekkuklēma. *Exeunt* Pylades, Elektra *and the* Libation Bearers *into the palace. Doors close.*

Notes

1 Much of Orestes' speech, perhaps originally around thirty to forty lines long, has been lost, since the first page is missing from the only surviving manuscript of *Libation Bearers*. However, quotations in other authors allow us to restore over nine lines before the manuscript resumes at 10 and so provide a playable prologue.
2 Text corrupt; I print a possible reconstruction.
3 165 relocated to after 123.
4 Omitted (see Theatrical Commentary, p. 174)

> 205–10. Here is a second sign – some footprints! Look.
> They match, and they are similar in shape to mine.
> These are the outlines of two pairs of feet,
> those of the man himself and of some friend;
> and as I measure them the heels, the contours of the tendons, all
> are in proportion with the prints I made!   210

5 228: 'and when you followed in my footsteps like a hunter' omitted.
6 *prosthodomois*, 'in front of the house' is corrupt, and impossible to retain, since it implies that Klytaimestra buried Agamemnon near the palace, which she would never have done after mutilating his body. See further note in the Theatrical Commentary, pp. 177–78.
7 The text is corrupt, and I translate West's suggestion.
8 439–43 transposed to before 434–8 to give motivation – the fact that Klytaimestra mutilated Agamemnon's corpse – for Orestes' outburst.
9 Many editors divide this speech between Elektra and Orestes. This is wrong; Elektra needs her plangent swansong before being reduced to a silent character in the remainder of the play.
10 Some editors transpose this and the next stanza, so that Klytaimestra's deed comes last. But the main part of the Choros should end with the worst of all crimes committed by females, the massacre on Lemnos.
11 The whole of Choros 5 is very corrupt in the manuscript, and there are a good number of conjectures in this translation.
12 The whole of Choros 7 is very corrupt in the manuscript, and there are a good number of conjectures in this translation.
13 A line cited in an ancient commentary on Euripides' *Orestes* has been restored.
14 986. A spurious line is omitted.
15 The transposition of 991–6 is necessary, as the focus on the net needs to be completed before Orestes turns to speak about Klytaimestra in 991ff.
16 Menelaos is clearly mentioned in the manuscript of this line, which is otherwise corrupt and needs restoration.
17 A conjecture fills a gap in the text.

Eumenides

CAST (IN ORDER OF APPEARANCE)

Priestess of Apollo
Apollo, god of prophecy
Orestes
A dream-image of Klytaimestra
The Furies
Athena, goddess of wisdom
Herald (trumpeter)
Eleven male jurors (silent roles)
Women and girls of Athens

110   *Oresteia*

The façade represents a temple.

Scene 1 (a)

Enter Priestess, *left.*

Priestess: First of the gods I honour in this prayer
      the Earth, first prophetess. And then Themis,
      goddess of Right, the second – so the story tells –
      to sit here on her mother's throne of prophecy. The third –
      and by consent; there was no use of force –
      was yet another Titan daughter of the Earth,
      Phoibe, who gave this oracle, the day that he was born,
      to lord Apollo, who inherited from her his other name, Phoibos.
      He left the marshy lake and rocky isle of Delos,
      beached his ship on Pallas' busy shores,   10
      then came up to this land, where Mount Parnassos lies.
      He was escorted with great reverence by Athenians,
      who tamed a savage land and smoothed the way for him.
      When he came here, the people greatly honoured him;
      so did the king, Delphos, the helmsman of this state.
      Zeus breathed the heavenly skill of prophecy
      into Apollo's mind, and set him as fourth prophet on this throne.
      He is called Loxias – the prophet of the Father, Zeus.
      These are the gods I honour now, in my first prayer.   20

      Pallas Athena, she whose shrine is near this oracle,
      deserves my reverence; and the nymphs, whose cave of Korykis,
      beloved of birds, the gods frequent.
      Dionysos also rules this place – I don't forget –
      since he led out an army of Bacchantes, and contrived
      the death of Pentheus, ripped to pieces like a hare.
      I call upon the streams of Pleistos and on lord
      Poseidon; last, I pray to Zeus, the great accomplisher,
      and now I go, to sit as prophetess upon the throne.
      May the gods grant this session be my best   30
      by far; if any Greeks are here, they may come in –
      draw lots first for your places, as the custom is.
      All that I utter will be as the god directs.

Exit into the temple.

Re-enter Priestess *from the temple, crawling on all fours.*

      A sight too terrible to see or speak about
      has sent me back out of Apollo's Hall.

Eumenides 111

I have no strength, I cannot stand –
I run, but on my hands and knees, not on my feet.
When frightened an old woman's nothing, just a child.
As I was going to the inner shrine, where laurel hung with
      wool adorns
the temple, I saw on the very navel of the earth   40
a man abominated by the gods, posed as a suppliant.
His hands were dripping blood; he held a new-drawn sword, also
a branch of olive, bound up reverently by a long band
of shining wool; about this I can speak with clarity.
But just in front of him there sleeps
a terrifying crowd of women resting on our seats.
Not really women – they were more like Gorgons;
but I cannot truly liken them to Gorgons
nor to Harpies – for I saw a picture once
of Harpies stealing Phineus' feast, and they   50
had wings; but these have none, and they are black
and horrible in every way. They're snoring,
and the stench around them is unbearable.
Disgusting streams of filth
pour from their eyes. Their garments are unfit to be
worn near the images of gods or in the homes of mortal men.
I've never seen the tribe from which this band of predators
has come, nor can I guess how any land could nurture them
and live unscathed to tell the tale without regret.

What happens now will have to be the care   60
of Loxias himself, the mighty master of these halls;
he is a lord of healing, he can read prophetic signs,
and he has often purified the homes of other gods and men.

Exit Priestess, *left.*

Scene 1 (b)

Enter Orestes *from the temple in anxiety and haste, followed by* Apollo.

Apollo: I will not betray you; I will guard you to the end;
both when I stand near by you, and when far away,
I never will grow soft towards your enemies.
So now you see these rabid creatures overcome;
they've fallen into sleep, the loathsome virgins –
haggard, aged children, whom none of the gods,
no man nor beast, has ever mingled with.   70
For evil they were made, and evil is that gloomy

112   *Oresteia*

Tartaros where they hold sway beneath the earth;
they're hated by mankind and by the gods.
So much for them. You must escape, and not grow weak;
for they will drive you through the length of Greece.
You must stride on across the earth, your wanderings will tread
        it down
over the sea, and to the island cities which the sea surrounds.
Do not grow weary; tend this labour
like a herdsman – only rest when you have come
to Pallas' city; clasp her ancient image in your arms.   80
There we will have men who can judge this case,
and words to charm them; we will find a way
to free you utterly from all these sufferings.
For I persuaded you to take your mother's life.

Orestes[1]:   Lord Apollo, you know better than to harm your suppliant;
with all your knowledge, do not harm him by neglect.
Your strength for doing good is worthy of men's trust.

Apollo: Remember that; do not let terror conquer you.

Exit Orestes, *right.*

Now brother, son of my own father,
Hermes, guard him! Answer to your name;   90
be his escort, tend my suppliant as if you were
his shepherd, as you lead him back into the world of men;
for Zeus reveres an outcast's sanctity.

Exit Apollo, *into the temple.*

Scene 1 (c)

Enter A Dream-Image of Klytaimestra, *right.*

Klytaimestra: You wish to sleep? Hey! What use are you asleep?
Because I get no help from you, the other dead reproach me
        ceaselessly;
I wander in disgrace! I tell you that
I bear a heavy burden for their deaths.
These grievous torments were inflicted by my own blood-kin   100
and yet no god is angered by my fate,
though I was slaughtered by the hands of my own son!
Look at these wounds, and let them strike your heart;
for when it sleeps the mind has eyes![2]

Eumenides 113

You have lapped up my many offerings –
wineless libations, soothing draughts.
I've given many solemn feasts for you
beside the fiery hearth at dead of night, the hour that's yours alone.
And now all this is trampled underfoot;   110
he sprang into the air and vanished like a fawn.
How easily he leapt out from the middle of
your tightest nets and made great fools of you!

Now you have heard me speak about the very life-blood
of my soul: awake to wisdom, goddesses of Earth below;
I am Klytaimestra, and in your dream I summon you.

Furies: *(from inside the temple; moaning)*
Klytaimestra: You may well moan; but he has now fled far away.
    The suppliant is not devoid of friends.
Furies: *(moaning)*   120
Klytaimestra: You sleep too much, you have no pity for my suffering;
    I am the mother murdered by Orestes, and he has escaped.
Furies: *(groaning)*
Klytaimestra: You groan, you sleep; get up at once!
    What other duty have you but to cause him pain?
Furies: *(groaning)*
Klytaimestra: Hard work and sleep are powerful conspirators;
    they've drained off all the deadly venom from the snake.
Furies: *(moaning, twice as loud)*
    Get him, get him, get him. There!   130
Klytaimestra: You're hunting in a dream! You're barking like
                    a sleeping dog
    that can't forget its need to kill.
    What are you doing? Up! Do not succumb to toil;
    do not let sleep make you ignore what has been done to you.
    Let my complaint torment your hearts; the honest soul
    is spurred to action by a justified reproach.
    Blow out your bloody breath against that man,
    waste him away with blasts of inner fire,
    pursue him once again until he drops!

Exit, right.

1 Fury: *(in the temple)* Wake up! And now wake her as I have
                 woken you.   140
    Do you still sleep? Get up, and kick away your slumber –
    let's find out if that dream was false.

114 *Oresteia*

Choros 1

Enter Furies *in ones and twos, from the temple.*

1 Fury: (A1) Oh...! Oh...! We have been wounded, friends.
1 Fury: How many wounds I've suffered, all unjustified.
1 Fury: Now we've been wounded terribly; Oh, this is unbearable.
1 Fury: The quarry's leapt out from the trap and gone;
 sleep conquered me and I have lost my prey.

1 Fury: (A2) Oh son of Zeus, you are a thief!
 You are still young, and you have ridden roughshod over
 ancient goddesses 150
 by rescuing the godless suppliant
 who was his mother's bitter enemy.
 You are a god, and yet you stole the matricide away.
 Would anybody say that this is just?

1 Fury: (B1) While I still slept, reproaches came in dreams
 and struck me like a horseman with his whip
 in the belly, in the liver.
 I feel the chill, the heavy chill, 160
 the icy whip-lash of the executioner!

1 Fury: (B2) This is the sort of thing the younger gods all do,
 ignoring justice; I can see
 a throne that reeks of slaughter
 head to foot!
 Here, on the navel of the earth,
 the horrible pollution of fresh blood!

Furies: (C1) Prophet, you have of your own will defiled the shrine
 and brought pollution onto your own hearth; 170
 by helping him you have destroyed the gods' own laws
 and all the ancient ways of Destiny.

 (C2) I hate Apollo, and he will not help that man escape.
 Orestes never will be free, even below the earth.
 He is a murderer, and even there
 he'll bring a new avenger down upon his head.

Scene 2

Enter Apollo *from the temple, armed with a golden bow and arrows.*

Eumenides 115

Apollo:	Get out, I tell you, leave my house at once;
	you must be gone from this prophetic shrine 180
	or you will feel a gleaming arrow's bite
	winged on its way by my bow's golden cord.
	The pain will make you spit black foam
	and puke up all the clotted human gore you've quaffed.

It is not fit that you draw near these halls:
your home's the slaughterhouse where heads are lopped,
eyes are gouged out for vengeance, boys' young manhood is destroyed
by cutting off their testicles; where men are mutilated, stoned
to death, and groan with piteous cries
impaled on stakes. Do you not realize 190
it is because you love such hideous feasts
that all the gods spit you away? The way you look
tells the whole story; creatures such as you
should live inside the lairs of lions that feast on blood,
rather than grind pollution into soil as pure as this.
Get out, you flock without a shepherd; there's no god
who would delight in herding you.

1 Fury:	Lord Apollo, listen to us in return.
	You are yourself not just a part-conspirator in these events;
	in every way your actions show you are their cause. 200
Apollo:	How? You may speak long enough to tell me that.
1 Fury:	Did you not give an oracle that he should kill his mother?
Apollo:	That he should punish those who killed his father; what of that?
1 Fury:	You then stood ready to receive him with the blood
	fresh on his hands?
Apollo:	I did, and told him he must come here as a suppliant.
1 Fury:	And now you slander us because we follow him?
Apollo:	Yes, you're not fit to enter such a shrine.
1 Fury:	But this has been ordained; it is our task.
Apollo:	Oh, really? Let me hear it; boast about your splendid privilege.
1 Fury:	It is our duty to pursue a matricide from house and home. 10
Apollo:	Well, what about a woman who has killed her husband?
1 Fury:	She would not have killed a true blood relative.
Apollo:	Then you reduce to nothing and despise
	the sacred vows of marriage, sanctified by Zeus
	and Hera the fulfiller; you dishonour and reject Kypris,
	the goddess who gives humankind their closest bond.
	The bed, where man and woman are united by their destiny –
	Justice defends that even more than sacred oaths.
	And so if you are less than strict in your pursuit of murderers,

116   *Oresteia*

and don't exact a penalty or visit them with all your anger, then   220
I say you have no right to persecute this man;
for now I find that some misdeeds enrage you, while
on others it is obvious you take a softer line.
The goddess Pallas will watch over how this case comes out.

1 Fury: I will not ever let him go.
Apollo: Well then, pursue him. Give yourself more toil.
1 Fury: Don't try to cut my privileges down by words.
Apollo: I wouldn't want to have your privileges.
1 Fury: No; whatever happens you are held in high regard beside the throne
             of Zeus.
             But I – since I am driven on by mother-blood –   230
             will go in search of justice. I will hunt Orestes to the end!

Exeunt, right.

Apollo: And I will give protection, and will save my suppliant;
             the anger of a man who turned to me for refuge would be terrible,
             among both men and gods, if I could help, and failed.

Exit into the temple.
    *The playing space is empty. Preset a statue of Athena, centre. The façade now
represents a temple at Athens.*

Scene 3

Enter Orestes, *right.*

Orestes: Lady Athena, I have come at Loxias' command;
              receive this wanderer with kindness.
              I am not now a suppliant with unclean hands;
              no – my pollution's lost its edge; it has been worn away
              in other houses, other paths of men.
              I've crossed both land and sea, and all the way I've kept   240
              Apollo's orders in my mind; goddess, I now approach
              your temple and your holy image. I will stand guard here
              and wait until the outcome of my trial.

Enter Furies, *right.*

1 Fury: Look! Here's a clear sign of the man,
             a silent accuser; follow where it leads!
             We'll hunt him out the way a dog tracks down
             a wounded fawn – by following the trail of dripping blood.

Eumenides 117

1 Fury: This manhunt has exhausted us – our lungs
are short of breath. Our flock has roamed the earth,
and flown across the ocean fast as ships, although   250
we have no wings. I know he's cowering somewhere here;
the smell of human blood smiles on me now.

(Choros 2)

1 Fury: Look – and look again!
1 Fury: Look everywhere, don't let
the mother-killer flee unharmed.
1 Fury: Here he is – in safety!
Wrapped around the image of the goddess, now
he wants a trial to free him from his deed.   260
1 Fury: But that can never be. His mother's blood upon the ground
can never be recalled.
It soaked into the earth and vanished. In return
I will demand red clots to gulp
from your own living limbs; you are to be
my noxious drink, and when I've sucked you dry
I'll take you to the underworld
where you will pay with agony for all your mother's pain.
1 Fury: There you will meet the other criminals
who've shown no reverence to the gods,   270
to travellers or parents –
all receive the treatment that their deeds deserve.
1 Fury: Below the earth Hades the great accountant calls
all human beings to their final reckoning.
Nothing escapes his eye; it's all engraved
upon the tablets of his mind.

Orestes: My sufferings have taught me, and I know
what's right to do in many things, including when
to speak and to be silent. Now in this affair
a wise instructor's told me I must speak.
The blood I shed is drowsy now; it dies away and leaves my hand.   280
A matricide's pollution can be washed away.
For it was driven from me, while still fresh,
at the god's hearth; Apollo purified me by the ritual sacrifice of swine.
The story would be long, if I spoke now of all
the people I approached without inflicting harm.   285[3]
And now from a pure mouth I solemnly entreat   287
Pallas Athena, ruler of this land, to come
and be my helper; she will gain without a war
myself, my country, and the Argive citizens   290

118   *Oresteia*

as just and faithful allies for the rest of time.
She may be far away – perhaps in Africa,
her birthplace by the streams of Triton;
then, she may be marching or advancing cautiously
to help her friends; perhaps, bold general that she is,
her eye is turned upon the plain of Phlegra.
Goddess, come! For you can hear me, even far away;
become my saviour, free me from these creatures here!

1 Fury: Neither Apollo nor Athena's strength
will save you; you will wander as an outcast,   300
never knowing joy – a bloodless shadow,
feast for daemons.

1 Fury: Nothing to say? You spit away my words,
you who were nurtured for me, consecrated as my sacrifice?
No slaughter at the altar; I will feast on you
while you still live. Now, victim, hear
this song that binds you fast.

Choros 3

1 Fury: Come, let us dance;
we are resolved
to show you all our fearful power of song,
and tell you how we carry out   310
our tasks among mankind.
We say that we are fair;
when a man can show pure hands
none of our anger chases him,
he lives his life unharmed;
but if someone offends us like this man,
and tries to hide his murderous hands,
then we appear! We are the victim's ever-truthful witnesses:
we are there to help her; we exact
the final penalty for blood.   320

Furies: (A1) Oh mother who gave birth to me, oh Mother Night,
to be chastiser of the living
and the dead; hear this!
Leto's whelp has cheated me –
he stole away this hare,
my proper sacrifice to cleanse
the murder of his mother.

(A1a) This is a song
for the one who is doomed;
a blow to the heart that smashes the mind,   330

Eumenides 119

a song of the Furies to bind his wits,
a horrible sound to shrivel a man.

(A2) Destiny spun this, dealing death,
    as my unchanging duty, fixed for evermore;
    if any man uses his hands
    to murder kindred, then
    we follow him until he goes
    beneath the earth – and even dead
    he is not free of us.   340

(A2a) This is a song
    for the one who is doomed;
    a blow to the heart that smashes the mind,
    a song of the Furies to bind his wits,
    a horrible sound to shrivel a man.

(B1) These duties were ordained for us when we were born.
    We keep away from gods; we have
    no fellow-banqueters to join our feast.   350
    I do not share in their white robes
    or in their joyous company.

(B1a) For I have chosen overthrow of houses!
    When War becomes innate within a family,
    and kin strike down their kin,
    then we pursue the murderer;
    however strong he is, we make him weak
    till he is drained of blood.

(B2) I'm eager to remove these troubles from the world;   360
    my labours keep the gods immune
    from worry – they don't even have
    to start inquiries. Zeus has ruled
    that we are bloodstained, hateful, and
    may not approach his company.

(C1) Men's dreams of glory on this earth
    all melt and vanish underground, discredited,
    when our black forms advance   370
    and our feet dance vindictively.

(C1a) I spring high up;
    I bring my foot right down with crashing force.

120 *Oresteia*

My limbs are dangerous; I'll trip
the fastest runner, and his fate is death.

(C2) He doesn't know this – his pollution maddens him,
such is the cloud of filth that hovers round;
and people weep to tell
of the dark mist upon his house.

(D1) This stands forever; we are skilful,
and complete our task.
We do not forget the wicked, we are awesome,
we cannot be bribed.
We do the work the gods disdain,
that no god gives us credit for,
in sunless darkness; we are sheer and hard
for both the living and the dead.

(D2) So! Is there anyone who does not feel respect
and fear of what we do   390
when he has heard the final rights that destiny decreed
and that the gods conceded us?
I retain my ancient privileges;
no one has yet dishonoured me,
although I live beneath the earth
in darkness where the sunlight never falls.

Scene 4

Enter Athena *right, in armour and wearing her aegis.*

Athena: I heard your cry for help, though I was far away,
taking possession of the land beside Skamander, which
the leaders and the chieftains of the Greeks
made over to me roots and all for evermore –   400
by far the greatest part of all the wealth won by their spears,
a special gift to the Athenians.
My feet cannot be wearied; I flew here
without the use of wings, by brandishing my aegis.   404[4]

These visitors are new to me;   406
I have no fear, but wonder strikes my eyes.
Who are you? I am speaking now to all of you,
both to the stranger sitting at my image
and you – you do not look like any other race,   410
not kin to any goddesses the gods have seen,

Eumenides 121

nor are you similar in shape to mortal women…
But to speak ill of guests who've done no harm,
that is not right; it would be far from just.

1 Fury: Daughter of Zeus, you will learn all at once;
we are the everlasting children of the Night;
we are called Curses in our home beneath the earth.
Athena: I know about your ancestry, the names and titles that you bear.
1 Fury: Now you will quickly learn our role in life.
Athena: I would learn that if someone tells me clearly.   420
1 Fury: We hunt down murderers, and drive them from their homes.
Athena: Is there a limit to the killer's flight?
1 Fury: A place where there is never any thought of joy.
Athena: And now you're hounding him to such a fate?
1 Fury: Yes, for he thought he had the right to be his mother's executioner.
Athena: Was he forced to do it? Did he fear the anger of someone?
1 Fury: Where is the goad sufficient to compel the crime of matricide?
Athena: Here are two sides, but only half an argument.
1 Fury: He won't affirm on oath that he is innocent.
Athena: You'd rather be renowned for justice than be just in all
                    you do.   430
1 Fury: What do you mean? Show me, for you are wise.
Athena: I say injustice must not win by oaths.
1 Fury: Well, you look into it; find out which case is right.
Athena: Would you trust me with how your accusation ends?
1 Fury: Why not? We'll pay you the deserved respect for your respect for us.
Athena: Stranger, what do you want to say against this in your turn?
                Tell me your fatherland, your ancestry and all your sufferings,
                and then defend yourself against the charge they bring,
                if you sit there and guard the image near my hearth   440
                because you trust in justice, if you are
                a solemn suppliant like Ixion.
                Respond to all these points with clarity.
Orestes: Lady Athena, first I will remove
                the great concern expressed in your last words.
                I do not come unpurified; I did not take my place
                beside your image with pollution on my hands.
                And I will tell you a great proof of this;
                it is the custom for a murderer to stay
                in silence till someone with power to purify
                has cleansed him of the blood, by slaughtering a new-born
                    animal.   450
                This sacred rite was done for me in other places, long ago,
                with other animals than yours, and other flowing streams.
                And now you'll swiftly learn my parentage.

122   *Oresteia*

I am an Argive, and you do well to inquire
about my father, Agamemnon, gatherer of men of war,
with whom you made the city of the Trojans, Ilion,
into a desert. But when he came home
he died ingloriously; my black-hearted mother murdered him –
she trapped him in a many-coloured hunter's net   460
which still remains as witness of the slaughter in the bath.
When I returned (I had been long in exile), I
killed my own mother – I will not deny the deed –
to punish her with death for my own, dearest father's death.
And Loxias is equally responsible with me;
he spoke of torments which would be like lashes to my heart
if I did not do something to my father's murderers.
Now you decide the case – if I was right or not;
whatever happens to me here, I will be satisfied.

Athena: This matter is too large, if any human being thinks   470
that he could try it; even I have not the right
to judge the issue in a case of murder where hot tempers rage –
especially since you have come here to my halls
schooled by your sufferings, a pure and harmless suppliant,   474[5]
while they...they have a duty which we cannot simply
        disregard,   476
and if they do not win the victory
the arrows of their pride will come back afterwards
and fall upon our soil, a horrible and everlasting blight.
So that is how it is; to let you stay, or make you go –   480
either alternative is hard for me, and will bring harm.
But now, since this affair has fallen onto us,   482
I will choose blameless men of Athens,   475
judges of murder, faithful to their oath,   483
which I will now establish for the rest of time.
Then you must call your witnesses, and show your proof –
sworn testimony which will aid your case.
I shall select the best of all my citizens,
not led by unjust thoughts to violate their oaths,
and then return to give true judgement here.

Exit Athena, *left.*

Choros 4

Furies: (A1)   Now it would be the overthrow   490
        of our established laws
        if his outrageous case

Eumenides 123

for mother-murder won.
Mankind would then unite
in a new harmony of hands
ready for crime.
It's true!
Parents must then expect
that wounds will be inflicted by their offspring
evermore.

(A2) We are the watching maenads;
       but our wrath will cease to fall
       on those who do vile deeds.   500
       I will let every kind of death run wild!
       Crying out about their neighbours' woes
       they will search eagerly both far and wide
       for some relief from suffering –
       but in vain,
       with remedies that do not work.

(B1) Let no man call on us
       when he is beaten down by suffering, and cry out loud:
       'Oh Justice,   510
       Sacred Furies' –
       as perhaps a father
       or a mother who has just been hurt
       cries out in agony, because
       the house of Justice has collapsed.

(B2) There is a place where Fear is good,
       and needs to sit as silent guardian
       on watch over the mind;
       it's right that pain should teach good conduct.   520
       How could any man or any city that does not
       nurture an element of fear inside the heart
       still worship Justice?

(C1) It is wrong to praise
       the life of anarchy
       or that subject to tyranny.
       In all things God has given victory –
       whatever end they reach –   530
       to those who take the middle path.
       Let me tell you a word that matches this;
       Violence is the true child of Impiety;

124   *Oresteia*

a healthy mind will lead
to that prosperity which all adore
and long for.

(C2) I tell you this;
    worship the altar of Justice,
    don't kick it down with godless feet   540
    and dishonour it for gain.
    A penalty will come;
    the end is final, and it waits for you.
    Reverence your parents,
    welcome strangers, wait on them;
    so should you live.

(D1) The man who willingly serves justice
    will not lack prosperity!   550
    He will not be destroyed.
    But anyone who dares to stand against us lawlessly,
    and carrying the spoils of wickedness piled up,
    sooner or later he'll be forced to lower sail,
    the moment that disaster strikes
    and breaks his yard-arm.

(D2) There he is, struggling in the middle of the whirlpool –
    no one hears him!
    Then the god laughs, to see the man   560
    of fiery blood, who never thought he could be trapped,
    beyond escape, and so exhausted by his peril that
    he can't get clear.
    His lifelong wealth has foundered on the reef
    of Justice, and he perishes
    unseen and unlamented.

Scene 5

Enter Athena, *left, followed by a* Trumpeter.

Athena: Herald, gather my people;
    let the shrill Etruscan trumpet,
    filled with human breath, give out its piercing cry
    up to the heavens to summon them.
    Then, while the court is filled, there must be silence.   570
    I shall state laws which everyone must learn,
    both my whole city for the rest of time
    and those here now, so that this case may be tried well.

Eumenides 125

Fanfare. Enter Eleven Citizens of Athens*, left. They bring benches and a table with two voting urns.*

    Enter Apollo*, right.*

Athena[6]:   Lord Apollo, use your power only over what is yours.
     Tell us what part you play in this affair.
Apollo: I come to testify – for this man is my suppliant,
     he came to Delphi, took the ritual place before my hearth,
     and he was purified of murder at my hands –
     also to be his advocate; I am responsible
     for this man's murder of his mother. You, bring on the case;   580
     decide the outcome as you best know how.
Athena: I now bring on the case; it is your turn to speak.
     For if the prosecutor speaks first at the start
     then he can teach us truly what the issues are.
1 Fury: Though we are many, we shall not say much.
     You must now answer word for word.
     First tell us if you killed your mother.
Orestes: Yes, I killed her. No one can deny the fact.
1 Fury: Here is the first of the three wrestling throws.
Orestes: Don't boast; I'm not yet down.   590
1 Fury: But you must still tell us just how you killed her.
Orestes: Yes, I shall; with sword in hand I cut her throat.
1 Fury: Who then persuaded and advised you to do that?
Orestes: Apollo's oracle. And he is my witness.
1 Fury: The prophet counselled you to kill your mother?
Orestes: Yes, and till now I have not blamed my luck.
1 Fury: If the vote catches you, you'll tell a different tale.
Orestes: I have faith; from the grave, my father will send help.
1 Fury: So you put faith in corpses, mother-murderer?
Orestes: Yes, deep pollution touched her twice.   600
1 Fury: How? You had better tell the jurors what you mean.
Orestes: She killed her husband, and she killed my father.
1 Fury: So what? You're still alive, while death frees her from punishment.
Orestes: Why did you not pursue her into exile while she was alive?
1 Fury: The man she murdered was not her blood-kindred.
Orestes: Am I then kindred to my mother's blood?
1 Fury: Foul murderer, did she not nurture you
     inside her womb? Do you renounce the dearest life-blood
        given by your mother?
Orestes: Now you must testify, Apollo; give your counsel and explain
     if I had Justice with me when I took her life.   610
     I did it; that is true, and cannot be denied;
     but was the bloodshed just or not? What do you think?
     Give me your judgement, so that I can tell the court.

126   *Oresteia*

Apollo: You are Athena's mighty court of law; all I will tell you now
        shall be with justice. Then, I am a prophet, and I never lie.
        Not one word have I spoken from my throne of prophecy
        about a man's, a woman's, or a city's fate
        that is not by Zeus' order – Zeus, the father of the gods.
        Well now, think what a powerful point of law that is.
        I do advise you to follow my father's will;   620
        there is no oath which has more strength than Zeus.
1 Fury: So it was Zeus, you say, who granted you this oracle
        to tell Orestes that he could avenge his father's death
        with no account at all paid to his mother's rights?
Apollo: Yes. For it's not the same as when a man has died –
        a noble man, with royal sceptre granted by the gods –
        this at a woman's hands. She did not kill him with
        far-shooting, savage arrows like an Amazon,
        but in a manner which I shall tell you, Pallas,
        and you who sit with her to judge this matter by your votes.   630

        He had come from the war; his judgement had been good
        in most of what he did. She welcomed him with kindly words;
        she poured warm water in a silver bath, and then
        as he was stepping from it, at the end,
        she threw a robe right over him and struck him down –
        her husband, shackled by the close and endless meshes of the robe.
        There; that is how he met his end,
        a man revered by everyone, commander of the fleet.
        I've told you in this way, so all those people may be stung
        to wrath, who have been chosen to give judgement in this case.
1 Fury: According to your speech, Zeus gives the greater weighting
                     to a father's death,   640
        but he put his own aged father Kronos into chains;
        how can you reconcile these points?
        Jurors, I call on you to witness this.
Apollo: You utterly revolting beasts, hated by all the gods,
        fetters can be removed – there is that cure,
        and many ways in which release is possible;
        but once a man has died, and thirsty dust
        has sucked up his black blood, he cannot be restored to life.
        For this my father has produced no counter-song,
        although he turns and orders all things else   650
        at his desire with undiminished energy.
1 Fury: Beware; do not regard this as a valid plea for his release.
        Your client spilt his mother's blood upon the earth;
        will he then live in Argos, in his father's halls?
        Will he officiate before the public altars of the city?

Eumenides 127

What brotherhood will let him share their sacred rites?
Apollo: I'll answer that as well; mark how I tell the truth.
    The person called the mother is no real parent
    of a child; she simply nurses foetuses once they've been sown.
    The parent is the man, who mounts; the woman is a hostess   660
    who preserves a stranger's offspring – if they are not harmed by
         any god.
    Now I will show you living proof of what I say.
    A father can beget a child without a mother; see, right here
    as witness stands the child of Zeus himself;
    she was not nurtured in the dark depths of a womb,
    yet she is such an offspring as no goddess ever bore.

    Pallas, I promise now as best I can
    to make your city and its army great in many ways.
    That's why I sent this man to take his refuge at your hearth.
    so that he might be pledged to you for all the rest of time.   670
    You would gain this man, goddess, as your ally,
    and his heirs – and it would be so evermore;
    all his descendants would be faithful to the pledge made here.

Athena: Have you both said enough? Shall I request
    the jurors to consider and return their votes?
Apollo: For our part, every arrow that I have has been unleashed,
    and now I wait to hear the judgement of the court.
Athena: Well then, how shall I act and not be criticized by you?
1 Fury: You've heard what you have heard, and as you cast your votes,
    good citizens, revere within your hearts the oath you took.   680

Athena: Now hear the law I set for you, Athenians,
    as you cast the first judgement in a case of bloodshed.
    People of Aigeus, you will have this court
    of judges for the rest of time.
    Here they shall sit upon this rock, where Amazons
    once pitched their tents because they held a grudge
    against Theseus. They marched against us, built
    a high-walled rival to our citadel, and sacrificed
    to Ares, god of war. That's why it bears his name,
    this rock, the Areopagos, a place where reverence   690
    for all our fellow-citizens will soon become inborn, and so
    restrain injustice day and night alike –
    provided that the people don't destroy their ancient customs;
    if you allow polluted flows of muddy water in,
    you'll ruin your clear streams and never find a place to drink.
    Athenians, I beg you reverence and maintain

128   *Oresteia*

a life neither anarchic nor beneath a tyrant's rule –
and do not cast all elements of fear outside your walls;
what man stays just if he has naught to fear?
So if you reverence and fear a court like this   700
then you will have a fortress for your land, a saving grace
upon your city like no other men,
unequalled by barbarians or other Greeks.
This place of counsel, free from bribes,
inspiring awe, sharp in its anger, wakeful guardian
when others are asleep – I found it now.

That speech was my advice, extended
to our future citizens; now you must rise
and take your votes and judge this case,
in reverence to the oath you took. I have said all.   710

The Eleven Human Jurors *step up, one during each of the following speeches,
and cast their votes into the first, active urn. They discard the other pebble into
the second urn.*

1 Fury: We are a heavy burden on the land;
            I counsel you, whatever else you do, do not offend us.
Apollo: And I advise you hold in awe my oracles
            (they come from Zeus) and do not make them fruitless.
1 Fury: You've interfered in bloody murders which aren't your concern;
            now you'll give oracles from a polluted shrine.
Apollo: My father's judgement was in error, then,
            when he protected Ixion, the first suppliant murderer?
1 Fury: You've said it! And if I don't get fair treatment here
            I'll settle, as a heavy burden, on this earth.   720
Apollo: You have no credit with the older gods
            or with the younger; I shall win.
1 Fury: It's just the kind of trick you played at Pheres' house;
            you got the powers of Destiny to make a mortal live for all eternity.
Apollo: Was it not right to help a worshipper of mine,
            especially when he stood in need of help?
1 Fury: You plied the ancient Fates with drink, and then
            broke down the fundamental order of the world.
Apollo: You will not win this case; soon you will vomit out your poison,
            harmless to everyone, even your enemies.   730
1 Fury: You, though a younger god, are riding roughshod over me;
            so now I wait to hear the outcome of this case,
            still in two minds whether to vent my fury on this city.

Athena *has approached the urns with her voting pebbles in her hands.*

Eumenides 129

Athena: It is my task to cast the final judgement here;
  and I will give Orestes' cause this vote.
  There is no mother who gave birth to me;
  in everything I'm for the male with all my heart (except
  I would not marry one); I am the true child of my father Zeus.
  And so I will not give a greater status to a woman's death
  who killed the man, the guardian of the house.   740
  Orestes conquers, even if the judgement comes to equal votes.
  Now cast the lots out of the urns, quick as you can,
  those of the jurors who have been assigned this task.

The votes are counted.

Orestes: Phoibos Apollo, how will the contest end?
1 Fury: Night, my black mother, do you look on this?
Orestes: Here I shall die by strangling, or shall live and see the light.
1 Fury: And we shall wander outcast, or preserve our rightful role.
Apollo: Be careful, friends, in counting out the votes –
  and as you sort them, see injustice is not done.
  Without good care great damage might result,   750
  and just one vote can save a house.
Athena: *(after scrutinizing the ballots)*
  The man escapes the penalty;
  the votes are equal on each side.

Exit Apollo, *right.*

Orestes: Oh Pallas, you have saved my house,
  and have returned me to the native land
  of which I was deprived. The Greeks will say:
  'He is an Argive once again, and now he lives
  on his ancestral property; all this is due
  to Pallas, Loxias, and Zeus the third, the Saviour and
  fulfiller of all things' – for he paid tribute to my father's death   760
  and saved me, though he had to face my mother's advocates.
  Now I shall go back home – but first
  I pledge my oath to Pallas and her people
  for the future, for the whole eternity of Time
  that never shall the man who rules my city dare
  to lead our splendid army out against this land.
  I will use all my power, out of my grave,
  and will wreak havoc if there should be anyone to break
  these oaths which I swear now; I'll make their road
  a hopeless journey, blasted by counter-omens   770
  so they will regret their toil.

130   *Oresteia*

But if this oath is kept straight, and they aid
Athena's city by supporting you in war,
then I shall be more favourable to them.

So now farewell! Farewell to you and to the people of this place;
may you possess a wrestling-stance no enemy can beat,
so you'll preserve your city and gain victory in war!

Exit Orestes, *right.*

FINALE

Furies: (A1)   You younger gods, you override
                the ancient laws, and snatch them from my hands.
                We are deprived of all we live for; in our misery   780
                our anger will be terrible, and we'll let
                the poison fly out from our hearts
                to cause this country suffering in return –
                unbearable! The blight will drip
                to kill your crops and children.
                Justice! Justice!
                I will rush down to the plain, and pour into the earth
                the blight that will destroy all human life.
                I weep. What shall I do?
                They laugh at me. In Athens I have suffered terribly.   790
                We are the miserable, greatly suffering Daughters
                        of the Night;
                no one respects us, so we grieve.

Athena: Let me persuade you not to take the trial so heavily.
            You were not beaten – no, the case truly came down
            to equal votes, and took no credit from you;
            shining testimony was brought to us from Zeus,
            and he who gave the oracle stood as witness to the truth;
            Orestes had to do this and receive no punishment.
            So you should not cast down your heavy fury   800
            on this land; do not be angry, do not wreck
            our fruits with dripping poison from your breath,
            a deadly froth that will devour the seed.
            For I now promise you as fairly as I can
            a place below the earth to live, here in a land
            devoted to the cause of Justice; you shall rest
            on gleaming thrones beside the hearth, and all
            my citizens will pay you the respect that you deserve.

Eumenides 131

Furies: (A2) You younger gods, you override
the ancient laws, and snatch them from my hands.
We are deprived of all we live for; in our misery   810
our anger will be terrible, and we'll let
the poison fly out from our hearts
to cause this country suffering in return –
unbearable! The blight will drip
to kill your crops and children.
Justice! Justice!
I will rush down to the plain, and pour into the earth
the blight that will destroy all human life.
I weep. What shall I do?
They laugh at me. In Athens I have suffered terribly.   820
We are the miserable, greatly suffering Daughters of
the Night;
no one respects us, so we grieve.

Athena: You have not been discredited. You're goddesses, and
should not be
so furious with mortals, nor desire to wreck their land.
Besides, I have my confidence in Zeus, and (need I mention this?)
I am the only god or goddess who can open up
the chamber where his thunderbolt is sealed.
But we do not need that. Let me persuade you, and
do not inflict your reckless threats upon this land,   830
to make blight fall on all its fruit.
Please lay to rest the bitter force of that black wave of bile;
for you are deeply honoured here, and may soon share my
dwelling-place.
Then you will praise my words, since for the rest of time
you will receive the first-fruits of this splendid land
in offerings whenever there is childbirth, or a marriage solemnized.

Furies: (B1) Me to suffer this!
Ah! Me with the wisdom of old age
to live beneath the earth,
dishonoured and despised!
Ah!
I breathe out fury, and let loose my rage.   .   840
Ah! The pain beneath my ribs.
Oh mother Night!
I have been parted from
my ancient privileges by the clever tricks
of these deceitful gods; I am of no account.

132   *Oresteia*

Athena: I will tolerate your fury; you are older;
            then, in many ways, you are the wiser too,
            although I have a little wisdom granted me by Zeus.   850
            But if you go off to another, foreign land
            you will then long for Athens. I foresee – the flowing course
            of Time will bring greater renown
            to these my citizens, and if you have a place
            of honour near the palace of Erectheus
            an endless line of men and women will present to you
            gifts you would never get from any other race.
            This is my country; do not cast on it
            bloody strife that sharpens knives and causes wounds
            when young men rage in anger, maddened not by wine   860
            but by your venom; do not give them hearts that seethe
            like fighting-cocks by planting in my citizens a God
            who makes them fight each other, in the strife of civil war.
            Let war be with our enemies, it won't be hard to find –
            that war in which men will enjoy the fearful love of glory.
            Domestic, civil violence is no proper contest; so I say.

            That is the sort of gift that you may take from me;
            do well here, you will fare well here, and you will take your place
            with honour and reward; the gods all love this land.

Furies: (B2)   Me to suffer this!   870
            Ah! Me with the wisdom of old age
            to live beneath the earth,
            dishonoured and despised!
            Ah!
            I breathe out fury, and let loose my rage.
            Ah! The pain beneath my ribs.
            Oh mother Night!
            I have been parted from
            my ancient privileges by the clever tricks
            of these deceitful gods; I am of no account.   880

Athena: I shall not rest from telling you these blessings;
            you will never say that I, a younger goddess,
            and my citizens evicted you and made an older god
            wander away dishonoured and rejected from this land.
            So if the glorious goddess of Persuasion has some sanctity for you –
            she who gives to my words a honeyed and a soothing charm –
            you'll stay; and if you still don't want to, then
            you could not fairly let the scales of harm
            or anger tilt against this city, injuring its men of war.

Eumenides 133

	For here you have a chance to be part-owner of this land	890
	for ever, given all the privileges you deserve.	
1 Fury:	Lady Athena, what is this place you say I'll have?	
Athena:	One free from every kind of pain; please take it.	
1 Fury:	Well, suppose I do; what privileges will I have?	
Athena:	That no one's home may flourish unless you approve.	
1 Fury:	You'll really do this, grant me so much power?	
Athena:	Yes, I will give prosperity to those who reverence you.	
1 Fury:	And you will give your word on this for all the rest of time?	
Athena:	Of course; I would not speak of anything I will not do.	
1 Fury:	You seem to soften me; my rage abates.	900
Athena:	Then you will live under our land and gain new friends.	
1 Fury:	How would you have me bless this place?	
Athena:	With songs fit for a glorious victory;	

       blessings both from the earth and from the sea
       and from the heavens; pray for breaths of wind
       on sunny days to sweep across the land,
       and that the earth's fruit and abundant wealth of herds
       may never cease to flourish for my citizens,
       and human seed be fertile – and especially
       that of those people who revere the gods.   910
       For I am like a gardener, and I will cultivate
       the race to which these righteous men belong.
       All that is in your power; while I shall never cease,
       in any combat where men show distinction in the arts of war,
       to honour this city of victories.

Furies: (A1)   I will accept, I will live with Athena;
       I will not hurt the city
       which is ruled by Zeus the conqueror
       and Ares, guardian of the gods –
       the glorious city which defends
       the altars of the gods of Greece.   920
       I wish it well; I pray
       the bright light of the Sun will make
       the blessings of good fortune
       burst in abundance from their soil.

Athena: This I am doing because I love my citizens;
       I have inspired these goddesses both great and hard to please
       to settle here; for they have power
       in all affairs of men.   930
       If anyone encounters their hostility
       he doesn't even realize they've struck him down.
       For all the errors of his ancestors
       drag him into their net, and silent death,

134   *Oresteia*

for all his mighty noise,
grinds him to dust beneath their rage.

Furies: (A2)   Diseases will not blight their trees
(I tell you of the favours I shall bring);
no fiery heat will trespass here
to rob plants of their buds.   940
No terrible and crop-destroying plague
will creep up on them.
May Pan ensure
that their crops thrive,
and bring to birth twin lambs
at the appointed time.
This land is rich in minerals;
may its inhabitants always repay
with offerings the lucky finds
the gods have given them.
Athena: Guardians of the city, do you hear this,
what they are promising?
A Fury can do much, and has great power   950
both with the gods above and those below;
and in the world of men, it's clear they always work their will
right to the end – some they give cause to sing,
to others a life dimmed by tears.

Furies: (B1)   I say their men must not endure
untimely death.
Grant their lovely maidens
men to live with – all you gods who have that power,   960
especially the goddesses of Destiny,
my sisters,
powers of Right;
you have a share in every house's fate,
and you are seldom gentle;
but you never come without a cause,
and so you are the most respected of the gods.
Athena: As they fulfil these pledges
of such favour to my land
I'm happy, and I thank Persuasion –   970
she guided my speech
when they were angrily refusing me.
Zeus, God of the assembly, won the day;
and now we are competing to do good
we have the victory for evermore.

Eumenides 135

Furies: (B2) This is what I pray;
   that civil war, the most insatiable of miseries,
   will not rage here;
   so may the dust not drink
   the citizens' black blood   980
   through lust to take revenge,
   embracing ruin for the city by
   a mutual slaughter;
   may they give each other joy,
   may they unite in friendship,
   may they hate as one!
   That is the cure for many human sufferings.
Athena: Do you not see?
   They are trying to find
   words that will lead us on the road to good.
   From these terrifying faces   990
   I see great advantage for my citizens;
   for if you pay great kindness to these kindly ones,
   you will keep land and city on the path
   of Justice, and be glorious in every way.

Furies: (C1) Hail then, hail Athenians!
   You're destined to be rich –
   you sit close by the throne
   of Zeus' virgin daughter, her dear friends,
   wise at the proper time.   1000
   Zeus the Father reverences the people who
   live under Pallas' wing.

Enter Priestess of Athena, Women And Girls of Athens *left, twelve carrying crimson robes for the Furies, others bearing torches, and one leading a sacrificial cow.*

Athena: Hail to you too; I must go first
   to show you where your chambers lie
   as this escort lifts the sacred light.
   Go now beneath the earth; and we will speed you there
   with solemn sacrifice to keep
   destruction down below, and send us everything
   that will bring profit to the city
   for its victory. Now you,
   descendants of Kranaos, keepers of this city, 1010
   you must lead these honoured immigrants;
   the citizens must fully understand
   the good they do.

136   *Oresteia*

Furies: (C2)   Hail, hail, and now farewell;
               all of you – both men and gods
               who live in Pallas' city –
               as long as you revere your new-found immigrants
               you'll never have to blame what happens in your life.   1020

Athena: I praise you for these blessings;
               I shall escort you now, while torches shine and light our way,
               to those deep places down below the earth,
               with these attendants who keep watch beside my image;
               come to the heart of Theseus' land, oh famous ones.
               < These Furies I now name the Solemn Goddesses;>[7]
               clothe them in garments rich in crimson dye,
               and honour them; let fire advance
               so they may make their friendly presence felt   1030
               by giving us the glorious gift of manly strength!

Escort: (A1)   Go now to your home, oh great and honour-loving
               ageless daughters of the Night; we are your friends
               and we escort you.
               People of the country, keep silence.

       (A2)   In the ancient depths of the earth
               may you receive great honour,
               gifts and sacrifices.
               People of the city, keep silence.

       (B1)   Graceful to us, and strict in your goodwill,   1040
               Solemn Goddesses, rejoice as you go
               upon your way lit by our torches;
               raise a glad shout in answer to our song!

       (B2)[8]   These torches mark your everlasting bond
               with the Athenians. Zeus who sees all
               and Destiny came down to aid our truce;
               raise a glad shout in answer to our song!

Exeunt Athena, Priestess, Torchbearers, Solemn Goddesses, Jurors, Remaining
Women and Girls, *left.*

Notes

  1 Some scholars transpose Orestes' three-line response to precede Apollo's speech.
    For the reasons why this is wrong, see the Theatrical Commentary, p. 197.
  2 This is a great line and should not have been deleted by some editors.
  3 286. An interpolated line has not been translated.

Eumenides 137

4 405. An alternative line, which has Athena enter on a chariot, has been deleted as an interpolation for a later production which sought to make her entrance more spectacular. See Theatrical Commentary, p. 215 n.16.
5 475 relocated to after 482.
6 The assignment of this speech has been disputed. In our performances I preferred to give it to a Fury, but now I think this was wrong; there is a good case for Athena to rebuke her fellow god for his intrusion, and the Furies already know what part Apollo has played in this affair.
7 A line is missing, since Athena needs to give the Furies their new title before the Women and Girls of the escort name them as the Solemn Goddesses at 1041.
8 The last stanza of the trilogy is unfortunately corrupt in the manuscripts. This is an approximate reconstruction.

Theatrical Commentary

Agamemnon

Dramatic Structure and Form

Agamemnon is formed around the king's return from the Trojan War.[1] During the first half of the drama, Klytaimestra perverts all the normal customs which underlie a Greek homecoming. The hope of a successful return which the Watchman expresses in Scene 1 is progressively removed. We see the ever-increasing power of Klytaimestra, as her successive engagements with the Elders and the Herald establish her possession and control of the playing space. At the same time, we see the hope of a safe return for the Trojan expedition gradually diminished, and Agamemnon comes home alone, in just one ship, having lost Menelaos and all the rest of the fleet. Gods do react to human actions; the returning fleet was scattered by a mighty storm because the Greeks had pillaged their altars during the sack of Troy (338ff., 526–7, 648–9).

Aeschylus uses the Elders' songs/dances to blur the audience's sense of time, so the key stages can be presented consecutively, even though in real life the action of Scenes 2, 3 and 4 would have been separated over several days (between Scenes 2 and 3, perhaps weeks). Klytaimestra's actions create the Elders' complex blend of hope and increasing apprehension as they respond in Choroses 2 and 3 to the events unfolding before them. Their first ode describes the horrendous sacrifice of Iphigenia, which portends vengeance within the palace (150–3); Choros 2 ends with the bleak thought that 'the gods unfailingly mark out/those who've killed many' (461–2), and Agamemnon's arrival is immediately preceded, at the end of Choros 3, with the thoughts that 'ancient Violence always breeds/a new, young Violence' and '[Justice] cannot respect/the power of wealth when falsely stamped/with praise' (764–5 and 778–80). This development is ominous in the extreme for the king, who is the son of a murderer, killer of his own daughter and sacker of Troy.

Klytaimestra's triumph over Agamemnon at the mid-point, in Scene 4, is so effective – and the setback, when Kassandra refuses to obey her in Scene 5 and forces her to delay the sacrifice, is so telling – precisely because these scenes are the culmination of her intrigue. The gathering momentum of Klytaimestra's perversions of ritual, sacrifice and ceremony[2] gives a compelling feeling of tragic inevitability to the climax, the death of Agamemnon; by dramatizing all

DOI: 10.4324/9781032646992-7

142   *Theatrical Commentary*

this and adding on top of it the revelations of the Kassandra scene, Aeschylus fulfils his primary aim of explaining why the death of the king took place.

In *Agamemnon*, the *skēnē* building represents the house of Atreus, and Aeschylus exploits its resources: the flat roof in Scene 1, the threshold and the double doors from Scene 2 onwards and the *ekkuklēma* in Scenes 7 and 8.

The first half of the drama uses words, music and movement alone; the only props are the walking-staves on which the Elders lean. The absence of props symbolizes in theatre terms the emptiness of a kingdom without a king[3] and so reinforces the expectation and apprehension as everyone in Argos waits for Agamemnon's return. Klytaimestra's ever-increasing power is indicated by the fact that she alone enters and exits through the doors of the house of Atreus and does so at moments carefully chosen by herself for maximum effect.[4]

Then, at the mid-point of the drama, Aeschylus deploys in rapid succession two remarkable visual images: Agamemnon's return, alone in a carriage with Kassandra beside him, and then the robes which Klytaimestra orders her maids to strew between him and the entrance to the palace.

Scene 4 is focussed around the carriage, the robes, and the doorway to which they mark the path. The most important and dominant focus in the Greek playing space is normally the centre-point. Aeschylus now exploits the fact that when they are in use the double doors inevitably pull the focus back away from it and make the line from C to EBC the main axis for establishing presence.[5] (Actors are most powerful in an arena configuration when they advance down this line; they start to lose power only when they pass C and begin to advance towards EFC, as from C forwards the portion of the audience to whom the actor is not presenting his face increases rapidly.)

Then the robes are removed, and Scene 5, in which Klytaimestra attempts to persuade Kassandra to leave the carriage, is focussed around the now vacant space between carriage and doorway. The carriage is removed for Scene 6, in which Kassandra (who up until now, as she has stayed silent and motionless, could herself be regarded as another, very striking property) dominates the action with the first solo actor lyrics in *Agamemnon*. Although this scene uses the entire playing space, it increasingly focuses on Kassandra's interaction with the palace doors, which have remained open since Klytaimestra's last departure – and on the route, formerly marked out by the robes, which Kassandra must follow, in Agamemnon's footsteps, to meet her fate.

In the first half, the absence of properties allows Aeschylus to create a complex interaction between the past events recalled in the three wide-ranging choral odes and the developing situation in the dramatic present. After Agamemnon's arrival, the only two choral odes are brief responses to the specific situation in which the Elders find themselves at the end of Scenes 4 and 6; the remainder of *Ag* is focussed around the use of properties in the space and the power of the threshold. However, the pressure to which events have built up by this time permits Aeschylus to compose two intense lyric scenes for choros and solo actor (Scenes 6 and 7).

After Kassandra has gone in, the Elders are helpless; for the first time since Agamemnon's arrival, they are left alone in the playing space without a prop or person to interact with. They are rapidly relieved of their confusion; Klytaimestra appears on the *ekkuklēma* in triumph over the bodies of Agamemnon and Kassandra, and the last third of the drama crystallizes around her defence of, and the Elders' attack on, her deed. The corpses remain visibly present, and centrally in the thoughts of the characters and the audience, from the moment they are first displayed until the end of the play. The final third of the drama explores the consequences of the murder of Agamemnon, and fore-shadows the return of Orestes to avenge it, which is prophesied by Kassandra and hoped for by the Elders (1273ff., 1667).

Scene 1

This scene establishes the return of Agamemnon, and the reception which he will receive on his arrival, as the main action of the drama (cf. especially 34–5).

In Homer,[6] Aigisthos posted a Watchman to warn him of Agamemnon's arrival in Argive territory. Aeschylus significantly changes the story; Klytaimestra has set this Watchman at his post, and she transcends gender expectations in a way which the original audience would have found sinister and dangerous. She exhibits 'masculine' planning ability (10–11) and shows at once that the initiative will be with her and not with Aigisthos. It is Klytaimestra's purpose to know as soon as Troy has fallen, not just when Agamemnon's actual return to Argos is imminent.

Scene 1 lays down the fundamental emotional pattern of the drama.[7] It proceeds from expectation to the joy of fulfilment and then into apprehension. This pattern is replicated many times – most overtly in Choroses 1–3 – and it does more to establish the feeling of blighted homecoming than any other single aspect of Aeschylus' dramaturgy. Agamemnon's return is overshadowed, even before it has begun, by the Watchman's cautious but firm allusions to the 'masculine' strength of Klytaimestra's intellect (11), the Fear that will not leave him (14ff.), and the troubles in the house (18–19). He waits for 'release...from these sufferings' (1) – another recurrent verbal motif in the drama (and a sinister one; 'release from sufferings' was also a euphemism for death),[8] and he receives it; but the direction of his thoughts in 9–20 prefigures a reprise of his fears as soon as his first rejoicing is exhausted. In 36ff., the Watchman returns to the deeper reality which underlies the news that Troy has fallen; and his sudden, sinister withdrawal into silence does more than any further words could do to consolidate the final tone of apprehension for the future.

In several modern productions, the Watchman has stayed motionless throughout; but Aeschylus must have been alive to the potential for movement from side to side on a flat roof. The monologue should begin with the Watchman crouched down (cf. 2); but the text contains strong inducements for him to rise at 8, and walk from side to side, to indicate to the audience his restless anxiety,

144 *Theatrical Commentary*

at 12. Then his hope is illuminated effectively by bringing him to rest again –
perhaps stopping at one end of the roof – at 20–21.

It is very unlikely that a real beacon was kindled at this moment in Aeschylus'
performance. After a pause, the Watchman simply has to mime attention to a
distant spot, disbelief – and then celebration. He moves to just above the central doors for the outcry at 25, and rapid, excited movements can illuminate his
summons to Klytaimestra and his ecstatic victory-dance. Then the retreat into
ominous silence at 36ff. becomes a retreat also into a depressed body posture,
matching and exceeding the weariness expressed in the opening lines; the actor
then turns away as abruptly as is needed to convey the bitterness and finality of
39, before descending the internal stairs back into the *skēnē*.

Choros 1

It was a normal feature of Greek life for the city council to assemble to discuss
strange news; this became a convenient opening convention in dramas with
male choros characters.[9] The group played by the choros can meditate on
recent events, and expand on the background, before the main action gets
under way.

With the first entry of the Elders, many productions of the *Oresteia* lose the
audience (and give them a permanently distorted view of Greek tragedy as dull
and boring – what Peter Brook called 'The Deadly Theatre') as twelve grey-
beards totter on, take up almost fixed positions and start declaiming what
apparently is a long theological meditation on behalf of the author.[10] The use
of staves, an essential prop to characterize the Elders (and very useful in
the choreography), does not imply that they doddered around ineffectively
throughout the play, presenting an image of senile immobility. Athenian choros
members were young men at the peak of their physical ability, who rehearsed
the trilogy and its satyr-play for many months in preparation for the competition and trained as intensively as Olympic athletes; and the lyric images in
Agamemnon demand for their illumination some of the most evocative dance
of any surviving Greek tragedy.

There would have been nothing incongruous to Athenian eyes when
Aeschylus' team of young men, dressed and masked as old men, danced vigorously to match the verbal imagery; in classical as in modern Greek culture, men
danced actively right into old age (cf. Euripides *Herakles* 673–86, where
another choros of Old Men celebrate their dancing). Accordingly, I believe
that the convention of this play (and others where the choros play the parts of
old men) was that the choros members mimed the Elders' age and feebleness at
the few moments when the audience needed to be reminded of them for the
purposes of the plot – perhaps when they are first introduced at 72ff., at the
opening of Scene 7 after Agamemnon's death-cries, and in the confrontation
with Aigisthos and his bodyguards in Scene 8. Elsewhere, they moved at least
as vigorously as the Athenians would have expected their senior counsellors to
move – with a lot more sprightliness than we would perhaps imagine!

This is the longest choral ode in the surviving Greek tragedies and arguably also the most powerful. It is exceptionally challenging in performance; Aeschylus took a calculated risk when he asked his choros to sing and dance their most extended song in the entire trilogy immediately after they have warmed up.

Introduction (40–103). The Elders enter the playing space full of confidence, and the picture which must be evoked in the choreography is clear; for them, the expedition against Troy is to be seen as a legal act of justified vengeance to exact recompense for a violation of *xenia*.

This perspective is one-sided, and it is rapidly undermined, by the momentum of the chanted narrative itself, at 60ff. Now there are both favourable and unfavourable aspects to the expedition; the war is being fought for just one promiscuous woman, and it is the cause of Greek suffering as well as Trojan. (These are two major motifs which will be developed in Choroses 2 and 3.) The good was obvious at the outset, while the bad has stolen in as the Elders develop their theme. The pattern is identical with that of the Watchman's thoughts after the appearance of the beacon.

Then comes a remarkable conclusion (72ff.). Ostensibly only introducing themselves, explaining why they were debarred from joining the expedition, the Elders refer to the weakness of the marrow in their limbs – no stronger than a child's. The unsung implication is strong; only between childhood and age, in the prime of life, is man able to act; but we have already heard of the questionable nature of action, the sufferings it involves and the inexorable but unforeseeable consequences. The opening dance thus descends from the mime of heroic departure, of angry vultures bereft of young and the justified revenge for them, through the evocation of wartime suffering to the pathetic, hobbled gestures of old men.

The Elders have gathered before the palace because they have seen sacrifices all around the city; they are apprehensive and worried. In the absence of the king, they have come to the queen, who is acting as regent, to seek accurate news. When Klytaimestra declines to emerge,[11] they attempt to understand the past. They brood on the departure of the Trojan expedition, and their attempt ends in a disastrous evocation of the sacrifice of Iphigenia – another example of expectation-fulfilment-apprehension.[12] They thus immediately set before the audience a picture of Agamemnon so trenchant and memorable that it will underlie the first half of the drama. (The sacrifice is, significantly, thrown in his face by one of the Elders when he arrives, 799ff.)

Aulis 1 (104–59). The Elders retrace their path and embark upon a complex lyric narrative of the setting-out of the expedition; but much has changed since their opening presentation. The sons of Atreus are no longer sent out by the avenging hand of Zeus, but by the portent; and the complexity of the verse in these stanzas matches the way in which both the men at Aulis then, and the Elders in the dramatic present now, have to feel around in the dark, trying to see into an obscure and ominous future – which later becomes revealed and tragic.

146   *Theatrical Commentary*

In stanza A2, Kalchas interprets the portent. The eagles, he says, stand for the sons of Atreus, who are about to go to conquer Troy. We are to conclude for ourselves that the pregnant hare stands for Troy, and its young for Troy's inhabitants. Destiny will destroy Priam's city forcibly, with the expedition as its medium; but once again, the reassuring note is qualified. Kalchas fears lest some divine anger may overshadow the army – for Artemis 'hates the eagles' feast'; and if we translate the symbolism of the portent, she is angry as the protector of all the young innocents who will be destroyed when the sack of Troy avenges Paris' crime. As his vision flows on, into the *epode* A3, Kalchas is able to see the future – to predict, and fear, the winds. More obscurely, he is also able to see, though dimly, the goddess' eagerness for monstrous sacrifice and the consequences for the house of Atreus – an implacable hatred (which the audience should interpret as that of Klytaimestra) which will await Agamemnon on his return home.

As the Elders narrate these events, a refrain steals in ('Cry sorrow, sorrow – yet may good prevail!' 121), focussing on the moment of suffering and the optimism of the hope that the outcome will be better. Repeated and transformed, as a disastrous outcome is more and more seen to be unavoidable, it becomes a recurring verbal motif to express the tragic cadence of the drama, the widening chasm between men's hopes and what actually happens in the real world. At first, it simply appears, gently, as the Elders' own comment to round off A1; it is then repeated, as an outcry by Kalchas, at the end of A2 – adding emphasis and anxiety to his reading of the omen; and finally, when the perils of the expedition are complete in Kalchas' prophecy, the Elders join their voices 'in harmony' with those of all the men at Aulis; their own emotions now are fused with those of the others, ten years ago.

In the lyric verse of Greek tragedy, *strophe* responds to *antistrophe*; the metrical pattern of matching stanzas (here A1 and A2) was exactly the same in the original. In this group, there is also an *epode*, A3, in the same metre, but different in detail from A1 and A2. The parallels between matching stanzas cannot be brought over into English, since no translator can locate every key word at exactly the same point in the line as in the original; indeed, it is usually not even possible to translate matching stanzas with corresponding English verse patterns and remain faithful to the sense of such complex stanzas. But if some of the main points of relationship are preserved, the choreographer can devise suggestive parallel patterns of choreography for responding stanzas which will bring out the aspects of the Greek playwright's meaning which this patterning expresses. For example, in this sequence, Aeschylus places the Elders' narrative in A1 in parallel with Kalchas' in A2, setting their sense of their own authority to describe the portent in parallel with his authority to interpret it. After matching Kalchas' opening to theirs, Aeschylus then enforces the parallel between the portent and the army whose fate it interprets, by matching all the details of the description in A2 to that in A1. Then he ends by bringing the act which symbolizes why Artemis is angry (the eating of the hare, 119–20) into

Agamemnon 147

alignment with Artemis' pity for that act (134–5), and he reinforces the convergence of meaning at this point by repeating the refrain.

Aulis 2 (160–257). The full burden of the prophecy which they have just reported is obscure to the Elders, even in the dramatic present, since Klytaimestra's hatred of her husband is still concealed from them. Aeschylus needs a pause between Kalchas' prophecy and the implementation of the first thing that he feared, to measure and reflect the time which elapsed at Aulis, before it became plain exactly what Artemis' demand was.

It is appropriate that in the darkness of this moment the Elders turn to Zeus, for he, they believe, is the only source by whose agency vain burdens of reflection may be cast away. But a subtle irony undermines their attempt to find comfort. The praise of Zeus leads them on at 182–3 to confront an aspect of his powers which is highly, and unpleasantly, relevant to the situation which they are in the middle of describing. Zeus has given Agamemnon the great gift, or favour, of sacking Troy; but such favours are dangerous to mortal men; the gods may well demand a price. And because his gift from Zeus exacts so much from others who are under her protection, the goddess Artemis demanded such a recompense from Agamemnon.[13]

This sequence of thoughts explains how, with a seamless transition, without change of metre – indeed, in the middle of a strophic pair – the Elders shift their focus from their meditation on the power of Zeus to the situation of Agamemnon at Aulis; and here again the matching responsion of the danced stanzas makes the point. The powerful connection at 183 'ranges the special case under the general law'[14]; we see the sufferings of the Greeks, as they languished at Aulis, danced to steps in C2 parallel to those which accompanied the pain inflicted by the favours of the gods in C1.

Then the narrative flows seamlessly into its final phase. Once again, strophic patterning is central to the meaning. In D1, the Elders first sing of the suffering which the gale inflicted on the expedition and then of the terrible remedy which was Artemis' demand. This is matched in D2 by the way in which Agamemnon's agonized indecision is followed, in the second part of the stanza, by his movement to accepting that remedy. Aeschylus then emphasizes the madness of the deed by setting the E2 account of the sacrifice in parallel to E1, the Elders' fierce denunciation of Agamemnon's state of mind. But Artemis' demand of his daughter's blood if he is to fulfil a mission ordained by Zeus leaves him with a choice which is no choice, precisely described as such when 'he put on the harness of necessity' – *inevitably choosing* a deed which will doom him at the hands of Klytaimestra. (Compulsion by a god or, as in this instance, two gods does not excuse a human being from responsibility in mid-fifth-century ethics.)

The account of Iphigenia's last moments runs directly onward in mid-sentence into the F stanzas (a rare writing technique in Greek tragedy) and sets the choreographer the challenge of devising related movements to evoke both the appalling pathos of the picture evoked in F1 and the reckless abandon of the Elders in F2 as they attempt to retreat from that picture into unjustified

148 *Theatrical Commentary*

optimism. The extended choral dance comes through to a highly ominous conclusion.[15]

Scene 2

Klytaimestra's part in the first half of *Agamemnon* is conceived in theatrical terms, as a series of rehearsals for the return of Agamemnon – a commanding performance, which is finally frustrated and upstaged by Kassandra, when Klytaimestra attempts to create the climax of the drama after Scene 4. The power struggle between Klytaimestra and a succession of men begins in Scene 2; as Agamemnon begins his return home, his wife tests her ability to think and act as strongly as a man against the chief citizens of Argos – and she succeeds. The Elders are left at the end with nothing but their scepticism, which will be undermined at the start of Scene 3.

Aeschylus pours into the confrontation the bitter fruit of ten years of growing mutual antagonism and political conflict. Lines 258ff. make it plain that the Elders tolerate Klytaimestra's political position as regent only because they are obliged to; 270 can be played as expressing the totally feigned public emotion of the politically subservient in the face of an official statement which, inwardly, they totally disbelieve.

The Greek theatre shape is very effective in illuminating the ebb and flow of a confrontation. This is evident in Scene 2 from the moment the doors open, framing Klytaimestra as she steps into the playing area. She comes out for the first time in the play to confront the Elders, and they retreat. Wherever Klytaimestra goes during 264ff., the Elders have to advance towards her one by one during the *stichomythia*, only to be swept away as she breaks out from the locked-in confrontation and drives them back towards the perimeter with the opening words of the beacon speech.

There are many possibilities for directing the rest of the scene. One promising approach is to take advantage of the fact that in an arena theatre the line from EBC to C is the most commanding axis; BC and C can be used as Klytaimestra's resting places for those moments in the two long speeches when she is at her most emphatic. Then, by contrast, she can range around the playing space during those passages where the speech flows more freely, annihilating the Elders' attempt to maintain their own physical solidarity in the space. The movement should visually complement the command of geography in her rhetoric.

Klytaimestra's second speech, her response to the studied insult to her intelligence in 318–9, is an enigmatic performance. In terms of movement, it is perhaps best seen as an appeal to the Elders to become emotionally involved in a situation whose exact parameters and relevance are opaque to them. The spatial metaphor then remains similar to that in the first speech; once again, BC or C are the most effective positions for the key points of rest (especially the crucial warning at 338ff.). Her sallies before that point are, however, quite different from the triumphant circling appropriate to the beacon speech; here, by contrast, she should quit her commanding position to seek the Elders' involvement, coming forward towards them in gestures of appeal as she explores emotionally the fate of the victims – and prefigures the dangers that await the conquerors (341ff.).

She will head towards the palace, of course, for the last three lines – but, ironically, she prepares to depart by deprecating herself as (merely!) female and echoing the motif 'yet may good prevail'. She should then exit at once, not waiting for a reply,[16] and so undermines by her contempt both an Elder's grudging concession of victory and the attempt at sarcasm in 352.

Choros 2

The Elders embark on their official celebration of the sack of Troy in fulfilment of the duty which they have twice promised to Klytaimestra, but the rejoicing quickly turns sour. This ode presents one of the most striking manifestations of the play's underlying pattern: expectation met by fulfilment and then by apprehension. The Elders brood on what Klytaimestra has told them, trying to focus their feelings on an analysis of the ways in which the capture of Troy has fulfilled the traditional belief that Zeus himself protects the rights of hosts and guests. They prove this to their satisfaction, but their thoughts lead them on to a very different perspective, in which the conquerors of Troy are almost as overshadowed by the potential consequences as the defeated Trojans.

In the choreography, the prelude and epilogue must be marked off clearly from the three strophic pairs, in which there should be a continuous pattern of movement to match the seamless development of the Elders' thoughts. Severe, abrupt images of power are appropriate in the prelude, as the Elders evoke Zeus while taking up their positions for the dance proper. Then the A stanzas invite a highly complex and subtle response from the choreographer, who must match both the remarkable sequence of the imagery and the ways in which the tentative initial picture in each stanza gradually develops towards a terrible certainty in the last four lines. This mood must be continued, with gathering clarity and power, in the B stanzas; each dance here opens with an image of gentleness and subtlety and ends in the desolation of personal loss.

Stanzas C1 and C2 call for choreography of even greater intensity and gravity, leading to an extremely ominous conclusion, as the Elders' celebration finally reaches its denouement in apprehension. Then this choreographic sequence suddenly dissolves, in the epilogue 475ff., into dislocated, sudden individual movements.[17]

Scene 3

Following normal practice, Agamemnon has sent a Herald ahead to the city of Argos on his landfall at the port of Nauplion, while he sacrifices to the gods of his homeland. The Herald's arrival instantly punctures the fantasy with which the Elders tried to escape in 475ff. from the burden of their reflections.

150   *Theatrical Commentary*

Klytaimestra was right, and all they can do is hope that the more ominous implications of the sack of Troy will not be fulfilled. (They will be; cf. 527–8.)

The build-up to the Herald's entry is of unusual length, and it gives the opportunity for the Elders to break up, individually and slowly, from the defiantly bold positions which they have taken up in the epilogue to Choros 2. They now cluster hopefully around and behind the one of their number who has crossed to near the right entrance to tell them about the Herald's imminent arrival.[18] But a pattern for the scene is set at once by the way in which even this functional speech has a dying fall built into it. The speaker shies away in 499ff. from the fear of disaster, and this must be brought out in the movement. He should turn away from the right entrance and carry his meditation into the rear centre of the playing space. This establishes a mood-pattern which can then be developed when the blocking later reflects the ways in which the Herald also tries desperately to hold onto his unwarranted optimism – and loses it.

In preparation for the arrival of Agamemnon himself, the Herald first arrives to take possession of the playing space and is then driven by Klytaimestra to the perimeter. In our production, the Herald entered at a run and then collapsed, exhausted, at front centre as he delivered his opening line. He rose gradually, first to his knees and then to his feet, during the ensuing greetings to the earth, the gods and the heroes of Argos. Then he began to assert possession of the space, moving up the centre-line (obviously) towards the palace before and during 518ff. and turning to face forward as he addresses the Elders from 522. Whether he moves again during 527ff. or not, the last section of the speech must be played as an attempt from a static, commanding position to persuade the Elders, culminating in the triumphal declaration of 532ff. The Herald's confident view should then be systematically undermined. After retreating from their initial curiosity in the face of his aggressive, rhetorical address to them, a few of the Elders can draw closer, one by one, for 538ff. The Herald naturally moves towards them too, reaching out to them in a dialogue during which both partners truly attempt to communicate with each other. However, a chasm grows between them; in his political naivety, the Herald – after finally, at 549, getting the point at which they are driving – then misses it totally, when he misunderstands 550 and uses it as the springboard for a second optimistic speech. In our production, the Elders at this point broke up their increasingly close concentration around the Herald – the first contact by the people of Argos with the returned expedition – and retreated in disgust to positions around the front perimeter.

Their retreat forces the Herald to address the first of his appeals (555ff.) to their turned backs. In what follows, the Elders can slowly overcome their reluctance, turning to face him one by one in response to the increasing pressure of his rhetoric and of his movement around and between them. At 568ff., as he tries desperately to recreate the joy of victory, his mood changes, and the Elders can all turn to follow the flow of his speech. Lines 572ff. play well with the Herald at a distance from the Elders, as he builds up to the climactic declaration at 577ff. and then approaches the Elders to address to them the admonition of his last three lines.

Finally, he turns back again and begins to advance towards the palace. This accords with a familiar practice; it was customary for the bearer of good news to convey it in person and receive a reward from the king or queen. But this Herald is interrupted. Klytaimestra appears, as if by magic, at the exact moment when she can subvert his move towards the house; she deprives him both of the fulfilment of his duty and of his reward.[19]

Her sudden entry disrupts the pattern of triumphant Herald and attentive Elders. She drives them all back to the perimeter of the playing space by the vehemence and speed of her entry and subsequent movements, as she delivers an astonishingly bold and challenging speech, which she uses as a second, even more aggressive rehearsal for the control of the space which she will exercise – and now the grand hypocrisy which she will raise on the basis of that control – when she greets Agamemnon himself. She then departs as swiftly as she came, before the Herald or the Elders can muster a reply.

This dynamic, whirlwind speech is best played fast and with violent contrasts between the sections in which Klytaimestra is still and those in which she is on the move. Much of it is an attack on the Elders, though two small parts (598–9 and 604–7) are addressed to the Herald; one section (607–12) can be played as an open boast, which in an arena theatre should be played over all their heads to the air, the sky – and the audience.

The Herald now has no choice but to suffer interrogation by the Elders on the one subject that he was hoping to avoid. An Elder makes a derisive comment at 615–6 on Klytaimestra's performance, which is lost on the Herald; then they take an assertive new tack. Accordingly, the final *stichomythia* should be blocked to express the Herald's various attempts to escape and the ways in which the Elders corner him. Lines 652–3 can then be played as a last, futile attempt to turn away from their interrogation before he settles down to the narrative, in which Aeschylus makes creative re-use of Menelaos' story, in *Odyssey* 4, of what happened after the fall of Troy.

In the last speech, the Herald's syntax becomes increasingly complex in order to express his continuing reluctance to speak; the movement must reflect this. The speech begins in a very elevated tone, with the Herald perhaps circling around in fragmentary patterns as he tries to convince the Elders (who may now have retreated to the perimeter) that they do not really want to hear his story; but at 649, almost by accident, he blurts out the fact that there was a storm. After this, the narrative settles down, and 650–66 can be delivered virtually from one spot (e.g., BC).

More movement is helpful in the closing section, after 667 – especially at 675ff., when the Herald approaches the Elders (who should now have come in a little and re-formed, to express their involvement in the disaster he has described). He attempts to impose his hopefulness upon them, but their silence (aided in production by motionlessness) speaks louder than his words, and he circles, turning to no avail inside their formation. The audience realizes that Agamemnon will now return alone, without an army to protect him from the conspirators. After 662, the Herald's optimism sounds far more hollow (674ff.),

152   *Theatrical Commentary*

and the echo of the play's recurrent theme 'yet may good prevail', as he attempts for the second and last time to make a closure, is full of irony. He is obliged to exit[20] with no response to his ringing, optimistic assertion of truth.

Choros 3

The Elders pass, for the first time without prelude or introduction, into a depressed, introverted mediation on the sheer scale of the disaster caused by Helen; and they arrive as Agamemnon is about to enter at their fullest illumination yet of the general truth that all actions have their inexorable consequences. The last example is the furthest, in both space and time, from the action of the drama – for the final image is of the avenging Fury settling in Troy on the arrival of Helen; but the last statement is the most detailed and the most universal as well as being the one most applicable to the present situation in the house of Atreus – which is now seen to be parallel in many respects to the royal house of Troy.[21] The Elders' final words are ominous in the extreme for a 'sacker of cities' whose house bears the *miasma* of ancestral crime.

This third and final Choros of recall is also the most direct; it takes the pattern of almost irresistible flow from subject to subject, already established in Choros 2, to its furthest extent. The argument again exploits the parallelism of *strophe* and *antistrophe*; the A stanzas pair Helen, as destroyer, with Troy and the way that city incurred the wrath of Zeus by accepting her into a bigamous marriage. Then the B stanzas figure Paris' nature through the parable of a lion cub and set its loveable behaviour when first born in a hideous contrast with the terrible destruction that it wreaked when fully grown.

Finally, the C stanzas break up this patten. The Elders return in the *strophe* C1 to the event which started all this destruction, the settling of the Fury in Troy when Helen first arrived; but the *antistrophe* C2, instead of pursuing this theme, launches into a generalization. On the basis of all that they have seen and heard in the drama so far, the Elders dispute the old, fatalistic belief that prosperity in itself gives birth to violence and misery. It is *crime* that brings down destruction on wealthy homes. Aeschylus then allows them to hint in the D strophic pair at the past of the house of Atreus – the previous impious acts which threaten the destiny of the surviving king (a part of the legend which will not be openly heard in *Agamemnon* until Scene 6).

The choreography has only one task: to match the ever-continuing flow of the argument, from the meditative opening to the lapidary conclusion, with images of ever-increasing power and force. Paradoxically, we found that angular movements of almost military precision, set in deliberate opposition to the flow of the words, achieved a better outcome than attempting to match the movement style to the verbal content.

Scene 4

This famous scene makes powerful use of the arena playing space. At the midpoint of the drama, Agamemnon arrives back in front of his palace and places his carriage in the central position appropriate to the power that he believes is his due; Klytaimestra then converts that position to powerlessness as she first demonstrates that the remainder of the space is her territory and then fills with robes what has now become its most significant part, that which lies between Agamemnon's carriage and his threshold.

Aeschylus uses his first props single-mindedly to illustrate the only theme which concerns him at the moment: the subversion of Agamemnon's home-coming, as Klytaimestra proves that she is the stronger, conquering the con-queror of Troy. When the gods' eyes are on him (cf. 461–2), she persuades this 'man who has killed many' to incur their jealousy (924, 947ff.), trampling over crimson (to be exact, brownish, blood-red)[22] fabrics. He voluntarily wastes fine property, part of the substance of his *oikos*, and walks over a sea of blood into the house of Atreus – evoking all the bloodshed for which he himself is respon-sible from the sacrifice of Iphigenia to the sack of Troy. And he does so simply under the influence of Klytaimestra's persuasion, enacting the pattern set out by the Elders in 369ff. There are other overtones;[23] but the verbal combat between Klytaimestra and Agamemnon is the primary focus of Scene 4, and the movements implied by the text illuminate it continually. The two substan-tial properties enable a detailed reconstruction of the action to be made.

Agamemnon comes into the view of the stage-left spectators during the final stanza of Choros 3 – words which are ominous for him – and at the moment when the Elders finish singing (782), his carriage enters the playing space.[24] It was accompanied by at least one attendant, to hold the horse(s); possibly – but probably not – also by one or two foot-soldiers.[25] The main visual image which needs to be established at his entry is that Agamemnon's triumph as conqueror of Troy is less than total, reinforcing the Herald's narra-tive of the loss of the fleet.

Agamemnon's opening speech shows that he is blind to the wider implica-tions of the sack of Troy and deaf to the Elders' guarded warning. He is firmly confident in the gods' support and his own ability to resume power at Argos. The carriage therefore comes to rest with Agamemnon in the most command-ing position in the playing space – at the centre-point; his arrival forces the Elders into the front left quadrant. (Any position for the carriage L or R of centre is unsatisfactory because it would necessitate an asymmetrical layout of the robes as well as taking Agamemnon away from the centre of attention; he must be placed somewhere on the centre-line between EBC and EFC. A loca-tion behind C unacceptably truncates the space to be covered by the robes, but one in front of C constricts the action since Agamemnon, in the carriage and facing forward, can only interact naturally with people to his front and right [actor left], namely FC and FL.)

Klytaimestra's power is then shown by the ease with which, on her entry, she upstages Agamemnon and converts his position of dominance into one of sub-servience by controlling his attempt to enter the palace. She should enter after 851 – not 855 as Taplin (1977a: 306) and most translations – and walk imme-diately down to FC; she needs to be within Agamemnon's field of vision as he completes 854, to stop him leaving the carriage, presumably by a gesture;

154   *Theatrical Commentary*

a commanding appearance at the doors of the palace is not enough, *pace* Reinhardt (1949: 94). When she arrives at FC and begins to speak, she has a captive audience, with the Elders ahead of her and to her right and Agamemnon to her left. Agamemnon is trapped between her rhetorical performance in front of him and the robes behind him, which will cover the dominant movement line from C to EBC.

Klytaimestra's speech breaks down into five parts[26]:

(1) 855–75. Klytaimestra turns her back on Agamemnon and establishes her total control over the front portion of the playing space in vigorous, sweeping movements. She dominates the Elders by hyperbole and brazen hypocrisy and approaches Agamemnon only as if he was the illustration for a lecture to them, a specimen under examination, at 866ff.

(2) 876–86. Klytaimestra addresses Agamemnon for the first time. This section needs to be played quietly, close to Agamemnon – perhaps even as a quasi-aside, with Klytaimestra deliberately turning away from the Elders – to establish a contrast with the rhetoric that follows.

(3) 887–94, played to the Elders and including Agamemnon only by a half-turn at 890, the springboard for

(4) 895–901, the climax of the speech, directly addressed to Agamemnon from left of FC. At 919, Agamemnon implies that Klytaimestra has prostrated herself full-length before him in the homage which the Persian monarchs required of their subjects and the Greeks found deeply offensive. The best place in her speech for this to happen is at the culmination of the rhetoric, which then reaches its climax in a contrived swoon into total self-abasement after 901.

(5) 902–13. Klytaimestra recovers from the outrageous climax of her homage and calmly prays for the daemon Jealousy to stand far away – after which she immediately proceeds to ensure that Jealousy will be present here and now, and hostile to Agamemnon, by persuading him to walk across the robes. Crossing to close by the rear of the carriage, so she can be seen by the maidservants beside the doors, she finally gives her permission for Agamemnon to approach his own halls, but only over the finely woven robes.

The Elders are ignored after 904; the scene is now set for a total confrontation – the first interchange between two solo actors in *Agamemnon*. Given the king's position facing forward in the carriage at C, this can be achieved only by placing Klytaimestra at front left by 930. This shows that she has the confidence to begin the argument with her back to the Elders, who are at EFL; Agamemnon's vulnerability is acutely symbolized by his position, trapped with the robes behind him and Klytaimestra directly facing him on his opposite side.

The text seems to suggest that Agamemnon should leave the carriage at 957, when he verbally accepts her command (904ff.). But this creates two practical difficulties: first, 951ff. play very awkwardly if Agamemnon is right beside Kassandra in the carriage; the introduction of Kassandra is a counterattack against Klytaimestra, and Agamemnon needs some playing space to make it

Agamemnon   155

effective. Second, Agamemnon cannot step at the end of his speech out of a central carriage directly onto the robes and then walk towards the palace doors. A crucial moment in the action would then be obscured from the view of a large portion of the audience, since the horse and carriage would debar everyone except those in the front right (audience left) segment of the *theatron* from seeing the moment at which Agamemnon first places his foot upon the robes.

Both difficulties are removed if Agamemnon has his own small moment of rebellion and steps from the carriage to the ground at the end of 949. It should then be moved immediately towards the left exit, to free the central point as a usable position for the actors.

Agamemnon must have entered the palace by 972. Just before that, Klytaimestra delivers fifteen lines of superbly focussed rhetoric. Most commentators imagine or assume that he begins to walk at 957 and completes the walk by entering the *skēnē* at 972; but her speech is far too long for that purpose unless Agamemnon creeps over the roughly ten metres of his direct path to the door at a comically inappropriate place or Klytaimestra rushes through some of her finest lines.

There are no lines in the middle of the speech which could be played as suddenly overpowering Agamemnon's hesitation and motivating him to walk over the robes. So one possibility is for Agamemnon to be seen as firmly committed – walking without hesitation as soon as he has expressed his intention to obey Klytaimestra (956) – but submissive enough to pause at the threshold and listen passively to her final, climactic celebration of his return (perhaps from 966) before making his exit into the house. This pause is weak.

Another blocking makes more exciting and effective theatre. Agamemnon advances at 957 to the brink of the robes, but then hesitates at C, and does not move until after 972. (This staging was also adopted by Karolos Koun.[27]) Klytaimestra is then obliged to create the speech, with its outrageous comparison of their household's wealth to that of the sea, as desperate rhetoric to persuade a still reluctant Agamemnon. To do that, she must move on the first lines, crossing in front of Agamemnon by the beginning of 962 to a position (BR) from which she can confront him directly.

Lines 973–4 are, of course, delivered after Agamemnon has gone into the palace. The whole first half of the play has led up to this moment, at which Klytaimestra, having made Agamemnon enter the household on her own terms, attains her supreme triumph, aligning herself (correctly) with the will of Zeus as she is on the point of fulfilling her design. The moment demands a position commanding the whole theatre. For this reason, and to avoid obliging Klytaimestra herself to walk on the robes, the maidservants must remove them, and disappear inside, as soon as Agamemnon has completed his walk and passed into the house.

Klytaimestra advances to C while they do this. She is then able to deliver the last two lines from the position of maximum strength before she departs, asserting her own total domination by striding from C to EBC – over the same line, now free of coverings, which Agamemnon has just walked under her control.

156 *Theatrical Commentary*

Choros 4

After what they have just seen and heard, the Elders are no longer capable of offering a lengthy Choros of narrative and argument. The homecoming which they have desired throughout the first half of the play has happened, but still they cannot suppress their fears. Here is the final development of the pattern which the Watchman began: the fulfilment of their expectations has plunged the Elders into an extreme apprehension. (Note 1019–21, the sinister thought, generated by the image of the blood-red robes, which dominates the close of this drama and the start of *Libation Bearers*; the possible solution offered in the B stanzas provides no release.)

After Scene 4, Agamemnon's death is almost inevitable. But the Elders do not express any premonition; they simply brood on their fears. If he were to die now, the implications for the future would be unclear. The events between Agamemnon's exit and his death-cry will generate the action of the next drama and so propel the narrative thrust of the trilogy.

Aeschylus signals that Agamemnon's death will not happen immediately simply by leaving the Trojan prophetess on the carriage, motionless, wordless, and still unidentified. In Aeschylean drama, nothing is introduced without a purpose, and the conventions of the Athenian theatre are broken only for good reasons.[28] Agamemnon's death therefore cannot take place until Kassandra has taken part in the action.

The continuing presence of Kassandra and her carriage also constricts the choreography of Choros 4. For the first time, the Elders are obliged to sing and dance in a physically restricted space; and the position of the carriage BL virtually confines them to stunted, introverted movements in the front half of the playing space, matching the mood of the text.

Scene 5

Kassandra knows exactly what Klytaimestra is inviting her to. With the carriage now in an angled position BL, Kassandra is staring directly past Klytaimestra at the open doorway which will lead to her death; and her immediate reaction is a defiant silence, accompanied now by quivering spasms of terror, at the latest by 1062–3, in preparation for the sudden explosion of dance and song at 1077.

Visually, Aeschylus opposes Kassandra's unrelenting refusal to respond, let alone leave the carriage, to the angular movements which illustrate Klytaimestra's consuming desire for revenge and her frustration. This is Klytaimestra's first rebuff – an indication, even before the murders, that her power is not absolute and she too will be brought down. She can make a male, a great Greek king and the conqueror of Troy cross from the carriage to the threshold and over the robes at her will; but she cannot make a foreign, female slave obey her command.

Agamemnon 157

The first speech must be played as by a woman on edge, using all her strength to submerge her seething, devouring need beneath a veneer of gentle persuasion. Klytaimestra's impatience then becomes explicit, as Kassandra's refusal to respond exasperates her beyond endurance, and increasingly agitated movements illuminate her feelings. In our production, Klytaimestra broke away suddenly at 1055, moved back slightly to face Kassandra at 1059, then wheeled around at the start of 1064, to turn in fury on the Elder who spoke 1062–3. Then perhaps, as one effective way of ending, a lunge down towards ERC as 1064 is completed, a vigorous cross towards the back during the next three lines, the exit line 1068 hurled back at the Elders from between BC and EBC – and Klytaimestra, temporarily defeated, is gone as swiftly as she came.

Scene 6

Kassandra's terror and agony are those of a seer – the only human character in the trilogy who possesses true insight into the past, the hidden present and the future. Aeschylus interweaves the three elements closely. In the past lies the 'first-beginning crime' (1192), the adultery of Thyestes, and the consequent murder of his children by Atreus, whom he had cuckolded. Kassandra's vision of this introduces for the first time a past crime in the house, explaining Aigisthos' part in the conspiracy and adding another direction from which Agamemnon's life is threatened, since Kassandra sees in the hidden present the other children's avenging Furies summoning Aigisthos. In the immediate future lie the deaths of Agamemnon and Kassandra herself; but as the scene unfolds, Kassandra sees further and realizes that they too, like the children of Thyestes, will be avenged; the fatal consequences of Klytaimestra's deed are brought before us before she has even done it.

Kassandra's prophecies cannot be believed (1202ff.), so we watch the Elders groping towards a truth which they do not want to hear. They cannot overcome the barrier imposed by Apollo's punishment, even when in desperation she prophesies the death of Agamemnon directly (1246). But by the end, as they watch Kassandra accept her fate, they have come as close as Apollo's curse permits to believing her. The doors remain open after Klytaimestra's exit; so Kassandra's outcries as she peers into the darkness inside the palace begin to establish the threshold as a visual metaphor for passing into Hades.

Part 1 (1072–1177). Kassandra leaps from the carriage (it must then be withdrawn, by the left exit),[29] and her long silence erupts into lyrics. This unexpected scene unfolds on the largest scale since the introduction of lyrics suspends time between Klytaimestra's furious exit and Kassandra's final departure to meet her fate.[30]

In this part of the scene, Kassandra sings – initially with extreme emotion, as her visions show her that Apollo has brought her here to die[31]; this is reflected in the short-lined, repetitive lyrics. Gradually she calms down, and the stanzas become longer and more lucid. The Elders attempt to contain their anxiety by

158 *Theatrical Commentary*

defensive, pedestrian (and twice downright comic) responses to her agony; but at 1121, her reminders of the bloody past of the house of Atreus and her vision of Klytaimestra's preparation for the murders provoke them from individual spoken responses into unison lyrics. The dance must reflect the initial violence (the metre in Greek of all these lyrics is the extremely agitated dochmiac), the increasingly expansive thrust of Kassandra's visions, and the sudden passionate involvement, against their will, of the Elders. Kassandra's last stanzas are relatively meditative and gentle, but 1172 is well illuminated if, after the line, she collapses for a few moments as the Elders bring the dance pattern to an end.[32]

Part 2 (1178–1330). Now Kassandra tries to explain in spoken words what she can see. Each of three speeches is followed by a four-line response from one of the Elders and then by a *stichomythia* exchange with several of them. An onset of prophetic pain, imposed by Apollo to prevent her from communicating closely with the Elders, twice suddenly regenerates the sequence; but during the third pattern, Kassandra frees herself from the constraints of the god, and the final section, after her last outcry at 1307, is written in a loose combination of dialogue and speech, to express the freedom that she has achieved.

Until 1264ff., when she throws away her emblems as his prophetess, Kassandra is struggling to communicate with the Elders through the barrier of Apollo' curse; only after that does she fully regain her human dignity, as she gathers from her prophecy at 1279ff. the courage to face her fate. She knows that neither she nor Agamemnon will die unavenged, and even her death has a place in the long sequence which will end only after Orestes' deed. The closing mood of her last long speech is triumphant, as we see the mortal young woman emerge from under the terrible possession of the god, which has made her at once superhuman in her clarity of vision and subhuman in the bestial subjection of her prophetic agonies. Then, conscious of her fate and therefore hesitant, she recreates the last walk towards the doors of the house of Atreus which Agamemnon made freely and blindly.[33]

Aeschylus establishes a strong contrast between the possessed movements of the first two speeches, in which Kassandra ranges over most of the playing space – coming forward to escape from the horrors which she sees inside the palace and driving the Elders back to the perimeter with the intensity of her conviction – and the brief points of rest during the Elders' four-line interventions and the subsequent dialogue. This leads forward to the contrast within the third speech between the initial activity, in Kassandra's final moments of possession, and Kassandra motionless in the visionary closing section (1279ff.).

Kassandra needs to begin her final walk after 1290 at C to replicate Agamemnon's path. The opening section of the third speech must therefore be enacted in the front half of the playing space. 1279ff. play well if addressed not directly to the Elders but forward, facing from FC into the centre of the audience – like the corresponding moment (*Eu* 681ff.) at which Athena sees into the future.

For the last section, the Elders can best form two rows to flank her journey on both sides as if in a guard of honour. That journey has now become a theatrical metaphor for the gradual acceptance of death, as Kassandra moves slowly towards the doors, twice recoiling and twice hesitating. The script implies these movements:

1286	At FC, turns towards the façade to address the Elders
1290	Moves slowly towards C
1291	Kneels at C facing the doors
1295–1301	Rises, advances to BC
1305 and 1307	Recoils (e.g., towards L)
1313	Resumes the centre-line and again walks up past BC
1315	Above BC, turns to the front and addresses the Elders
1320	Resumes her movement towards the doors
1322	At EBC, turns to face forward to address her last words to the Sun
1330	After the last word, exits swiftly. Doors close.

Kassandra reaches in her last words a mood which is unique in surviving Aeschylean tragedy. Poised just before the climactic moment in *Agamemnon*, the death of the king, both playwright and character stand back as she accepts her fate, inviting us in 1327ff. to seek a bitter, momentary comfort in the transitory condition of humanity as a whole.[34]

Choros 5

The Elders now have virtually no doubt that Agamemnon will die. They sum up the issues which have dominated the drama in twelve pivotal lines: a fast, trenchant summary, chanted in anapaests in the original, of the hazardous implications for all humankind *if* (the keyword; 1338) that happens. The Elders can surge forward as they chant, perhaps tossing the lines from speaker to speaker (they divide easily 4,3,5) to create as much distance as possible from the doors by the end of the stanza, to prepare for the immediate, abrupt opening of Scene 7.

Scene 7

The Elders alone. The death-cry is heard at once. The tragedy dissolves into farce as the Elders are first paralysed into immobility[35] and then scurry comically around the playing space, talking about the importance of not talking in the aftermath of Agamemnon's death.[36]

Aeschylus' company have just performed one of the greatest scenes in surviving Greek tragedy – and are about to plunge into another. He therefore separates the Kassandra scene clearly from the confrontation between Klytaimestra and the Elders, by inflicting two drastic changes of tone in as

160 *Theatrical Commentary*

many minutes: from the high pathos of Kassandra's exit and Choros 5 into the increasingly absurd dithering of the Elders and then into Klytaimestra's speech of exultant triumph.

The contrast at 1371 is acute between the Elders, who as the chief men of Argos should be in a position at least to determine what to do, and Klytaimestra, who has already acted and, as the rest of the scene makes plain, is totally aware of what she needs to do next. It is so great and so striking that the *ekkuklēma* must have been employed to provide the requisite sudden transition from empty space to tableau, thrusting the dark events from the interior into the full public light of day.[37]

The agōn *with Klytaimestra.* This is the climax of *Agamemnon.* Here, and in the deliberately anticlimactic final scene, Aeschylus discharges all the energies which he has built steadily since Scene 1. The macabre tableau of the bodies of Agamemnon and Kassandra remains in sight right to the end, to remind both the Elders and the audience of the utter finality of Klytaimestra's act (she should be covered in blood; cf. 1388–90). Now the focus turns inexorably from the deed itself to its consequences, and Klytaimestra's position becomes completely undermined. Though she begins in absolute triumph over the bodies, she is obliged to retreat from her stance. After Kassandra's death has proved her veracity, the Elders are armed with all that she has said; they add that knowledge to the wisdom they have gained from their own earlier meditations on the pattern implied by the sack of Troy. They find the power to counter much of Klytaimestra's self-justification and make her see that her deed is merely one link in what now threatens to become an unending chain of vengeance and counter-vengeance.

The conflict also brings deeper knowledge to the Elders. At first, they denounce the deed as monstrous and insane; Klytaimestra must have been high on drugs to dare such an act (1407ff.). But this is not an adequate viewpoint any more than her initial conviction that she is wholly justified. In two powerful speeches, Klytaimestra puts before them the depth of the affront to her womanhood when Agamemnon slaughtered Iphigenia, the humiliation of her husband's many infidelities, and the crowning insult, Kassandra. Nor will she shirk conflict; with Aigisthos as her consort, she is prepared to meet any and all opposition.

This forces the Elders to reflect more deeply. Klytaimestra's command of language and of the situation is total, and she is clearly not insane. They must seek further if they are to find the true causes and make an adequate response to the death of the king. By the end of the scene, the Elders come to apprehend fully the powers at work in the situation. Klytaimestra too has some right on her side; the daemon is indeed present, and the house is falling, under the threat of retribution and incessant shedding of kindred blood. Their summary at 1560ff. contains no hope; violence has now become endemic in the house of Atreus, and there is no prospect that it will leave.

Part 1 (1372–1447). Like Scene 6, this massive scene is carefully structured to mark out the stages through which the confrontation passes. Klytaimestra

Agamemnon 161

begins her speech of orgasmic triumph (NB 1391–2 and cf. 1447), whose impact must be total, over the bodies on the *ekkuklēma* (see 1379); but clearly she does not remain there. EBC is not the strongest position in any theatre shape, even when the focus of attention is pulled there by a striking tableau; and Klytaimestra's verbal challenge to the Elders contains some of the most powerful imagery in the entire drama.

She therefore quits the tableau after a short time, like other users of the *ekkuklēma* in later plays, and advances to interact with the Elders, who will have retreated to the front perimeter under the impact of the tableau. Klytaimestra then comes forward down the centre-line soon after 1379 – perhaps to BC on 1382. She must complete the advance to the most dominant position, C, during 1391–2, so as to command the playing space from there for the final, totally defiant challenge to the Elders in 1393ff.

The aggressive elaboration of her position in 1401ff. goads them out of their shock; after a relatively muted, spoken first response, they attack her vigorously at 1407, in the heightened intensity of song (in the original Greek in the dochmiac, the most emotional lyric metre). Their initial reaction should provoke a further series of commanding movements from Klytaimestra during her second speech – perhaps back up to near the corpse, so she can exhibit it like a specimen in 1404–5, before returning to the centre-line to accompany the absolute finality of 1406. The movements for both characters must be intensely powerful and confrontational from 1399 right through to 1438ff., where Klytaimestra concludes her final speech back by the bodies. Her absolute control of language in the four speeches must be matched by a complementary control of space, to establish the commanding nature of her triumph, before it is undermined in the second part of the scene.

Part 2 (1449–1576). Klytaimestra's power is now so great that the Elders do not attempt to counter her but ease at 1448 into a meditative, despairing mood. Agamemnon's more questionable actions are forgotten, expiated by his death, and he now begins to be rehabilitated, in preparation for the unequivocally favourable view which his surviving children and the Libation Bearers will take in the second drama.[38]

The B1 stanza is followed by an *ephymnion*, a lyric pendant in which the Elders brood on the destructive power of Helen; but this spurs Klytaimestra to the greater emotional intensity of *anapaests* (unlike Kassandra, Klytaimestra never expresses herself through the uninhibited emotionalism of full lyrics); the rest of the scene is a chanted/lyric interchange between solo actor and choros.[39]

Slowly, as they begin the new dance after 1448, the Elders should repossess the bulk of the playing space, isolating Klytaimestra and provoking her into argument. In 1462ff., she challenges first what was sung in the first stanza and then the *ephymnion*; if the quiet opening has been sung by two soloists (as is appropriate to its mood), Klytaimestra is forced to turn to answer first one of the dancing Elders and then another – and then a third, after the singer of the B2 stanza rounds on her (preferably from a distance [e.g. from EFC] to make

162   *Theatrical Commentary*

the most of 1471). And the fact that she is here on the defensive is signalled by her progression from spoken words (up to 1448) to the higher intensity of chant from 1462.

Throughout all this, Klytaimestra should remain fixed to one spot, near the tableau (cf. 1472–3); part 2 reverses the roles played by the characters in part 1. Klytaimestra, although she comments as if from a position of authority on the truth or falsehood of the Elders' diagnoses, is now on the defensive, while they move increasingly freely.

After 1489, the Elders begin an *ephymnion* of mourning for Agamemnon, and the text implies that they establish a close physical relationship with the body; they have therefore by now extended their possession of the playing space back into the extreme rear segment, passing around and beside Klytaimestra.

This motivates her vehement (and outrageous) counterattack at 1497ff., which animates the Elders' reflection in the next stanza and so precipitates the closing movement. When they repeat the C *ephymnion*, she counters by reminding them once more of the sacrifice of Iphigenia, so powerfully that by 1530ff. (D1) the Elders feel totally helpless. The dance winds down into an exhausted half-truce; the Elders no longer attack her for her outrageous boldness, although in 1551ff. her bitterness against Agamemnon reaches new heights of sarcasm, preparing us for the revelation in *Libation Bearers* (439ff.) that she mutilated his corpse before she buried it and spurring the Elders in 1560ff. (D2) to a fierce, final summary.

Klytaimestra's proud exultance, her firm self-justification, and even her bitterness towards Agamemnon have all disappeared. It is the measure of her weakness now that she agrees (1567ff.) with what the Elders have said and voices a modest wish to make a pact with the daemon. Even this is utterly futile. Scene 6 and now Scene 7 have made it clear that the act of violence in which she has gloried will itself be avenged. But there is no vision of how the cycle of ever-continuing violence may be averted. The drama has run down to an unresolved conclusion, which Aigisthos does nothing to change.

This closing section could be realized by having the Elders increasingly draw apart from her, suggesting that their meditations on the scene become more inward as they consider the future, while Klytaimestra remains isolated by the bodies to emphasize how her vision remains backward-facing almost to the end of the scene. It is, however, better to devise a bold image which will embody the situation just before Aigisthos' arrival. In our production, Klytaimestra advanced towards the centre of the playing space during 1551ff. to match the vehemence of her irony in this speech. She was then gradually surrounded by the Elders during 1560ff.; at the end of the stanza, they raised their staves to a horizontal position, with the ends all touching; Klytaimestra delivered her final stanza kneeling, as if imprisoned. An image like this embodies Aeschylus' meaning more effectively than the alternative and also explains how Aigisthos, with his guards, can enter down the left *eisodos* and begin to speak without being noticed by either Klytaimestra or the Elders.[40]

Scene 8

Aigisthos is expected, but his belated appearance both confirms the accuracy of Kassandra's prophecies ('a wolf-coward', 1224) and fulfils (albeit ironically) Klytaimestra's claim that he will be her protector. Scene 8 also answers the political question which the murder has created, as Aigisthos dismisses the King's Elders, usurps Orestes' throne, and establishes a tyranny in Argos, suspending constitutional rule.

On a deeper level, Aigisthos is superfluous. His glorious claim to Justice is undermined by cowardice. His tearful but banal account of the Thyestean banquet is fatally coloured, both for the Elders and for the spectators, since Kassandra has already told this appalling story, in appropriately intense language and without omitting the first crime, the adultery of Aigisthos' father Thyestes. Aigisthos' brash self-righteousness contrasts so completely with Klytaimestra's justified passion in her defence that Scene 8 becomes a parody of Scene 7. Both begin with an avenger entering in triumph, to be challenged by the Elders; both end with a weary truce and the issues unresolved. Only this time the descent is deeper, and *Agamemnon* ends in a snarling, bitter conclusion without parallel in any other surviving tragedy.

Aigisthos' absurdity is patent in the linguistic inadequacy of his opening speech. The justice of his hereditary feud against the house of Atreus is fatally compromised by his bombast, self-righteousness, and frequent descents into cliché (beginning with 1577!). He also sometimes loses control over his syntax, unlike any other *agathos* in the *Oresteia*.[41] The speech invites extravagant movements and gestures, to reflect his over-developed self-image, and the low opinion which the Elders and the audience soon form.[42]

The Elders must fall back to the far right side of the playing space before the military strength of the bodyguards, as they follow Aigisthos in and deploy themselves in the left section[43]; this permits him to use most of the playing area to match the expansive thrust of his rhetoric. In the course of his narrative, Aigisthos needs to face in several directions – addressing the opening apostrophe to the heavens at large, but then inspecting the body of Agamemnon (1580–3), and telling the story of the Thyestean banquet (1584ff.). This narrative plays much better if parts of it are delivered rhetorically out towards the audience rather than to the Elders (whose disdain remains total throughout the speech); he then turns finally in self-justification towards the Elders at 1603.

The Elders counterattack at 1612ff., moving as far against Aigisthos as they dare (given the presence of his bodyguards) during the cut and thrust of the following exchanges. They should gradually advance in the right segment until Aigisthos, Klytaimestra and the guards possess only the left half of the playing space. This move forces Aigisthos from the centre and cuts him off from the house of Atreus, which he has come here to occupy. Aigisthos' increasing paranoia, as the argument develops, is then explained in visual terms, as is his sudden threat at 1649.[44] Here Aeschylus increased the intensity of the scene, in Greek, by changing the metre from iambic trimeters to trochaic tetrameters;

164 *Theatrical Commentary*

modern productions must reflect that lift in intensity, which remains for the rest of the play, perhaps by adding music and staging the confrontation vigorously as well as increasing the intensity of the spoken dialogue.

There is a case for making Klytaimestra cross a substantial space before she can intervene in the ensuing conflict, so she begins to move around 1650–1 and arrives by Aigisthos only just before she tries to soothe him. (Audiences will not miss the irony of 1656 if it is spoken, as in our production, by a Klytaimestra whose clothes are covered in blood.) Clearly, she must then also be between the contending parties, so she can turn easily first from him to the Elders at 1657, then for the deeper reflection of 1659–60 away from both groups, before turning back to face them all as she delivers 1661 – a line which reflects her full, rueful awareness that now, after Scene 7, she has been far reduced from her earlier ability to combine the strengths of both genders and is ('just') a woman.[45]

Nothing is resolved at the end of *Agamemnon*. The choral exit is unparalleled in any other surviving drama: in opposition to the principal characters and without any comforting words sung in conclusion. The Elders' last words are a series of angry taunts, verbal protests against the physical brutality of the new regime, which are effectively underscored if they depart in successive small groups during each individual Elder's speech after 1665, so that Aigisthos has to shout his defiant counter-threats at their departing backs.

To gain access to the interior of the palace, Klytaimestra and Aigisthos must step past the bloody tableau on the *ekkuklēma*.[46] This indignity undermines both the victorious defiance which Klytaimestra attempts to impose by her closing couplet and the triumphal procession in which she leads Aigisthos to cross the threshold of the palace which she has now made his.

When all the actors have gone, the tableau can stand for a moment before it is withdrawn, as a silent, implacable statement of the shed blood which cannot be recalled; it demands and will inevitably receive revenge.[47]

Notes

1 The pattern of the *nostos* or homecoming story in *Ag* is discussed in Ewans 1982a. Note the parallel with Sophocles' *Women of Trachis*, in which, as in *Agamemnon*, the king sends an advance Herald on to the palace while he makes a sacrifice to the gods of his homeland at the place where he has landed.

2 Compare Zeitlin 1965.

3 Conversely, the use of props and extras can be used to communicate the presence and power of a king, as with the suppliant Priest and children who come to call on Oidipous to help them in the opening scene of Sophocles' *Oidipous the King*.

4 See below. The importance of Klytaimestra's dominance of the threshold in *Ag* was first perceived by Taplin 1977a: 299–300.

5 For the notation system used in this Commentary, see p. 33.

6 *Odyssey* 4: 521ff.

7 Compare Ewans 1975: 18–9 and Stanford 1985: 122–3.

8 Compare, for example, Sophocles *Women of Trachis* 1171ff.

9 Compare, for example, Aeschylus' *Persians*, Sophocles' *Antigone* and *Oidipous the King*.

Agamemnon 165

10 Neuburg 1981: 163ff. and 210ff. rightly stresses that the narrative is the Elders' response to the sacrifices that Klytaimestra has organized, their own in-character re-living of Aulis, not Aeschylus' authorial account.

11 Performances both ways have shown that Taplin 1977a: 280–5 was right as against the psychologizing approach of, for example, Pool 1983, who would have Klytaimestra enter to respond silently to this address. The people whose psyches are affected by the narrative of Aulis are the Elders and the audience, not Klytaimestra – who resolved long ago to murder Agamemnon (1577–8). In our production, the Elders first turned in formation towards the palace, came to a despairing close as the chant drew to an end unanswered, and then turned forwards – after a pause – into a new formation as the song began at 104ff. Neither the actress playing Klytaimestra nor any of the Elders felt a need to have her come on at 83 and pull focus either by 'stage business' or by watching the rest of Choros 1. On the contrary, her entrance after 257 became highly effective – with a moment of pointed silence when she was seen for the first time, as she stood just outside the doors of the palace and coldly confronted the Elders. Address to offstage characters by the choros is common in Greek tragedy.

12 The patterns of this ode are discussed in more detail in Ewans 1975 (cf. Lattimore 1964: 40–1).

13 It is often said that their remark that Zeus 'made it law that men/will learn through suffering' (177–8) 'lies at the heart of the trilogy' (Goward 2005: 61). I cannot see that this is true. Orestes is the only character to whom this thought might apply; see *Eu* 276ff.

14 Wecklein, quoted by Fraenkel 1950: II. 114.

15 Space does not permit me to discuss correspondences between *strophe* and *antistrophe* in detail for every choral ode in the trilogy. It is hoped that this discussion of *Ag* Choros 1 will encourage practitioners to examine other choral odes from this perspective and consider using matching patterns of movement in their choreography for corresponding stanzas. Also, see Wiles 2000: 139–41 for an analysis of the strophic correspondence in *LB* Choros 7.

16 Taplin 1977a: 290. He is also, of course, right to take Klytaimestra off at the end of this scene; his arguments are not damaged by Mastronade 1979: 21.

17 These could prefigure, on a much smaller scale, the much greater chaos into which the Elders will be plunged by the death-cry of Agamemnon at the start of Scene 7.

18 This sequence works so well in the theatre that there is no need to bring Klytaimestra back on to speak these lines – spoiling the effect of her sudden entry at 587 (see below) – simply because there is no 'parallel' in the very small number of surviving ancient Greek tragedies for such a long speech by a choros member; *pace* Dale 1969: 215.

19 This theatrical effect, which will be replicated at 851, justifies Taplin 1977a: 294–7 and 299–300 in firmly rejecting all attempts to have her present earlier in this scene.

20 Which side? If he is to obey Klytaimestra's instruction (604ff.) and take a message back to Agamemnon, then he should return the way he came and exit right; but it seems better to have him leave by the left exit, as if that command had been forgotten in the last part of the scene, and he goes on into the city to rest after his journey.

21 Compare Kitto 1956: 12–9.

22 Goheen 1955: 115ff., rightly emphasized by Vickers 1973: 366ff.

23 Compare the fine discussions by Easterling 1973: 7ff., Vickers 1973: 363ff., Taplin 1977a: 310ff., and Winnington-Ingram 1983: 88ff. More recent work has largely focussed on details; compare, for example, Lee 2004 and Bakola 2018.

24 Taplin 1977a: 303–4 writes as if sudden entry down an *eisodos* is possible. It is not.

25 The presence of soldiers is problematic. Where would they go, and what would they do after Agamemnon's exit into the *skēnē*? And Agamemnon has come 'quick as he

166 *Theatrical Commentary*

can' (605) – and is therefore vulnerable (Meineck 1998: 31). The practice of making Agamemnon's entry more spectacular with Kassandra appearing on one of several extra wagons laden with the spoils of war dates back at least to Hellenistic times (Anon. *Hypothesis to Agamemnon* 8–9). It is still prevalent (cf. e.g. the BBC's 1979 production of the *Oresteia* under the title of *The Serpent Son* and Hall's 1981 National Theatre production) but is rightly opposed by Taplin 1977a: 304ff. Kassandra must be in the same carriage as Agamemnon, to establish visually the intimacy between them which motivates Klytaimestra's determination to kill her (1440ff.). Rehm 2017: 98 rightly notes that the image of a man and a woman standing together in a carriage evokes Athenian wedding customs; and Klytaimestra does not fail to note that Kassandra is her husband's concubine (1440ff.).

26 For a more detailed analysis of the speech, compare Ewans 2023: 82ff.

27 In his National Theatre of Greece production at Epidaurus (1980), preserved on YouTube: "Ancient Greek Theater Performance – Oresteia Aeschylus".

28 The puzzlement caused by Kassandra's silence and the delay in identifying her are well discussed by Taplin 1972: 77–8 (cf. 1977a: 305–6).

29 This lyric scene requires the whole of the playing space, and when Aeschylus is staged, any property should be removed as soon as its purpose has been fulfilled.

30 Compare Taplin 1977a: 322.

31 In Greek, Aeschylus puns at the outset on the similarity of sound between 'Oh Apollo' and *apōlesas me* ('you have destroyed me').

32 For a more detailed analysis of the first part of this scene, compare Ewans 2023: 126ff.

33 Compare Reinhardt 1949: 101–4 and Taplin 1977a: 321. Rehm 1985: 89 notes parallels in the language used of Kassandra in her last moments and of Iphigenia in the description of her sacrifice at Aulis.

34 Compare Stanford 1983: 152.

35 Lines 1343–7 are in trochaic tetrameters in the original Greek. This metre expresses greater agitation than regular iambic dialogue (cf. 1649ff.). There is also something slightly comic, at least to my ear (and A.E. Housman's, cf. *Fragment of a Greek Tragedy* 1989: 238), in Agamemnon's ability to utter two perfectly formed verses as he is being pierced three times with a sword. (Contrast the inarticulate cries normally uttered by victims in tragedy; e.g., Aigisthos at *LB* 869.)

36 It was a very rare effect for the choros to enter the *skēnē* during the course of a play (in surviving tragedy only in Euripides *Helen* (330ff.) and by a subsidiary choros in the fragments of his *Phaethon* (245ff.)) The dramatist could, however, generate suspense by threatening to do this and then escaping from the situation by other means – as here (cf. Euripides *Medea* 1275, *Hippolytos* 782 and *Hecuba* 1041).

37 This is the majority view, though strangely, in view of the points made on p. 324, Taplin is undecided 1977a: 325–7.

38 Compare Vickers 1973: 383.

39 The Elders counter the vividness and power of Klytaimestra's rejoinders by thrice adding to their sung stanzas another *ephymnion*: after each of the C stanzas a short, identically repeated refrain of mourning for the dead king and then finally after D1 a lament that they should have lived to see her murder her own husband.

40 In the Greek theatre, his arrival (with bodyguards) would have been seen by an ever-increasing number of spectators on the right as he drew near the playing space during the closing part of Scene 7. Like Agamemnon's, this cannot be a 'surprise entry', *pace* Taplin 1977a: 327.

41 Compare only the Herald and Kilissa in *LB*.

42 Rosenmeyer 1982: 73, wrongly supposing that Taplin agrees with him, has Klytaimestra exit at the end of Scene 7 and re-enter before 1654. However, 1576 does not provide a cue for an exit, and 1654ff. are far more natural if Klytaimestra has been visibly present, watching the development of the quarrel before her

anxious intervention; and the omniscience which she showed in appearing 'on cue' from inside to prevent the entry of both the Herald and Agamemnon into the house is part of the 'masculine' powers which she has lost as a result of the events of Scenes 5 and 7. Finally, an effective point can be made if she is present from the outset of Scene 8 as an alternative focus but is ignored by Aigisthos as he attempts to take all the credit for the death of Agamemnon.

43 The entry in Peter Hall's production of a full hoplite phalanx, with helmets, shields, spears and body armour, made exactly the right effect.

44 Lines 1617–8 have sometimes been pressed into service as evidence for a raised stage (cf. Introduction, p. 6 ff.). However, the dramatic point is precisely that Aigisthos does not have the commanding physical position which his nautical metaphor implies.

45 Compare Vickers 1973: 387. She will remain in this diminished role on her two appearances in *LB* (cf. especially 672–3); meanwhile, the Elders have stigmatized Aigisthos' cowardice by reducing him to female status (1625; cf. Orestes at *LB* 504–5).

46 It is probably best for the Guards to follow the Elders downtown, by the L *eisodos*.

47 Compare Reinhardt 1949: 110.

Libation Bearers

Introduction

The murder of Agamemnon has locked the action into the house of Atreus. The death of the king and the godless rule of the usurpers are wounds so serious that the outside world recedes, not to return to our sight until *Eumenides*. This short, intensely powerful drama is the dark night, the winter at the centre of the trilogy, in and through which the quest for a new light must be pursued.[1]

This atmosphere is established almost at once, in Choros 1. The Libation Bearers return insistently to the motif which dominated in the last two scenes of *Agamemnon*: 'How can the house be purified, once blood's been shed?' (48). The shed blood of Agamemnon has confined the action to this house because only there can a cure be found for its self-inflicted wound (cf. 471ff.).

Only children can save a man's glory, after he is dead. His descendants are duty-bound to pay honour to his grave. A male heir must avenge his murdered father, or his father's Furies will turn their anger onto him; and legitimate power descends, with spiritually cogent force, from father to son. *Libation Bearers* reflects completely these basic features of Greek belief. Only Agamemnon's heirs can lift the veils of *miasma* under which this house now lies; only when Agamemnon's son removes the tyrant Aigisthos and takes his rightful place on his father's throne will its greatness be restored.

This is a drama of sharp contrasts, developed from the acrimonious division between the Elders and Aigisthos in Scene 8 of *Agamemnon*. Here, people and their actions are judged by only one criterion: do they remain true to the natural order, or do they not? Are they the real *philoi* of Agamemnon, or have they become the instruments of Aigisthos and Klytaimestra and so his enemies? Even physical objects, such as the lock of hair which Elektra finds on Agamemnon's grave, are subjected to this test.

Orestes declares at the outset his resolve to avenge Agamemnon (18–19, cf. 297–8); this is no drama of Hamlet-like indecision. Gradually, there gather around him the powers, both human and divine, that will aid him; like Klytaimestra in *Agamemnon*, he slowly obtains the strength that will make his success inevitable. The difficulties of his task are firmly stressed; the Libation Bearers are only foreign slave women, his sister is treated like one, and he has

DOI: 10.4324/9781032646992-8

Libation Bearers 169

only one male companion. They are all exiles or outcasts, attempting to overthrow a regime which has abolished political processes and governs by force.

But we sense at once that Orestes' approach is very different from his mother's. Here is a man whose determination is calm and measured and whose stance towards the gods is far from reckless. And this is why the relative weakness of Orestes' human allies is steadily counterbalanced, as the first half unfolds, by the ever-increasing aid which he is able to summon, as he comes to deserve it more and more, from the gods, both above and below, and from his father's shade. In Aeschylus' world, the gods help those who help themselves.

The choros members now play characters on the side of the protagonist; the Libation Bearers take a central role in developing the audience's expectations. As Orestes nears his deed, they increasingly sing of the light that he will bring (809ff., 863ff., cf. 131); and after he has killed the usurpers, they break out into unrestrained rejoicing (Choros 7).

To avenge Agamemnon is inevitably, after Aeschylus' treatment of his murder, to take the life of Klytaimestra. The threat that Orestes' vengeance for Agamemnon – and his restoration to the throne of Argos – will involve matricide is present even in Kassandra's first vision of his return (*Ag* 1279ff.); but Aeschylus deliberately underplays it in the early stages of *Libation Bearers*, then makes it resurface powerfully just before the half-way point and overshadow the remainder. We are not allowed to know the nature of Klytaimestra's terrifying dream until it is right for Orestes to read it (523ff.).

At the climax, son confronts mother before our eyes, in a scene almost unparalleled in Western drama,[2] and Orestes finds himself in a position as monstrous as that of Agamemnon at Aulis. Klytaimestra's femininity and her motherhood are placed fully before him; against them lie his duty to avenge his father, and the command of the gods. Once again, like Agamemnon's, this is a real choice that is also no real choice, for the Furies will attack him – a father's or a mother's – whatever Orestes may do (924–5). By that point in the drama, we expect that he will take his vengeance; when Orestes decides that Pylades' advice is right, he satisfies the deepest expectations of the audience. But once again, just as at the end of *Agamemnon*, his deed is overshadowed – and far more terribly, because Klytaimestra's Furies rise almost immediately from her shed blood.

Dramatic Structure

To point up the similarities and differences between Orestes and Klytaimestra, Aeschylus dramatizes the story of Orestes' return through a structure parallel to that of *Agamemnon*. As in the first play, the action reaches its climax in the murders, which take place about two-thirds of the way through; and once again, the last scenes present the avenger appearing triumphantly on the *ekkuklēma* over the bodies of two victims – a man and a woman who have been lovers – only to be reduced, by the end, from triumph to apprehension as the murderer is overwhelmed by the prospect of vengeance.

170   *Theatrical Commentary*

Also as in *Agamemnon*, there is a structural division at the mid-point; but in *Libation Bearers*, it is far more marked. The drama is divided into two fundamentally opposed halves, around the scene-change which lies at the centre of the play and the trilogy. First a slow section, framed around the grave of Agamemnon at the centre of the playing space, with a steady and unified development, during which Orestes and Elektra are reunited and gain the support from Agamemnon and the gods which they need for their attempt at vengeance; then a rapid, suspense-filled second part set before the palace, in which Orestes deceives to get access and eventually succeeds in overcoming the usurpers.

The difference between the two halves is marked in several different ways. In the first half, set in the countryside, the grave pulls the focus forward, and the façade and doors are not in use. There are only two scenes and one full choral ode. Scene 2 is the longest scene in Aeschylus' surviving tragedies and is given monumental shape by the massive *kommos*, the invocation to the spirit of Agamemnon, which is the most substantial lyric actor–choros interplay in all surviving Greek drama. There are also only two speaking solo parts, two entrances, and no exits until the end.

In the second half, this steady build-up is replaced by constant surprises. The façade once again represents the house of Atreus, and since its double doors are in frequent use, the focus is often pulled towards the back of the playing space. This allows for many sudden entrances and exits, and there are five short scenes, divided off from each other by equally short choral odes. Their brevity maintains the pace, as the unity created in part 1 by interweaving sung and spoken parts is replaced by a marked alternation between the two modes. There are no actor lyrics – only the Libation Bearers sing; and while Elektra is reduced to a silent part, five new speaking characters join Orestes.

The reunion of Orestes and Elektra at Agamemnon's grave, the invocation to gain his support and the plotting to subdue the tyrants are all conducted in an atmosphere of ever-increasing confidence; this is symbolized in part 1 by the Libation Bearers' confident possession of the playing area, especially when they envelop the heirs and the grave in the *kommos*.

In the second part, the Libation Bearers no longer participate in the action on equal terms; their involvement in the conspiracy is used to generate an air of suspense. There are violent contrasts, as they begin each ode from a position of retreat, dispersed to the perimeter of the playing space in a feigned conformity to their proper social role. Four times they suddenly resume control of the playing space for a brief and intense choral lyric. This oscillation culminates in the sequence after Choros 7, a triumphant and hopefully a final repossession of the entire space, followed immediately by the horror of the tableau on the *ekkuklēma*, which drives the Libation Bearers back to the perimeter. Orestes himself then loses his command of the space to the Furies, and after he has been possessed and driven from the scene, the closing song is brief, hesitant and anxious.

Libation Bearers 171

Setting

Scenes 1 and 2 cannot be set in front of the palace. Klytaimestra had mutilated the corpse of Agamemnon so that its power to harm her would be diminished (439ff.); and she would have buried him as far away from her residence as possible. (She did not dare to take offerings to his grave herself, even after a very ominous dream.) So these scenes are set in the countryside, and the *skēnographia* panels would be designed to reflect this. (On the change of scene after 584, see pp. 177–8.)

No other position than C for the grave of Agamemnon is natural, or indeed practical, since it is danced around during Choros 2 and the *kommos*.[3] It was not represented by an altar placed at the centre-point[4]; this would not have enough space on it for the offerings and, in any case, would not look like a grave. Nor would it have been a monumental stone tomb with a *stēlē* beside it, as on many vase paintings of this scene. Aeschylus' Klytaimestra buried Agamemnon away from the palace, having mutilated his corpse to prevent its anger from reaching her; she would not have given this man she hated a noble tomb. Line 154 suggests a low mound of earth (cf. 722-4); it should be set at the centre of the space and with its long side parallel to the façade.[5]

Scene 1

Kassandra prophesied that Orestes would return from exile to avenge his father's death (*Ag* 1279ff.). *Libation Bearers* opens at the moment when her prophecy is fulfilled. The sole descendants of Agamemnon are about to be united at the one place where they can enlist the support of their dead father's spirit and of the gods who protect his interests.[6]

Scene 1 shows Orestes return and establish a relationship with his father's grave. Agamemnon was buried in the absence of his son and heir (8–9); we learn later that Klytaimestra mutilated his corpse, to hobble the dead man's spirit in the hope that his anger against her would be less potent (440ff.); the burial was performed by Klytaimestra alone, as she threatened at the end of *Agamemnon* (*Ag* 1551ff.); and the dead king was denied lament either by the citizens of Argos (429ff.) or by his only daughter (444ff.). In this scene, Orestes begins to gather round himself the powers that will make possible his own restoration to his rightful place.

Orestes must first establish his possession of the playing space, which represents the soil of Argos, and then focus more on building a close relationship with the grave itself, at which he must claim his inheritance.[7] He should therefore perhaps stand motionless just inside the playing space, facing the grave, for a few moments after his entry. This action offsets the initial image of desolation presented by the isolated mound; his return gives some prospect of a solution to the problems of the house.

He could circle the grave and then should kneel facing forward in the most dominant position possible, immediately behind the mound, when he offers the locks at 6ff.

172   *Theatrical Commentary*

Traditional commentaries neglect the role of Pylades because he says nothing until his crucial lines in Scene 6. But Pylades is present in every scene, except the brief Scenes 4 and 5, and his role goes far beyond the three spoken lines. Pylades is Orestes' silent guardian or protector. At the climax, he can credibly speak almost with the voice of Apollo because he has earlier witnessed, and given his silent approval to, everything done by Agamemnon's heirs. His positioning in Scene 1 must establish this role from the outset. One way to do this is to have him follow into the playing area only after Orestes has moved forward for the opening line. Pylades can then move almost immediately to, say, CR, observing and overseeing Orestes' interaction with the grave.

The approaching women become visible to Orestes and the spectators in the right-hand side of the auditorium just before line 10. Orestes springs back to join Pylades, and both men then look across the grave towards the left entrance. Orestes needs to move a little from BR towards BC as he looks more closely at the women during 12–13; Pylades meanwhile can move, after Orestes' final invocation to Zeus, to join him BR during 20–21 in preparation for their exit after 21 to conceal themselves. The most obvious and effective place for this in the ancient Greek theatre would have been the mouth of the right *eisodos*; they shelter just outside the playing area, under the lee of the auditorium's retaining wall.[8]

The manuscript in which *Libation Bearers* was transmitted through the Dark Ages begins at what is now line 10 of our texts; by great good fortune, some of the lines from the missing opening have been preserved in quotations by other ancient authors. Lines 1–5 are cited in Aristophanes' *Frogs* (1126–8, 1172–3; although the quotations are separated by dialogue, there is no good reason to doubt that the lines are consecutive). However, lines 6–7 and 8–9 are presented consecutively in this script only for the actor's convenience; they are preserved to us in separate sources, and the fact that 8–9 follow on neatly from 6–7 is no guarantee that they did originally follow without a break or indeed that the two couplets are presented in the order in which they originally appeared.

Though the surviving lines play well, there is one important element missing from the scene as we have it. In Scene 2, Elektra is rewarded with the sight of the locks of hair that speak of Orestes' return only when she has affirmed her loyalty to Agamemnon and prayed for an avenger to return. Similarly, Orestes should use the lament in 8–9 as the springboard for a firm declaration of his readiness and resolve to avenge his father; he would then be rewarded at once with the arrival of Elektra and her companions. If lines to this effect originally preceded 10, 18–19 would become a closing, recapitulative invocation to Zeus.[9]

Choros 1

Klytaimestra has buried Agamemnon far from the palace (22) to blunt and avert the anger of the king she has murdered. But during the very night that Orestes returned to Argos, the gods have sent Klytaimestra an ominous dream.

Libation Bearers 173

Agamemnon's anger from the grave has power – indeed, it has brought Orestes back, and the crucial day is at hand. This terrifying dream, together with Orestes' return, generates the plot of the first half of the drama. The success of the vengeance is due to Klytaimestra's fear (42ff.) and her lack of *philoi* apart from Aigisthos (revealed by the lie at 717). She must send the libations that she needs to appease Agamemnon's spirit by the hands of slaves who hate her and a daughter who is easily persuaded, at the start of Scene 2, to follow her own true loyalties. Coming together at his grave near the frontier of Argive territory, Orestes and Elektra are joined by both gods and slave women (the highest and the lowest strands of the Greek social order); together, these provide the heirs with the strength to overthrow the tyranny.

Elektra and the Libation Bearers enter by the left *eisodos*.[10] They begin to move before line 10; Orestes and Pylades withdraw into the opposite entrance after 21, and the Libation Bearers begin to sing at 22 as they step into the playing space. Elektra enters before the choros members, carrying garlands for the grave of Agamemnon, and takes up a neutral position (e.g. BL) for the duration of Choros 1. (Members of the choros bring on the pots and mixing bowl for the libations, as per the play's title, and might place them beside the grave during the dance movements of the first stanza or retain them for interesting choreography throughout the ode.)

The choreography must reflect the structure of the lyric; a strophic pair as introduction, creating a violent contrast between the women's torment and Orestes' calm[11]; then two pairs of stanzas which present the central theme of the play and a brief concluding *epode*. The dance must also show the tentative but firm relationship which the Libation Bearers establish with the playing space and the grave.

Scene 2

Part 1: Elektra's offering (85–164)

> [The Libation Bearers] encourage her [Elektra] to turn the weapons against the inventor by offering the libations as if from herself, with a prayer conceived in a directly opposite sense to that which Klytaimestra intended…The attempt was monstrous, and it has failed; the libations have been restored to their proper office; and Agamemnon's wrath, instead of being propitiated, has been aggravated by his child's prayer…That which Klytaimestra, in insult or fear, has denied to Agamemnon for years is conceded at last, and being entrusted to the hands of others is turned to the very purpose she would most have deprecated.[12]

Elektra's offering is the next stage in the queen's downfall. It matches Orestes' lock of hair; the spirit and the manner of the address which Elektra makes are parallel to his[13]; and she speaks 124ff. in the same place, behind the grave at C, to stress her affinity with Orestes.

174   *Theatrical Commentary*

The staging of this section is straightforward. Elektra must first establish her relationship with the grave; given the importance of her first speech, she should move to it as early as possible (perhaps to the L end of the grave during the opening lines, then around to C directly behind it on the strong lines 89–90). Next (100ff.), she must engage more closely with the Libation Bearers, preparing for the *stichomythia*; Elektra turns towards various members of the choros as she delivers the appeal.

This *stichomythia* is probably best played between Elektra and one member of the choros since the text implies an increasingly close mutual involvement.[14] The speaker's movements towards Elektra (106, 117, 119) are also movements towards the grave, establishing in spatial terms its importance to the Libation Bearers.

Elektra's speech at 124ff. is beautifully modulated, providing a fine opportunity for an actress to control her audience through the power of pathos and rhetoric alone. The key to the delivery is to take a diminuendo from 130 and treat the central section from 135 as a close and intimate address to the corpse. This then allows a steady build from 142 to the climax at 148.

Choros 2 is a short lyric in one single stanza. After the first four lines, it was composed in dochmiacs, the most violent Greek lyric metre; it requires an agitated outpouring of grief, to discharge the rhetorical emotion built up in Elektra's speech into the other world of lyric. The choreography must both evoke the act of ritual lamentation and express the intensity of the Libation Bearers' desire for the avenger; but it must not obscure the audience's view of Elektra as she pours the libations and then sees the lock of hair; most of the dancing should therefore be in the rear half of the playing space.

Part 2: The reunion (165–305). The main role of the lock is to establish the oneness of Orestes and Elektra (221) before they meet. The primary element is the divine guidance which leads Elektra to the lock,[15] and to mental anguish based on the fear that the lock may be his, but simply sent from exile, then to the reunion of Agamemnon's heirs at his grave.

If Elektra has poured the offerings at the L end of the grave, the lock of hair will naturally be discovered by her attention moving right, and she should go close to it during the last lines of Choros 2. The Libation Bearers would then come forward during 169–70 to cluster round Elektra just behind the grave. She picks up the lock during 170 (she will use this prop throughout 183–204) and should immediately break forward, to get enough distance from the choros to play the rest of the *stichomythia* and the monologue effectively. (Elektra still holds the lock at 230. We solved the problem of disposal by having her gently throw it to the ground behind her as she advances towards Orestes after 234 – a marvellous moment; she no longer needs his token after she has finally recognized the man himself.)

Some spurious lines (which must have been added before Euripides made fun of them in his *Elektra*, 508–46) imagine Elektra seeing a second token, some footprints. Strong arguments have been made against retaining these lines.[16]

Libation Bearers 175

Line 211 can be delivered FC facing forward; this allows Orestes to surprise Elektra as he enters rapidly, advancing to just R of the front of the grave. When they see him, Elektra starts back a little towards FL, and the Libation Bearers should retreat much further back, to EBC-ECL.

The recognition *stichomythia* can now become a slow repossession by Elektra of the area in front of the grave, which she has just abandoned to Orestes. Line 220 implies a move away from him, but from 224 onwards she gradually comes nearer and nearer to him, so that they are almost touching at 234, when he has shown her the piece of weaving.[17] After the recognition, they are close together, facing forward just in front of the grave, for Orestes' prayers at 247ff.

Pylades should be kept out of focus up to this point (e.g. at ERC). At 269, however, he can come into his own, countering a Libation Bearer's fear in 264ff. by coming forward to give Orestes strength and provide him with a springboard for his speech of confidence in Apollo.[18]

Lines 269ff. are another major speech, setting out at length the powerful forces which demand that Orestes should accomplish revenge for his father. In retrospect, these words also preview what his mother's Furies will threaten to do to him, even before we have been squarely confronted with the reality of his coming act of matricide. Its rhetorical variations cry out to be complemented by quite a lot of movement.

Part 3: the invocation (306–509). For the Greeks, the spirits of the dead inhabited a shadowy, ill-defined underworld. They are within the power of the gods below, in Hades. But they are also in their graves. The dead are present when a dirge is sung for them, and they are aware of what is done beside their tombs. This murdered man would have had the power to haunt his murderess had she dared to come near; and he has the power to help his children now that they are assembled at his grave. He can both profit from the *timē* paid by those who owe it to him and suffer, losing respect among the other dead if he does not receive his dues. But the senses are dulled by death, and strenuous effort is needed to ensure that a prayer or offering truly reaches the dead.

Out of these basic conditions of belief, Aeschylus created the lyric invocation, or *kommos*, in which Agamemnon's reunited heirs attempt to gain his attention and seek his aid and that of the gods. It is – or should be – one of the most powerful scenes in Greek tragedy. It should not be abbreviated, as it is all too frequently in modern productions.[19]

The heirs and the Libation Bearers pass through an intense psychological drama. Orestes begins with little hope, despairing of ever communicating with Agamemnon. The opening mood is slow and solemn, as both he and his sister dwell on the miseries of the past; their first prayers are hopeless, impossible wishes that Agamemnon had met a better fate or had not been killed at all. But the *kommos* must become faster and more impassioned for Elektra's outcry at 363ff.; and then suddenly, under the prompting of the Libation Bearers' optimism, hopes for the future start to overcome despair (372ff.). After a slight rallentando at 405ff. there is a moment of equipoise at 410–17; and then there

176   *Theatrical Commentary*

are no more doubts. The tempo picks up gradually to 428. Elektra's anguish is there in 418ff, but so too is her savage determination; and so, as the second section begins (423ff.), the Libation Bearers increase their emotional intensity, from chant to full song.

The murder of Agamemnon can now be recalled in all its horror (rallentando again 429ff. but with ever-increasing intensity to the climax at 456ff.). Orestes states his resolve directly to his father (434ff.), and brother and sister confront all that their mother did – including even (439) the mutilation of Agamemnon's corpse in an attempt to deprive his shade of the power to take vengeance.

The *kommos* itself transcends her attempt, and as it reaches its fierce, elliptical climax (456ff.), we hear no more of hopes and fears. The past has been consumed in the intensity of the scene, and Agamemnon's heirs now confront the present and immediate future firmly and with disciplined and solemn emotion. After the *kommos*, Orestes takes total command of the vengeance.

For the Greeks, a fated thing will inevitably occur – but the precise time at which it will come to fulfilment is not fixed. The right appeal, at the right time, may make it come. So too with this act of vengeance, prophesied by Kassandra in *Agamemnon*; the *kommos* has made now the right time – and for a few moments the power of their achievement fills the Libation Bearers with awe (463–5).

This lyric invocation, cast in the form of a highly complex pattern of responding stanzas,[20] requires a use of space which will reflect both its ritual solemnity and its ever-increasing dramatic intensity. The relationship and interaction between the Libation Bearers, Orestes and Elektra are vital. A regrouping is needed to mark the beginning of the *kommos*, either before or during the introductory stanza. Orestes and Elektra must take up their basic positions for the scene, which are clearly at the head and foot of the grave. Pylades, since he takes no active part in this section, should move to a position where his role as overseer may be communicated to the whole audience (e.g. EBL).

The placing for the Libation Bearers is more conjectural. The concept finally adopted in our production was for them to begin the invocation equally spaced in a circle around the perimeter of the playing space, facing inward, and to make their way successively, in the choreography of the choral stanzas, towards the centre, ending the scene in a close ellipse around the grave (incorporating Elektra and Orestes in this pattern) and kneeling facing the grave for part or all of the final section (463ff.). This has three main advantages: (1) two ritually complete formations are placed at the start and end of the *kommos* – the opening one spread out and tentative in its approach to the grave, and the last one in a close relationship with it, with an incomplete, transitional pattern in between to symbolize the struggle and anguish during the intervening lyrics; (2) the Libation Bearers can easily address both the grave and one or other of the heirs; and (3) it leaves plenty of room for the heirs to make their own movements and gestures.[21]

Libation Bearers   177

Emotionally, 479–509 form a cooling-off period, a calmer representation in spoken verse of that which was earlier conveyed to Agamemnon in the passionate intensity of song. Scott[22] imagines the choros as withdrawing from the grave, leaving the heirs close beside it. This fits in with his view that this section is the climax of the invocation scene (though the pause while the twelve choros members withdraw is messy). Some repositioning after the lyric *kommos* is clearly called for, but the better alternative is to move the heirs, leaving the Libation Bearers in their position close around the grave. The *stichomythia* and the speeches at 497ff. both gain power if Orestes and Elektra are now together facing the grave in unity rather than separated. Accordingly, we moved them during the choral epilogue to stand BR; the oblique angle to the grave, with Orestes and Elektra now together and facing the bulk of the audience, gave the required variation from the *kommos* positions while still making possible an effective interaction with the grave.

Part 4 (510–84). Orestes needs to be brought forward, away from Elektra, for the reading of the dream. This is achieved by selecting the speaker of 510ff. from between the C and L positions around the grave. (Her intervention goes well if it is spoken over the grave to disrupt the unity of the heirs.) Orestes has to come round towards FC during his response, and the Libation Bearer who speaks in 523–53 crosses to between L and FL to engage with him. Orestes is then near the grave at 540ff., and Pylades should come down from EBL to join him at the end of this speech, in view of his increased importance from 561.

Orestes' plan requires an interaction with both Elektra and the Libation Bearers. It plays well with the bulk of the action in the front half of the space and the Libation Bearers – with the one exception, who is now FL – still in their ellipse around the grave but now turned to face Orestes.[23] As Orestes quits his interaction with the one Libation Bearer, he can move towards FR during 554ff. Meanwhile, Elektra needs to come down to CR to be given her instructions. Lines 560ff. are then animated by small movements of Orestes in the FC area, with Pylades coming down to join Elektra and Orestes during 560–3.[24]

Line 579 is addressed to Elektra, close to her between R and FR; from this position, Orestes has an easy turn to address the remainder of the speech to the Libation Bearers and finally to the god Hermes.

The directions after 584. In the first half of *Libation Bearers*, the façade and its doors are not used; the grave of Agamemnon is imagined, for obvious political, psychological and religious reasons, as not being anywhere near the palace.[25] At 653, Orestes knocks on the doors, establishing that they now represent the entrance to the house of Atreus. A change of scene therefore takes place before 585, since the last two stanzas of Choros 3 are designed to accompany Orestes' entry to begin the attempt at revenge.

A scene-change in Greek tragedy requires that everyone – especially the choros – leave the first location before anyone enters in the second location; so the Libation Bearers must exit after 584 along with Orestes, Pylades and Elektra. It also requires a change of props.[26] Dale (1969: 119), Taplin (1977a: 318–9) and Garvie (1986: xlv) all believe that a scene can 'refocus' without exit

178 *Theatrical Commentary*

and re-entry of the choros and removal/addition of a prop. There is a simple practical problem with this; if left in the space for the second half of the play, the grave would prevent the characters from using the full playing area. It would also be totally unrealistic to play scenes set in front of the palace with the grave in plain sight about 10 metres away from the doors (see above, 'Setting'). And Greek tragedy was realistic in such matters (cf. Ewans 2023: 32–4).[27]

Accordingly, stagehands must strike the grave of Agamemnon after all the actors have left. While this is being done, the actors would have moved round behind the *skēnē*, on the lower level out of sight of the audience; in a modern production, they can simply cross backstage. They have made their exit left, to show that they are going away from the grave towards the city, but must enter right in the new location, to show that they are coming to the palace from the country. Meanwhile, the *skēnographia* panels representing the countryside would be removed, to disclose under them the panels representing the palace which were familiar from *Agamemnon*.

Orestes has ordered Elektra (554, 579) to go home and play a part, inside the house, in the action of the vengeance attempt. Most translators and commentators assume that she vanishes from the drama after Scene 2 – primarily, I believe, because she never speaks again. But her mute presence in Scene 3 is very effective, and in Scene 7 virtually essential (see below), and if Elektra comes out of the palace for either or both of those scenes, then logically she should have been seen to return to it from the grave. If she returns from the right, knocks and is admitted through the doors of the palace façade, this establishes, before the re-entry of the Libation Bearers for Choros 3, that it is now in use. It also prepares the audience for Orestes' entry and makes a nice contrast between Elektra's ease and his difficulty in gaining access to the house.

Choros 3

This is an inner dialogue between the Libation Bearers, placing Klytaimestra's crime in the full focus of other unnatural crimes which have been caused by the readiness of a woman seized by passion to take risks (A2). It widens the focus of the play, bringing in mythical examples in a way which is appropriate both for the mid-point of the trilogy and for the central ode of a drama which is otherwise focussed relentlessly on the fortunes of this house alone. They also begin here their attempt (which develops through the next two songs to a climax in Choros 6) to impose the view that Orestes is completely justified and may commit even matricide in the cause of avenging Agamemnon without deserving any consequences. This prepares, by contrast, for the sensational undermining of Orestes' defence in Scene 7.

The initial mood is philosophical and reflective; in our production, mindful of the approach of nightfall (NB 660–1), the Libation Bearers entered individually and collapsed exhausted around the perimeter of the playing space. Then the choreography began with one of them rising slowly to dance and sing

Libation Bearers 179

the first stanza. The song gains intensity and momentum through the B and C stanzas, until it achieves directness and power in the final strophic pair, by which time the Libation Bearers have summoned all the strength they need to welcome Orestes and Pylades.[28]

Scene 3

After the Choros ends, in two stanzas whose choreography should be a triumphal hailing of the returning hero, there is a complete contrast. As Orestes and Pylades approach the doors, the Libation Bearers retreat to the front perimeter,[29] feigning non-involvement for the first – but by no means the last – time.

The scene begins with a remarkable shift in tone, a sequence which has surviving parallels only in comedy.[30] The house at first completely ignores its rightful master – fulfilling Orestes' prediction of the maimed state of the *oikos* (566ff.). He has to knock three times before a servant emerges,[31] grumbling the first half of his line from inside the palace, and delivers the rest of it reluctantly through a partly open door. The regime has withdrawn into the palace; the outside world is now dangerous territory, viewed with suspicion by Klytaimestra and her followers.

Orestes' speech begins as a direct response to the Servant, but he soon opens out, first into the expansive rhetoric of 660–1 and then (663ff.) into speculations which are better addressed to Pylades, as a confidential aside. This allows for two further effects: first, the Servant can retreat in disdain before Orestes' affected, ornamental imagery (closing the doors precisely so as to undermine 662); then, Klytaimestra can enter early at 665 (not 668) to overhear the last three lines of Orestes' speech – directed, as a man-to-man confidence, to Pylades – and then score a rich, ironic point when she speaks her opening line.

Klytaimestra's entry disrupts Orestes' expectations. It is not simply that Orestes expected Aigisthos (554ff., 656); the vehemence of the language of the murder fantasy at 571ff., when taken now together with the evasive, sexist phrasing of 664ff., indicates that he actively wanted to meet Aigisthos first. Instead, he is forced to confront his mother at once.

This is the first scene after the doors in the façade have come into use, and it is therefore played largely towards the back of the space. Orestes begins his interaction with the Servant up by the doorway but leaves him and comes forward in a leisurely way with Pylades during the rhetorical amplifications at 658ff. However, as Orestes' tale unfolds, Klytaimestra will inevitably be drawn forward around 686ff., in preparation for the great outburst at 691ff., in which she temporarily breaks out of the web of Orestes' schemes. The substantial move here, clear into the front sector of the playing space, is Klytaimestra's only sally into a public arena which is increasingly controlled by her enemies.

Klytaimestra is clearly attended (cf. 712ff.) – but by whom? Some scholars have assigned to Elektra Klytaimestra's central speech at 691ff.[32] I am sure that this is wrong; it is *Klytaimestra's* reaction to the news of 'Orestes' death' that we want to hear at this point; she cannot be silent, and the speech is in any case

180 *Theatrical Commentary*

inappropriate to Elektra. The idea has unfortunately led almost everyone[33] to discount the possibility of Elektra's re-entering, now played in the original production by a 'silent face', or extra.[34] If Elektra does re-enter, it shows up the grand lie with which Klytaimestra ends the scene, even in advance of Scene 4, where the only person she can find to take her message to Aigisthos is an old Nurse totally loyal to Orestes. To receive Agamemnon, Klytaimestra came out in total command, symbolized in the theatre by the maidservants ready to do her bidding as well as by her free use of the whole playing space. Now she does not control the playing space, and to receive Orestes and Pylades, she can call upon no one but the daughter who hates her to act as her attendant.[35] Klytaimestra's every move is undermined by Elektra's presence at EBC, literally upstaging her and performing exactly the role which Orestes asked of her at 579.[36]

The meeting between Orestes and Klytaimestra is portrayed with great psychological subtlety; Klytaimestra is not now the monster whom the Libation Bearers portrayed to us in Choros 3. Even if there is a macabre irony when she offers 'warm baths' to Agamemnon's son, Klytaimestra is hospitable. She remains, as in the last scene of *Agamemnon*, firmly within the traditional limits of a proper woman's role (672–3).

Orestes therefore has to deceive a Klytaimestra who is receiving strangers correctly and properly. So his speech at 674ff. begins hesitantly, perhaps with head averted, and only takes flight – once again, in clichéd rhetoric – at 685ff. Then Orestes makes a sudden, vicious attack (690) and receives in reply not the hypocritical reaction which both he and we might have expected but a sincere meditation on the troubles of the *oikos*. Though she fears her son's return, Klytaimestra, when she first hears of his fictive death, sees it as yet another undermining of the household. (We will only be told later, by the hostile nurse Kilissa, that her second, secret reaction was rejoicing.)

Orestes overrides the pathos of 699 with the direct thrust of 700 – unfair even if he only refers to material goods and outrageously insensitive when delivered by a man purporting to bring the news that an only son is lost. In what follows, he continues to play the travelling Daulian – note, for example, the facile rhetoric of 702–3. But his hypocritical speech allows Klytaimestra time to recover, and with a sudden new energy (710ff.), she welcomes her murderers into the house.[37] She does this with sincerity; and she tells only one lie – in the final line, as she attempts to conceal the total isolation of the usurpers, which in the next scene will undo them.

Choros 4

The Libation Bearers now express an active desire to help in the deception. They call on Hermes to help Orestes,[38] and they call on Persuasion to come and help themselves, correctly sensing that the crucial moments of the action, which are happening now, may give them an opportunity. They are praying for 581–2 to be fulfilled; in the next scene, their prayer is answered, and they save Orestes.

Libation Bearers 181

In this ode, the Libation Bearers express their increasing anxiety, their suspense as they hope that they can guide or direct the action, and through that the fact that the drama is now nearing its climax. Given their starting position on the front perimeter, the structure of the words implies a rapid flow towards the centre during the first three lines, vivid gestures of invocation from a position surrounding the centre during the four-line prayer, and then a rapid movement away from the centre, which must be completed during the last three lines. Then they must freeze quickly in position the moment the doors begin to open.

Scene 4

The gods answer their prayer immediately and from a totally unexpected direction.[39] This scene begins with one of the Libation Bearers interrupting Kilissa to prevent her from leaving the playing space directly by the left *eisodos*. The contrast between the section up to 742 and what follows is easily established if Kilissa delivers the opening of her speech from one position (e.g., just forward from BC) and then comes forward to engage the Libation Bearers at 743–6. The movements must exhibit throughout the contrast in tempo between Kilissa's almost comic garrulity and their increasing impatience, with Kilissa perhaps circling around individual members of the choros to give visual form to her rambling discourse. She then disengages partially from them as she concludes.

By 763, Kilissa should have reached the centre, in view of the importance of what is to follow. One of the Libation Bearers intervenes to change the message[40] – an action unparalleled in surviving Greek tragedy; even the Furies themselves, for all their power in *Eumenides*, do not have the ability to change the course of the plot. The Libation Bearer who speaks to Kilissa can initially be at some distance; a substantial cross during 763ff. brings the audience's full attention onto her intervention. The dialogue needs to be played with urgent intensity until 775 and then eases back until 778–9, in which the speaker feigns detachment; the Libation Bearers could close in a little towards Kilissa from 763 and then finally yield outwards again. This allows Kilissa to make directly for her exit left, watched by them all. Choros 5 begins as soon as she steps out of the playing space.

Choros 5

As the action nears its climax, Aeschylus varied the pattern of short, intense astrophic odes between the scenes with this longer lyric. He reinforced the impression of spaciousness by opting for an unusual Greek metrical scheme, with the strophically responding stanzas interspersed by *mesodes* in a contrasting metre, which do not respond to each other (A1a, B1a, C1a). Each *mesode* intrudes, with disturbingly stronger content, on the regular pattern. Though the argument of the text continues through them, each *mesode* is an intensifying, heightening element in relation to the two matching stanzas which frame it.

182 *Theatrical Commentary*

And A1a is a diversion which qualifies what is otherwise a steady, serene development throughout the ode, reflecting the constant emphasis on the absolute rightness of what Orestes will do. The choreography must flow – perhaps beginning in a stately manner, but with a gradual rise in intensity and speed through the prayer to Zeus in the A stanzas; then with an overall calm, on a new level of emotion, during the address to the gods in the B stanzas; finally with a firm pattern for C1 acting as the foundation for an increasing level of emphasis through to the end.

Circular patterns, with much use of interweaving of choros members and of gesture, are appropriate for the first six stanzas with their sequence of supplications and their overall feeling of completeness. The C stanzas call for a much more direct, angular treatment to complement the combination of confidence and anxiety with which the Libation Bearers turn from the gods to address Orestes directly (presumably facing towards the palace during much of the last three stanzas).

Scene 5

Aigisthos enters 'summoned by a messenger' (838) – and we know how the Libation Bearers reshaped that message. Deception and treacherous persuasion are clearly working, and once again the Libation Bearers take extraordinary action. Just as there is no surviving parallel for their intervention in Scene 4, so too there is no parallel for a character played by the choros luring someone to his death.

Aigisthos' step from the mouth of the *eisodos* into the playing area is the cue for a violent transition – from expression of their true emotions to feigned subservience – which is the most important aspect of the Libation Bearers' part in Scenes 3–6. In our production, they moved suddenly at this point from an erect posture, with arms extended in salutation of Orestes' imminent triumph, to the total submissiveness of an Oriental salaam, in an echo of Klytaimestra's homage to Agamemnon in *Ag* Scene 4.

This short scene[41] allows the director to consolidate the atmosphere of political menace under the tyranny of the usurpers. In the speech, the actor can establish not merely the hypocrisy of Aigisthos' condolences on the 'death of Orestes' but also the sinister, decadent character into whom power has corrupted the self-justified poseur seen in *Ag* Scene 8. There is also the dynamic tension between the Libation Bearers, apparently weak and cowering before their tyrant – but in fact strong – and Aigisthos, who is the exact reverse. We tried to express all this by having the Libation Bearers kneel and prostrate themselves in a supposedly reverent – but in fact menacing – ellipse in the rear part of the playing space. Aigisthos delivered his speech circling nervously around the centre of this ellipse, pausing only to ruminate (841–3) on the implications of the 'death of Orestes'.

Aeschylus crystallizes the contrast between Aigisthos and his deceivers around a central issue of the trilogy – gender conflict. Aigisthos pours scorn on

Libation Bearers 183

Klytaimestra's message in 845ff., and these lines remind the audience both of Orestes' confidential aside to Pylades at 665ff. and – more directly though over a larger span of time – of the Elders' sudden distrust of Klytaimestra's beacons at *Ag* 475ff. Those parallel essays in male sexism, though subjected to almost immediate deflation, were at least addressed at the time to men alone; here, however, with supreme irony, Aigisthos is made to voice his distrust of women's words to a woman, who with consummate hypocrisy agrees with him. Aeschylus then takes the irony of the scene ever further; going to his death as blindly as Agamemnon, Aigisthos tells the woman who has duped him that 'My mind has eyes; it cannot be deceived'.

The movements and gestures here must establish the contrast between Aigisthos' false assumption that he has power and the true power of the slave woman who answers him and lures him to his death. For example, in our production, Aigisthos suddenly grasped one of the Libation Bearers by the chin at 847, jerking her half erect to make her answer his question; but she rose fully to her feet on 'we've heard' and delivered the rest of her speech standing, uncowed, after backing away slightly to assert her control over her own space. Aigisthos' transition from sadism to bemused acceptance was conveyed simply by his steady oblique move towards the doors in the next three lines.[42] It was then almost irresistible to play the last line as a parting address; Aigisthos turns back towards her at the doorway before a purposeful, unsuspecting exit.

Choros 6

Now the parallel with *Agamemnon* reaches closer. As the lesser victim, Aigisthos is technically parallel to Kassandra – though their difference in moral stature is shown by his being assigned the shortest scene in Greek tragedy, whereas she received a long scene, one of the greatest in surviving tragedy. The pattern of *Agamemnon* Choroses 4 and 5 is therefore replicated in the contrast between the two odes (5 and 6) which frame the Aigisthos scene. Here again, the excitement is whipped up after the victim's exit by a very short chanted sequence, which builds up steadily to a climax.

If the Libation Bearers are with one exception kneeling as Aigisthos exits, as was the case in our production, the only possible choreography – given the brevity of the ode – is for them to come successively to their feet, surging nearer to the palace and into a more and more excited stance as the words verge towards their final outcry.

This ode profits, even more than most, from division among individuals. Both the arch shape and the gathering momentum are reflected if the lines are divided 2/3/6/2/1, with the entire choros chanting the last line in unison.

Scene 6

Just as in *Agamemnon* after Scene 6, a victim has now passed into the house; the Choros has summed up, in a brief lyric outpouring, all the issues which are

184   *Theatrical Commentary*

at stake; the death-cry is heard from within, and the action breaks down into turbulent chaos in the immediate moments after the deed. But this chaos is not now stilled by the triumphant emergence of the murderer; here the male is the easier victim.

The impact of the climax is achieved by a startling change of pace. First comes the hectic, almost comic confusion created by the Servant in the moments after Aigisthos' death, followed instantly by Klytaimestra's brief reversion to male valour in the attempt to make a counterattack. But she is too late, and the restless action is stilled when Orestes appears and corners her. The texture of the verse changes completely at 892, and the issues are then exposed more slowly, in a confrontational *stichomythia* of remorseless power and economy.

Aigisthos rates only an inarticulate death-cry; as it rings out, the Libation Bearers respond with extreme excitement (870–1 are still in lyric metres). But their reaction turns rapidly from exultation to confusion and then to circumspection. This should be reflected both in the gradual falling-away of the excitement from their words and by dividing their two speeches between different members of the choros.[43]

The Libation Bearers need to be moved by 874 into a neutral position, so as not to pull focus from the climactic confrontation. This is the last and most important of their retreats from the action in the second half of this play. The most neutral place for the choros is in two groups, FR-EFR and EFL-FL.[44]

This leaves the Servant with the whole space to scurry around, articulating the frenzied energy of his panic in the face of the totally unresponsive, disdainful Libation Bearers.[45] Until 880, his speech is directed to them; then at 'Hey...', he turns away towards the back of the playing space, arriving BC in time for Klytaimestra to intercept him as she comes out.

The frenzied, almost surrealistic tempo continues with Klytaimestra's entry. She immediately engages the Servant in dialogue, turns briefly away from him for the recognition and meditation 887–8, and then back to send him off.

He cannot leave before 889, since this line motivates his exit.[46] Scholars have made strenuous efforts to preserve the 'three-actor rule' for Athenian tragedy, by making him leave earlier and postponing the entry of Pylades to give the actor time to change. However, performance experience shows that Pylades cannot enter at any other time except immediately after Orestes.[47] This leaves only two lines between the Servant's exit and Pylades' entry – far too little time for a change. A fourth speaking actor must therefore have been used.

This was a remarkable breach of convention.[48] The extreme surprise, when Pylades spoke the three crucial lines which seal Klytaimestra's fate, was caused not merely by his total silence up until this point but also by the fact that all three actors were apparently employed elsewhere, when a voice spoke from behind his mask. The audience would have had every reason, after the successive entries of the Servant, Klytaimestra and Orestes, to suppose that the mask and costume of Pylades are worn by a mute extra or 'silent face'. But Aeschylus has deceived them.

Libation Bearers   185

Does Klytaimestra bare her breast at 896ff.? Tragic as well as comic actors had false breasts when playing female characters, and the idea is perfectly plausible. Aeschylus ventured into realms normally confined to comedy three times in this trilogy: in Klytaimestra's obscene denunciation of Kassandra's sexual practices with Agamemnon on the return voyage from Troy (*Ag* 1440ff.), with the comic servant who answers Orestes only after he has knocked three times at the palace door (652ff.), and with Kilissa's musings on how baby Orestes peed in his swaddling clothes (753ff.). A tragic playwright that daring in words might very well have also used this startling action.[49] Edith Clever bared her breasts to great effect in Peter Stein's *Oresteia*.

Lines 892ff. must be played in a dominant position in the playing space. Orestes sees Pylades' intervention, when he himself hesitates, as one of two advocated pleas – the one which he accepts; Pylades' three lines match, answer and defeat Klytaimestra's 896–98. Orestes should not, however, be between Pylades and Klytaimestra, even though he is judging between their speeches. Pylades himself must be in the central position in the triangle, countering Klytaimestra's plea, to indicate how: 'in his one utterance we sense an awful authority, as if the god had possessed the seeming-mute and spoken through him'.[50] He then retreats instantly after 903, out of the way for the ensuing dialogue.

Aeschylus now presents another major actor–actor *stichomythia*, comparable to that by which Klytaimestra lured Agamemnon to his death in the parallel *Ag* Scene 4. The scene equals that dialogue in intensity and doubles it in length; only here she fails to persuade. As in *Agamemnon*, a relatively static blocking is desirable; only a few slight movements are required during 908–29.

Success in performance depends on a strong change of pace and tone at 922. Up until that point, the exchanges are cumulatively faster and more intense as Orestes' rebuttals are implacable and ruthless. But then, after Klytaimestra's realization that she is doomed, she once again threatens him with a mother's Furies; and now he does not simply brush that aside, as he did at 913, with a superficial tit-for-tat, but gives the fullest possible answer, revealing in 925 all the tragedy of his position. Here, Aeschylus undermines the hope (805–6) that there may be no more bloodshed and prefigures the consequences of Orestes' impending act – the combat for his life between Apollo and the Furies, which dominates *Eumenides*.

Accordingly, solemnity is needed from here to the end. With his father's Furies set in the balance with his mother's, Orestes has placed against Klytaimestra all the forces which bound him to do the deed (cf. 272ff.); and this final recognition, that faced with two evils he must inevitably choose his mother's death, is matched by Klytaimestra; as she reads the dream, she accepts its meaning and recognizes that she is doomed.

Once again, as in *Agamemnon* Scene 6, the open palace doors have become a metaphor for the mouth of Hades. Orestes shows his mastery at this point by understatement, concluding the 1–1 *stichomythia* simply by speaking two lines; unlike Klytaimestra in *Agamemnon* Scene 4, he does not need – and would not

186 *Theatrical Commentary*

employ – a pyrotechnic display of rhetoric to conquer his victim. She advances up the centre-line to the doorway, controlled by Orestes with his drawn, blood-stained sword.

Choros 7

As if to lay to rest the fear explicit in their sober, muted closing comment on Scene 6 (931ff.), the Libation Bearers embark on an ode of rejoicing, composed in the original Greek in dochmiacs, the most frenzied metre. The lyrics of this play have so far been metrically unified. The unity is now violently broken, to show the Libation Bearers' extreme emotion. However, we found that choreographing this Choros with regular patterns of movement, rectangular blocks and straight lines, worked well, with the exultation left to the gestures as the Libation Bearers take over the playing space, totally confident now for the first time in the second half of the play that that space is truly theirs.

Clearly, this is in retrospect premature rejoicing, expressing an almost desperate need to see Orestes' act as the end of a chain of violence. But the traumatic effect of the final scene does not completely undermine what they sing; on the contrary, Choros 7 reminds us of truths which could otherwise easily be forgotten in Scene 7. Orestes has indeed come back as the instrument of Justice; Apollo has given victory to Justice; and the house of Atreus has been purified. Only 969–72 express a premature hope.

Scene 7

Now comes a total reversal: the Libation Bearers retreat towards the front extremity of the playing space, abandoning the final, triumphant posture of Choros 7 in a horrified response to the tableau.

This is a remarkable 'mirror-scene'.[51] As Kassandra virtually prophesied (*Ag* 1316ff.), here again is a triumphant avenger standing over two bodies, one of each sex, and speaking in self-justification before horrified witnesses; and once again, their response forces the murderer onto the defensive.

Orestes maintains a reticent stance, not merely abstaining from such glorying in the deed as Klytaimestra indulged but actively rejecting it (1014–17, cf. 930). In return, where Klytaimestra was unequivocally overshadowed by the prospect of vengeance at the end of *Agamemnon*, Orestes receives Apollo's protection as his reward. At the end of this play, the mother's Furies have their victory, as they drive Orestes from the scene; but now there is something to set in the balance against them.

Once again, the scene is designed to exploit the theatrical power of the *ekkuklēma*. The continuity required, to achieve the effect of shocking contrast and suddenly undermine the Libation Bearers' rejoicing, could not have been attained if Orestes' attendants had to bring the bodies on slowly, and Orestes had to walk on and take up his position, before the first speech.

Libation Bearers 187

On the platform would have been extras, wearing the clothes and masks of Klytaimestra and Aigisthos, and placed under the net-like robe in which Klytaimestra entangled Agamemnon, the first actor playing Orestes with bloodstained hands and sword (1056–7),[52] and at least two attendants to display the net at 983. (It is theatrically weak to use any of the Libation Bearers; separating them from the tableau makes their chant of distress [1007ff.] and Orestes' need to come forward and defend himself more effective.) Orestes cannot make the violent gestures required to realize the latter part of his first speech if he is encumbered not only by his sword but by the wreath-crowned olive branch, symbol of his hope for the future, which he needs to take to Delphi (1034ff.). There is great advantage in bringing on Pylades[53]; if Apollo's representative carries the branch and hands it to Orestes during the third speech, the tokens of supplication take on a greater significance.

The other attendant is Elektra (see 991–4). These lines work superbly if Orestes turns to his sister and visibly allies himself with her; and the whole tableau is enhanced if Orestes is supported by two *philoi*.[54] This makes another strong contrast with Klytaimestra in *Agamemnon*; her only *philos* was a lover so cowardly that she had to kill, and defend her act of murder, alone.[55] By contrast, even the support of the two people closest to him is not enough to save Orestes now.

The first speech begins with Orestes in a dominant position on the *ekkuklēma*, behind the bodies; and as it proceeds, he establishes an ever-closer relationship with them (e.g. by crouching at around 977, to deliver the sick irony of 979 directly). He then rises, picking up part of the death-robe, as he begins 980; Pylades and Elektra must stretch it out at 983 – perhaps with the Libation Bearers refusing and shrinking back, in preparation for their muted, horrified response at the end of the speech.

The intensity increases: Orestes must advance to the front corner of the *ekkuklēma*, on the side where Klytaimestra's body is placed, at 991, and his speech builds to a climax at 996, before easing off; perhaps he could deliver the last two lines detached, at a short distance – off the *ekkuklēma*, but still EBC/BC.

The anguish and the strength of the prophecy in the chant at 1007ff. arraign him at an imaginary bar (cf. 987ff.) – as if he were already debating with the Furies. Orestes is forced on the defensive and suddenly seizes the bloodstained robe again. He drops this, however, after the first four lines; 1016–7 need a visual image of his vulnerability, best achieved by moving Orestes forward, away from his supporters.

Once again, the Libation Bearers, as they face towards him and the gory tableau behind him, concentrate remorselessly on the suffering which they foresee; and now Orestes cannot offer a counter. Lines 1021ff. are best played motionless, to prepare by contrast for the intense movement when the actual madness sets in.

Pylades advances towards Orestes at 1030, hands him the wreathed olive branch ritualistically during 1034–5, and returns by 1038 to his original place.

188   *Theatrical Commentary*

That leaves Orestes free to advance a little down the centre-line, past BC, during the closing phases of the speech.

As in *Agamemnon, stichomythia* is used to raise the intensity in the last moments. The Libation Bearers now gain authority as Orestes loses it under the pressure of the consequences of kindred murder.[56] Given that Orestes must leave by the right *eisodos*, the Libation Bearer who intervenes should be drawn from FL and advance at least half-way to him during her first four lines. Orestes then sees the Furies over her shoulder. He jumps back from BC towards BR; she follows him, perhaps taking his arm in 1051ff. But her ideal is impossible; the Furies are now more real to Orestes than Argos. They hurl him first around the playing space and then out of his city.

Choros 8

A brief, grim choral chant sums up the balance which the action of the *Oresteia* has now reached: on the one hand, the hope of Apollo's protection in the future; on the other, the prospect of Orestes' death at the hands of his mother's Furies. Just as Zeus, the third great god, is the saviour (cf. *Ag* 160ff.), so Orestes – also the third – can be seen as a saviour; or will the curse never end? In the even balance between these two prospects, the final lines pose the question which will dominate in *Eumenides*.

During this Choros, the dance takes the Libation Bearers from the front of the playing area back towards the palace. This final repossession of the space is muted as well as brief. The *ekkuklēma* is withdrawn with the tableau, Pylades and Elektra, taking with them 'the sad abandoned relics of this awful deed'[57]; then the Libation Bearers leave, also going into the palace with their heads down; all that they have supported throughout the drama is now, for the moment, defeated.[58]

Notes

1 Peradotto 1964 rightly noted the centrality of this progression from light, both literal and metaphorical, in the images surrounding Agamemnon's return through images of darkness in *LB* through to the new, secure light of the torchlit procession at the end of *Eu.*

2 The only example is Taneyev's loosely Aeschylus-based opera *Oresteia* (1895; see Belina and Ewans 2010); the confrontation between mother and son takes place offstage in Sophocles' and Euripides' Elektra plays and in all subsequent dramas based on this myth. In *The Revenger's Tragedy* (4.4), the audience is aware in advance that Vindice and Hippolyto are only threatening to kill Gratiana and do not actually intend to do so.

3 Reinhardt 1949: 110–1. *Pace* Arnott 1962: 59–61, Walton 1984: 115 and Garvie 1986: xliii.

4 So Marshall 2017: 29. There was an altar at the centre-point of the *orchēstra*, but it must have been removable during performances as the centre-point is the most important position in the playing area and, if not used for a central prop such as Agamemnon's grave, was the natural position of dominance for an actor. Compare above, pp. 152–3 on *Ag* Scene 4.

Libation Bearers 189

5 Compare the Barnard College 2014 production, discussed in Ewans 2023: 169–70.
6 Compare Adkins 1970: 66ff.
7 Compare Vickers 1973: 389.
8 Taplin's argument for the doorway of the façade (1977a: 355–6) should be rejected; the space in front of the doors is part of the acting area, and actors standing there, apart from being visible to Elektra and the Libation Bearers (!), would pull focus from them during Choros 1 and the start of Scene 2. Garvie's suggestion (1986: xlv) that Orestes and Pylades conceal themselves behind the grave is totally impractical, in view of the use which Elektra and the Libation Bearers make of it in the opening section of Scene 2.
9 The missing page in the manuscripts means that the prologue could originally have been anywhere between thirty and fifty lines long, according to the calculations of Brown 2018. So an additional ten to twenty lines have been lost.
10 Scott 1984: 82 and 201 does nothing to refute Taplin 1977a: 336. Choros entry through the doors, like all special effects in Greek tragedy, would not be made unless there is some point (as at *Eu* Choros 1). If the Libation Bearers entered through the façade, it would represent the house of Atreus and the grave of Agamemnon would be in sight of the house; neither is the case.
11 Compare Bowen 1986: 35.
12 Conington 1857: xv–xvi.
13 Compare Garvie 1986: 67–8.
14 Adverse *stichomythia*, as at the opening of *Ag* Scene 2, or that between the Furies and Orestes in *Eu* Scene 5 profits more from division.
15 Orestes left two locks, but Elektra always uses the singular. Does she ignore one or bunch the two up into one?
16 See Taplin 1977a: 237, Bowen 1986: 177ff. and especially Brown 2018: 219ff., adding to the arguments in Fraenkel 1950: II: 815ff.
17 It must be something which can be shown speedily – in our production, a belt with lions embroidered on each side of the clasp at the front, which has hitherto been concealed under Orestes' cloak.
18 In our production, this was symbolized by Pylades passing to Orestes the spear that he has been holding. Orestes then advanced to EFC, holding the spear vertical for 269ff., and tossed it decisively back to Pylades on 305.
19 For a summary of what the *kommos* achieves, see Marshall 2017: 66–7.
20 On the structure, see Garvie 1986: 124–5, and for the metres used in the original Greek, compare Scott 1984: 85–9. Marshall 2017: section 3.1 proposes a new arrangement of the responsion between stanzas. I am not sufficiently versed in the complex forms of Greek lyric presented by the *kommos* to know whether his arrangement is better than the one found in all modern editions of the text, and I have decided to follow Sommerstein's text in my parentheses.
21 These could include: 363ff. Elektra, in sudden rebellion against the picture that the others have built up in the two previous stanzas, breaks away from the mound (e.g. in the direction of EFR), returning to her place by 394; 380ff. Orestes addresses the mound more closely; 429ff. Elektra turns outward again, this time further, e.g. towards ERC, and goes back to her place at 444ff; 434ff, Orestes rises, apostrophizes Klytaimestra, then closes in; 461ff. Orestes and Elektra turn and face forward, to show that they have now completed their address to the spirit of Agamemnon and can confront the future directly.
22 Scott 1984: 94–5 (cf. 74–5).
23 The rear of the space is, of course, a possible position for them; but then they would all have to move during 510ff., which is undesirable.
24 Orestes might well use his sword as a prop to give vigour to the fantasy plans of revenge – drawing it at 575, miming the death-thrust at 576, and saluting the Fury at 577–8.

190   *Theatrical Commentary*

25 Lines 722ff. do not imply that the grave must be present in the second half of the drama, since a choral address to absent people is common in Greek tragedy; compare, for example, *Ag* 83ff.
26 Compare the scene changes in *Eu* (224ff.) and Sophocles *Aias* 814ff. (on which see Ewans [ed.] 1999: 191ff.). In both of those plays, where all cast members present leave before the scene change, including the choros, a prop is added at C, not struck as here in *LB*. But the principle is the same.
27 For these same reasons, I also disagree with the similar scenario envisaged by Marshall 2017: 87–92 and Brown 2018: 16–17 and 622–3 – for whom Orestes, Pylades and the Libation Bearers do not even exit; space cannot be 'condensed' in the same way as time. And I cannot accept with Meineck 1998: 95 that 'the exit of Orestes, Pylades and Elektra at 584, the preceding information, and the intervening choral song followed by the entrance of Orestes and Pylades onto the stage (*sic*) would have been sufficient to mark the scene change.'
28 Orestes and Pylades should therefore enter just before 639, not 653 – *pace* Kranz 1933: 165 and Taplin 1977a: 338.
29 Not up by the palace façade, *pace* Melchinger 1979: 100. Far from being 'almost invisible in their black robes', they would pull focus from the subsequent action around the doors. In an end-on theatre, they should probably retreat to the left and right sides of the front of the stage.
30 Bain 1981: 48 rightly notes the comic technique; compare, for example, Aristophanes *Frogs* 37ff.
31 *Pace* Taplin 1977a: 341 and Bowen 1986: 116, who suggest that the Servant does not appear at all. This is undramatic.
32 First in the Aldine edition. The case is made by Thomson 1966: 161–5, Winnington-Ingram 1983: 216–8 and Seaford (1989). Marshall entertains this possibility (2017: 99–101).
33 Except Fagles 1977: 206.
34 Compare Tekmessa in the later stages of Sophocles' *Aias* and Ismene similarly in the last phase of his *Oidipous at Kolonos*.
35 Line 715 is very imperious if addressed to an anonymous maidservant but plays well if designed to keep a rebellious Elektra under control.
36 Elektra perhaps carries a torch, to reinforce in visual terms the fact that night is drawing on during this scene (680ff., 710ff.). Torches could then become an important motif; one can be carried from the palace by Kilissa, and brought back by Aigisthos in the following scene, to remind the audience of the increasingly dark psychological atmosphere (in opposition to the literal broad daylight for the original performance) as Orestes' vengeance attempt comes nearer to its crisis.
37 Taplin 1977a: 343–4 would have Klytaimestra leave last, controlling the man's entry as in *Ag* Scene 4. But the last place now, without the triumphal exit lines which indicated her control then, is weak – the usher's position. Better to have Klytaimestra disengage from Orestes at 710ff., turn commandingly back towards Elektra, and then sweep out as she speaks 718, leaving the men to follow. It is her last, false victory; and the dramatic point at 930, where obviously she goes first, is to create a parallel not with this scene, but with Agamemnon's controlled, defeated final exit. Elektra will then be the last to leave here; escorting Orestes and Pylades into the house, she is once again doing exactly what her brother asked of her.
38 Kitto 1956: 51–2.
39 Aigisthos is away from the palace and needs to be sent for (672–3 and 718). It is probable that this will be done next, so the course of the action is not so entirely up in the air at this point as Taplin implies (1977a: 345). Kilissa is at the periphery of the action but gives reality to the central issue of the drama, the relationship between mother and son.

Libation Bearers 191

40 Her excitement makes the speaker break out of the regular *stichomythia* pattern for four lines at 770ff.

41 The shortest in surviving Greek tragedy. Scene 4 is the second shortest. Taplin (1977a: 346–8 and 351–3) rightly emphasizes the unrelenting pace of the events in Scenes 5–7.

42 He should not be allowed to replicate the dignified direct path from C to the doors walked by Agamemnon and Kassandra – and by Klytaimestra in Scene 6 of this play.

43 Perhaps there is even a case for splitting 870 and 871.

44 In an end-on theatre, they would have to kneel down to assist audience sightlines. Taplin 1977a: 348 proposes that they should retreat into the mouth of an *eisodos*. This is wrong because that movement would suggest that a scene change is imminent; because they would still be very visible to over half the audience and so pulling focus; and most importantly because the Servant needs someone in the playing space to address in the next section.

45 His panic includes asking the Libation Bearers to open up the bolts on the women's doors (877–9). This does not imply that there was a second door in the *skēnē* which he batters on and which Klytaimestra comes out from after 885, *pace* Sommerstein 2010: 168–9. the women's rooms would not have had a door leading directly to the outside of the palace, and anyway there was only one doorway into the *skēnē* (cf. Introduction, p. 10 + p. 27 n.38.)

46 Taplin 1977a: 353–4, *pace* e.g. Bain 1981:62.

47 Compare Taplin 1977a: 353–4, *pace* e.g. Garvie 1986: l, Marshall 2017: 120. Any later entry for Pylades pulls focus unacceptably from the intense dialogue between Orestes and Klytaimestra.

48 So rightly Taplin 1977a: 353–4, Bowen 1986: 147. Brown 2018:22. Note, however, that at no time are all four speaking actors on together. *Pace* Sommerstein 2010: 170.

49 So Sommerstein 1980: 74 and 2010: 169–70 against Taplin 1978: 61.

50 Jones 1962: 102.

51 Taplin 1978: 122–6.

52 Like Klytaimestra in *Ag* Scene 7 (*pace* Reinhardt 1949: 137). He carries this prop away with him, since *Eu* 42 makes plain that he still has it when he arrives at Delphi.

53 Compare Fagles 1977: 221.

54 Like the corpses, one of each sex; Aeschylus surely knew, though he did not use, the version of the legend in which Elektra subsequently married Pylades.

55 Elektra, Pylades and the Libation Bearers are the only people whom Orestes can refer to as his *philoi* (1026). Taplin 1977a: 357–8 rightly rejects the idea of a crowd of Argive extras.

56 Compare *Seven against Thebes* 712ff. Whallon 1980: 91 (cf. Marshall 2017: 4.7) would have the Furies enter around 1048, visible to the audience and to Orestes but not to the Libation Bearers, and pursue him from the playing space. This would pre-empt and ruin the whole careful build-up to their terrifying appearance in *Eu* Choros 1 (see below, p. 195–6). The audience must share the Libation Bearers' inability to see the Furies.

57 Bowen 1986: 164.

58 Melchinger 1979: 108 opts for the downtown, left *eisodos*. This is plausible and would match the Elders at the end of *Ag*. But the Libation Bearers are servants of this house, so it is logical that they enter through the palace doors.

Eumenides

Introduction

No other playwright ever dramatized the sequence of events which led to Orestes' deliverance from pursuit by his mother's Furies.[1] This phase of the legend was of special importance to Aeschylus, who wanted to explore the implications and consequences of Orestes' deed in depth.

The plot of *Eumenides* is dominated by the question whether Orestes deserves to be saved or destroyed. And the drama crystallizes around that question the two main issues which have emerged in *Libation Bearers*: to which parent does the son owe more, his father or his mother; and is there any remedy for blood spilt on the ground – can a house find release from the seed of violence, once it is sown?

In many previous versions of the story,[2] Orestes turned after the murder of his mother to the shrine of Apollo at Delphi and received there both purification and deliverance from the Furies. But there was a local legend that he made his way to Athens and was tried on the Areopagos. For Aeschylus, matricide is so extreme that taking refuge at Delphi and being purified are not enough to free Orestes; he must also supplicate Athena and her city before he finds complete release. The problem of determining Orestes' fate devolves upon the people of Athens.

This creates the last tragic dilemma of the trilogy. The Athenians are faced with an 'impossible' choice between equally undesirable alternatives – just like Agamemnon at Aulis. A suppliant's claim to refuge was a fundamental right in Greece, guaranteed by Zeus himself. Yet on the other hand, the Furies have their rights too and will make Athens feel their full destructive powers if they are not satisfied (470ff.). The way in which the Athenians make their decision and the reasons why they deserve to evade all retribution for the choice which they make are the main subjects of the second and third parts of this drama.

The Furies in this play are the only ancient chthonic deities, ill-omened powers from the realm of Hades, ever to appear in a surviving Greek tragedy (though Death, personified, has a part in Euripides' *Alkestis*); and the impact of their first entrance became a theatrical legend; 'Some say that when in the performance of *Eumenides* he brought on the choros individually, the audience

DOI: 10.4324/9781032646992-9

Eumenides 193

was so startled that children fainted and women gave birth'.[3] It was also a bold experiment, building on the success of the Danaid tetralogy in 463, to make the character played by the choros the central figure.

The decision to make the Furies materialize has a precise dramatic purpose. *Libation Bearers* closed with the Furies very much in the ascendant. This is natural; at that moment, in the immediate aftermath of matricide, our revulsion is so strong that we expect them to pursue Orestes and undermine his claim to full justification. But from the opening of *Eumenides*, the movement is in the opposite direction. The case in favour of Orestes' deed slowly makes up the lost ground until he obtains his release by a hairsbreadth.

The modern theatre could handle the subject-matter of *Eumenides* only with difficulty, using symbolism and expressionism. But the Greek vision, in which the boundaries of the human psyche are narrowed to the rational mind, and the gods intervene under the pressure of a moral crisis of this severity, meant that Aeschylus had available far more immediate means than ours; the gods themselves could become characters in the drama and fight out the issues. As we watch the contest, we must not hesitate to take a moral stance – just as we did with Agamemnon, Klytaimestra and Orestes in the previous dramas. We are intended to estimate the changing relative strength of their cases as the drama unfolds; the meaning of *Eumenides* is embodied in this process of moral flux.

The opening image is a simple one; Apollo, radiant young male god of light and Delphic certainty, is pitted against the Furies – hideous, old female daughters of the Night, loathsome creatures from the underworld. It would not have been difficult for the Athenian audience to take sides at the outset and favour the defender of Orestes. They were not cheated; Apollo's side gains ever-greater successes until finally it seems that Orestes just deserves to go free. Appearances are fundamentally not deceptive, and Aeschylus satisfies our hope that Orestes should gradually come to evade the Furies' binding power.

It would have been extraordinary if this expectation had not been fulfilled. In the surviving plays, Aeschylus does not inflict drastic reversals on his audience. But the pattern of expectation and fulfilment in *Eumenides* is distinctly different from that of *Agamemnon* and *Libation Bearers*, in which as the plot unfolded everything came more and more to point our expectations in one direction. These are Iliadic dramas, in which the deaths of Agamemnon and Klytaimestra represent a tragic outcome which is as deeply expected, when they happen, as the moment in Book 22 when Homer's Achilleus, killing Hektor in implacable revenge for the death of Patroklos, embraces as he does so the certainty of his own swift, inglorious death.

Eumenides, by contrast, is Odyssean. Here, just as in the battle in the hall on Ithaka, there is so much power deployed against the hero's quest for his deserts that his fate remains uncertain for the audience almost to the last – even after Athena has intervened and given her support.

As *Eumenides* unfolds, Orestes' side achieves an ever-growing prospect of success; but the Furies' case gains cogency as well. For Apollo is not simply the great god of prophecy, long and legally established on the ancient throne at

194 *Theatrical Commentary*

Delphi – though that is how his Priestess would have us see him at the outset. In *Agamemnon*, he punished the girl who broke her pledge with a hideous death; in *Libation Bearers*, he is ruthless once again, commanding matricide, warning of terrible penalties should Orestes try to evade it, and ordaining that Orestes must sink to treachery in order to achieve that end. Nor was his oracle, in real life, always above the charge of deviousness and trickery.[4]

Eumenides seizes on these facts. Apollo breaks the initial deadlock by trickery, drugging the Furies so that Orestes can escape; and he argues against them with more vehemence than logic. Then, at the trial, he cloaks the arguments of Orestes' defence in sophistry and specious rhetoric. The 'right' case – or at any rate the one which will prevail – is increasingly undercut. And so our certainty that his prophecies will be fulfilled is less than absolute.

Conversely, simple pictures of the Furies also lose their force. Apollo's abuse at 71ff. is corroborated by their physical appearance and by the terrifying verbal and dance images presented in Choroses 1–3. However, in Scene 2, even under a torrent of abuse and threats, they respond with courtesy to Apollo and claim no more than their rights. Then in Choroses 3 and 4, we come to see that there is substance in their claims; simple black-and-white moral pictures lose their force, and we become aware of complexity. Apollo is both a deceitful thief, as the Furies rightly sing in Choros 1, and also the guardian of the view of Orestes' deed which will ultimately prevail; so too the Furies are loathsome (as Apollo sees them) but also the incarnations of a profound moral law and a great benefit to any city which can acquire them. After the masculist thrust of *Libation Bearers*, a re-evaluation of the true strength and value of female powers takes place as the trilogy reaches its conclusion.

This aspect of Aeschylus' meaning is communicated primarily by music and dance. The initial images of Apollo and the Furies are conveyed by the costumes and faces; then this picture is gradually qualified. From their fearful opening song through to the radiant salutation of Athens in the Finale, the Furies change their aspect from goddesses of destruction and terror to goddesses of fertility and benediction, but without abandoning (indeed by building upon) the powers that make them so menacing to human beings (cf. 990–1). The unchanging costumes and faces enforce the continuity, reminding us of their underlying nature; the music and dance, based on the text of their lyrics, must show us the development.

When the two sides come to trial, they have equal force; the trilogy returns at its end to a moral crux as severe as that with which it was begun at Aulis, with a human life at stake. As the jurors cast their ballots, Aeschylus brings us once more to a paradox: Orestes both ought and ought not to be acquitted. This time, a resolution will be possible.

Dramatic Structure

The climax is still placed two-thirds of the way through the play, but the pattern of parallel structures is now broken, to mark off the special subject-matter and new dramatic mode of *Eumenides*. This drama divides into three parts, with relatively short first and third parts surrounding an extended central section.

In the opening scenes, set at Delphi, Aeschylus invents a unique structure for Scene 1 and deploys several special effects to establish at the outset the disturbance created by Orestes' matricide and the extraordinary new level of the action. The location then changes to Athens for the central section. This section follows first the story-pattern of supplication, and then in the trial-scene the format of an *agōn*.

From Orestes' arrival at Athens through to the end of the trial, the play proceeds by a regular alternation of dialogue scenes and choral odes, disrupted only by the brief song interjected into Scene 3. The drama concludes with a Finale for actor and choros, in which a lyric harmony between Athena and the Furies is established before Women and Girls of Athens enter to escort the Solemn Goddesses (as they have now been named) to their new home beneath the earth. The final section of the play is as unusual in its structure as the first part; but here the extraordinary images created in the interplay between Athena and the Furies are images of unity, to counterbalance the ever-increasing disunity between Apollo and the Furies over the span of the opening scenes at Delphi.

After the hostility and turbulence of Scenes 1–4, the half-circle of jurors (around the front perimeter, in front of the audience, in an arena setting) provides a point of rest in Scene 5. The trilogy then reaches its culmination at the end of the Finale when two full circles could be formed – jurors and female attendants surrounding the Furies, who themselves surround Athena. This can be the final image before the processional departure.

Scene 1

This scene is divided into three parts, postponing the entry of the choros by a sequence of disjunct solo entries. There are also several remarkable effects: the unparalleled re-entry of the Priestess on all fours; the hideous sounds from inside the *skēnē*; and the entry of the choros individually, in ones and twos, and not from a side entrance but from the façade of the temple.[5]

Aeschylus wrote this highly unusual opening sequence, as Taplin (1977a: 371) rightly observes, to create a continuous build-up of 'gradually mounting, threatening terror and horror' until the entry of the Furies after 142. In the previous drama, they were visible only to Orestes; now they have materialized, in the sacred temple at the centre of the earth. They are first described by the terrified Priestess, then spoken about with contempt by Apollo, and then supplicated by the dream-image of Klytaimestra. At this point, they manifest themselves to the spectators for the first time – but only as sounds from inside the *skēnē*; the audience does not finally see the Furies until after the dream-image has departed, apparently without success. The suspense caused by the invisible Furies moaning and groaning during Klytaimestra's address to them

196 *Theatrical Commentary*

(which works perfectly in performance, with her playing much of the scene towards the temple door) must not be destroyed by an earlier appearance of the Furies. And since Apollo has freed Orestes temporarily from the Furies' pursuit by drugging them (67ff.), he and Orestes can naturally come out from the temple for their dialogue. There is no good reason for spoiling Aeschylus' carefully calibrated and theatrically highly effective sequence by bringing some or all of the Furies on before 140. None the less, many scholars have imagined an earlier entry; either a 'cancelled entry' to form a tableau before the drama starts or an entry on the *ekkuklēma* at 64 by some or even, impractically, all of the sleeping Furies – together with Orestes, Apollo, twelve chairs and a terra-cotta replica of the *omphalos*![6]

In 1–19, the Priestess establishes that Apollo owns the space now represented by the playing area – the forecourt of his temple. The drama is energized after 33 by the interaction between the playing space, which in Scene 1 is still 'safe' for the forces of light, and the interior of the temple, now possessed by the Furies. Apollo can look, and move, back in confidence towards the doorway; the human characters (the Priestess and Orestes) turn that way only in horror.

Klytaimestra's dream-image, by contrast, plays 1 (c) in close interaction with the doorway. When the Furies enter, they transfer their possession from the inner shrine to the forecourt itself; all Apollo's energies are then required, in Scene 2, before they depart from his territory. By this sequence, Aeschylus sets out in spatial terms the opposition between Apollo and the Furies and establishes a visual image of how the Furies were treated at Delphi against which to contrast Athena's courteous reception of them at Athens.

1 (a) Since she has to establish the role of the façade as well as the playing space, the Priestess should probably not advance immediately to C on her entry from the left *eisodos* but should play her opening lines further back. Then the remainder of the first beat invites performance as one continuous sweep in which the Priestess claims possession of the whole of the forecourt, moving until line 19, where she could end up in a central position, with arms upraised.

The prayers to other gods in 21ff. are more animated, and once again this is a sweeping sequence, written for maximum use of the playing space. The Priestess should end at 28 as far as possible from the doors, so that 29 can be used for a long and dignified cross up towards them; 31–3 are to be played facing forwards, with a gesture to imaginary potential clients.

On her return in 34ff., the Priestess must move as far as possible away from the doors, and clearly the first four lines are designed to be delivered as she scuttles out. Then 38 provides a pause for breath, after which she slowly rises to her feet in 39ff. – the narrative which lays the foundation for the drama.[7] It gives us a picture of the deadlock which – as the Priestess herself makes plain in her parting remarks – Apollo will now have to transcend.

Eumenides   197

She moves towards the left exit on a slightly oblique route at first, heading up towards the façade on 60–1 to keep the temple in focus, ready for the last two lines. (Not, of course, right to it; she is very wary of what might come out of the open doors!) Then she should head directly for the exit, delivering 62–3 from a position beside it, facing forward towards FR to reach as much of the audience as possible – but perhaps including a side glance and gesture towards the temple doors before she turns abruptly and escapes from the scene.

1 (b)   The opening lines apparently imply that Apollo and Orestes entered in mid-conversation. There are no parallels for this in surviving Greek tragedy, so some scholars have argued that Orestes' last lines should be transposed up to here, to supply something for Apollo to respond to. But 85ff. are needed where they appear in the manuscripts, and 64ff. play well if Orestes makes a terrified, fugitive entry and Apollo follows calmly to reassure him. Orestes gradually gains the courage to draw closer (64–73) and perhaps even takes a tentative glance back inside the temple to satisfy himself that Apollo has indeed subdued his pursuers.[8]

Lines 85ff. show that Orestes is not wholly impressed with Apollo's hearty assurances – this is the key to the movement and gesture after 74. He can decline to set on his way when urged, then disengage from the god and move away – forcing Apollo to play the rest of the speech almost trailing after Orestes, in an attempt to overcome reluctance and scepticism.[9]

An extra playing Hermes is undesirable, as his presence would pull focus from the slightly barbed interplay between Apollo and Orestes.[10] Lines 89ff. play well if addressed to an invisible god; the confident circling movements needed to conjure him out of the air, and direct him towards Athens, give Apollo a chance to assert his possession of the space in front of his temple. This foreshadows his energetic response to the Furies in Scene 2.

1 (c)   Aeschylus now completes a contrast between Apollo – Orestes' loyal, active and mobile defender – and the sluggish, at first immobile Furies whom the dream-image of Klytaimestra can only arouse slowly, for all the plangency of her pathos-laden movements and appeals.

This sub-scene demands an extensive use of the playing space. The dream-image must first establish her relationship with the doorway soon after her entrance, perhaps circling round towards it during the build-up to the first climax at 104. But she can and should play 105–9 out, facing towards most of the audience, detached from a literal relationship with the place where the Furies are.

After the Furies have begun to respond,[11] the dream-image increases the pressure of her rhetoric (with its remarkable combination of abuse and invocation). Here, space is needed to establish by theatre metaphor the gulf between their inaction and her need. Accordingly, in our production, the dream-image came forward at 121 and once again addressed her reproaches to them from the front; she did not return to the rear half

198   *Theatrical Commentary*

of the playing space until the climax at 129. Then she was close to the doors for the plangent apostrophe at 131ff. and retreated from them only during 137–9.

Choros 1

Since the Furies entered individually, presumably they sang at least the first few stanzas as solos. The structure of the song reflects this. It is a powerful, straightforward Choros which sets out in alternation in the first four stanzas both their anger against Apollo (A1, B1) and their justified complaint against him (A2, B2). Then the Furies settle down in the C stanzas, now that they are all in the playing space, to sing first exactly what, in their eyes, he has done wrong and then how committed they are to dealing with it.

In our production, the choreography was a series of complex hunting and circling patterns generated by each individual entry, with the choros gradually moving during the B stanzas towards formation into one unit, so that the C stanzas could be delivered in unison as a direct attacking address from the centre-line towards the temple – as if challenging Apollo to dare to come out. (I could not resist swathing their entry in a knee-deep cloud of mist, and using half-light so the Furies were at first seen in silhouette, their ghastly faces and costumes only gradually revealed. Aeschylus' special effects in this Choros invite some complementary modern special effects.)

Scene 2

Apollo picks up the cue, and a powerful adversative scene follows, designed to set up in advance a contrast with Athena's reception of the Furies in Scene 4. Simple images of the contending parties now start to be undermined. The god of reason deploys a highly emotive argument, while the goddesses who so far have seemed to be nothing but angry feeling give lucid, logical responses which they present with courtesy and dignity. By the end, the situation is deadlocked; Apollo has accused the Furies of inconsistency in the case of Orestes, and the Furies have accused him in return of exceeding his proper powers. Both are right.

This short but complex scene divides into five beats, and up to 43 separate moves could be needed to realize its ebb and flow effectively in performance.[12] This is a possible scenario:

First beat: 179–84. Apollo threatens the Furies in an attempt to drive them from his temple. Here, Apollo takes the lead, brandishing his bow vigorously, disrupting the pattern of the Furies; he might well go close to several of them in turn and finally threaten one of them at close range with his bow.

Second beat: 185–97. Since the Furies have not been intimidated, Apollo tries to persuade them instead, but cannot maintain the calm which this requires,

Eumenides 199

and returns to threats. Apollo's bluff has been called, and he resorts to aggressively vivid rhetoric (to 190). The rest of the speech demands a continuous sequence of movements, less violent in the quieter central section 190–5 but then suddenly bursting out in a new threat at 196–7.

Third Beat: 198–212. The Furies begin a measured verbal response, gently advancing towards Apollo (perhaps one by one) and forcing him by 209 to retreat, to reinforce his irony by distance.

Fourth beat: 213–24. Apollo breaks out of the *stichomythia* with a new outburst of rhetoric – with wide sweeping movements away from them to give the speech room to flow – and ends with a disdainful turn on 224.

Fifth beat: 225–34. Apollo has proven to his own satisfaction that they are wrong and confidently abandons the argument. The Furies make their own equally uncompromising position clear before they leave – forcing their attention on a reluctant Apollo in the second *stichomythia* and then suddenly breaking formation at 230, moving swiftly to the mouth of the right exit, facing Apollo from there for the last six words of 231, and then leaving rapidly in a hunting posture. (To match this, Apollo too leaves suddenly after his own last words.)

Scene 3

The exit of the choros of Furies begins the scene change from Delphi to Athens. The doors are closed for the last time, and the change is completed by adding a prop, the image of Athena at the centre; this pulls the focus forward, away from the façade, which will not be used again. Since Orestes takes his refuge at this image, and the Furies then sing and dance their longest and most powerful ode, Choros 3, circling around him as he crouches there, the obvious and right place for it is at the centre of the playing space; like the grave of Agamemnon in the first half of *Libation Bearers*, this prop becomes the focal point for the action.[13] There is no subsequent scene-change: 'As for the present scene, at Athena's shrine, we are not told which shrine it is nor in what part of the city: the situation is deliberately left undefined in order that we may pass on to the trial without a further change of scene'.[14]

Eumenides now becomes a suppliant drama, a play in which one character takes up a position at the image of a god, or at an altar, in a foreign land, and begs the inhabitants for refuge and deliverance, while others come and demand that the suppliant be handed over to them. The dramatic issue then becomes whether the reluctant host country can resolve the dilemma without suffering harm. The act of arriving as a suppliant and the bond established between receiver and received were fundamental institutions in Greek society. The right to protection was guaranteed by Zeus himself; to grant or withhold it could make the difference between life and death.[15]

Orestes' first speech needs to be played as the fulfilment of an act of ritual, with Orestes standing reverently – or even kneeling – at the perimeter, as soon

200 *Theatrical Commentary*

as he enters Athena's sanctuary, to deliver the first two lines, then perhaps gradually circling round the image before moving in on 214 to take up his refuge there.

The Furies are trying to follow the scent of Orestes' 'dripping blood' like tracking dogs. Their heads are lowered almost to the ground, and there is a tragi-comic point (matching the bleak humour of 250–1) in the fact that they are now so exhausted that they do not see him until after they have all come into the playing space.

Aeschylus clearly intended them to enter slowly, dividing into two groups led by the two speakers in 144ff.; six Furies follow the path that Orestes actually took; the other group curves forward, so exhausted that they have lost the track and can only smell that Orestes is somewhere nearby.

Choros 2 is a short, violent one-stanza lyric, inserted into the course of a scene, like *LB* Choros 2, to crystallize and give expression to a particular moment of extreme emotion. In performance, it profits from being divided between several choros members. To match the development of the text, the choreography needs to be a sequence in which the Furies gradually close in on Orestes and surround him more and more closely as they advance (from 261), becoming both more menacing and more solemn as they reach 269ff.

Orestes' increasing confidence can be shown simply by having him first stand up and answer them – and then break out forwards through them, away from literal reliance on the protection of the image, at 278ff. This forces the Furies to turn and face him, as he now takes control of the events – following the plan which Apollo ordained.

After refuting their claim that he is still polluted, Orestes addresses a long-distance prayer to Athena herself. This subsection can be played properly only if Orestes has now left the image – he must be at a distance from it to make the prayer. Since Athena is away from Athens and will arrive for the next scene by the right entrance, it makes theatre sense if Orestes, after addressing the Furies at 280ff., begins at 286ff. from CL, facing towards the image and beyond it towards that entrance. Then he could, for 291ff., move a little in the direction of the rear section of the space to illuminate the broad sweep of his prayer. Finally, the Furies rise up during 299ff., threaten him, and drive him back to his original place beside the image.

Choros 3

The Furies possess the playing space completely for the first time; they are assembled around Orestes as he crouches at the altar. And the ode is very different in tone from their first two short, violent choroses. Aeschylus is preparing for the volte-face of 415ff., where Athena, by making an issue of their claim to be fair (312), talks them out of an absolute stance (427, 429) and beyond that for the resolution in the Finale, where these Furies, who now seem to be so sinister and threatening, turn out to be valuable and needed by any society which seeks to prosper.

Eumenides 201

Dance and song therefore need to establish a fine balance in this Choros. The movement may be as menacing as the choreographer can devise and the actors execute; it can be used, together with the visual appearance of the Furies, to impress upon the audience the terrible powers which they possess; but there is a strong case for making their music a lyrical composition which brings out the solemn, proud and dignified aspects of the Furies – those which evoke awe rather than terror.

To establish the air of ritual solemnity which the 'binding song' requires, Aeschylus supplied it with a substantial chanted introduction. Then there are four strophic pairs, of which the first three have a refrain, a *mesode* separating the strophe and antistrophe. The refrain of the first pair, the actual 'Song of the Furies', is repeated after the strophic pair for intensified effect.

The implications for the choreography are important. The fourteen-line introduction is 'cued' by 307 in a way rare in Greek tragedy; the Furies plainly use the introduction to form into a circle around Orestes, and the text implies that during the stanza the circle closes inwards towards him. Then the song begins. The singular forms in A1, A2, B1, B1a and C1a strongly suggest that to sing and dance some of these twelve stanzas, individual Furies broke away out and around the formation.

Scene 4

This is the crucial scene, in which the Furies alter their position. It also lays out the final tragic dilemma of this trilogy, the dilemma which now devolves upon Athena and the Athenians. So far, the Furies have been uncompromising; Orestes has undoubtedly murdered his mother and therefore must suffer at their hands (210ff., 360ff.). But when they meet Athena, they enter into a dialogue with her which closely resembles an Athenian magistrate's 'preliminary investigation'; at 435, they turn the case over to her for decision.

Athena speaks for eight lines without noticing the Furies.[16] This implies that they withdrew into the left segment of the playing space in reverence and respect when they saw her arrive and also that Athena should be characterized at the outset as regally single-minded, intent only on one thing at a time. She begins to speak to Orestes the moment she enters the playing area and does not stop to draw breath until after 404.

To make her failure to see the Furies plausible and create good positions for the ensuing interaction with them, we found it best to have Athena wheel round from BR towards FC in a continuous sweep, nominally addressing Orestes but in reality, after the very first line or two, turning outward to play the rest of the section towards the audience. Then before 406, she makes her first pause, to take the measure of the newcomers. At 410ff., she quietly comes closer to the Furies; at the end of 412, she perhaps suppresses an instinct to draw back.

In rich but economical language, Aeschylus establishes an immediate rapport between the Furies and Athena. Unlike Apollo, she restrains herself from voicing her repugnance at seeing them and treats them with the full courtesy

202   *Theatrical Commentary*

due to *xenoi*. So they interact with her at once. But when she learns about their mission, it seems to her to be far too absolute. She rightly detects evasion and one-sidedness in their responses at 425ff., and she upsets the Furies with her reproach at 430.

Athena is wise, female and courteous. She is worthy of their respect and trust and comes from a worthy lineage (435), so they have full confidence that she will be fair. Nor does it yet occur to them that a just decision in the case of Orestes could possibly go against them. And so they yield the decision to her.

Lines 415ff. precipitate a *stichomythia*, which must be blocked in visible contrast to that in Scene 2; the resolution of the drama's dilemmas depends on the contrast between Athena's courtesy and refusal to make hasty judgements and Apollo's partisan hostility. The reciprocal give and take between Athena and the Furies can be shown if the Furies pass the role of spokesperson between only two or three individuals and remain in one, non-adversative position (e.g., a loose ellipse) and if Athena avoids violent movements and disruptions of that pattern.[17]

After 445, the blocking must show how Orestes' speech involves Athena gradually in a complex dilemma. Orestes begins the speech hesitantly, perhaps fixed to one point. But he turns suddenly at 454 to involve Athena in what he is saying, coming much closer to her and perhaps even – if the production concept permits it – drawing her away into the R segment, away from the Furies, catching her up in his enthusiasm as he names his father, only to blight the picture, and place her in a dilemma, at 458ff.

This open admission delights the Furies. It is also the cue for Athena to disengage increasingly from Orestes – ready to pause, and go to the centre before 470ff., to convey the gravity of the situation. Orestes will be to her right, the Furies to her left, if she delivers the speech from just in front of the image, symbolizing directly and effectively how she is trapped in the middle between the two sides; this also prefigures the arrangement of the participants when the trial begins.

Athena should probably not move in this speech, after finally disengaging from Orestes during the first three lines, until she has completed the exposition of her dilemma at 482. After that, she moves decisively, to show that she has found a solution; 483ff. is a long exit cue, perhaps best played with some of the lines (the last four or just the last two?) delivered after turning back towards the contending parties, from just beside the mouth of the left exit, before she turns away again and leaves, headed for downtown Athens to fetch the human jurors.

Choros 4

The Furies now realize that in a court of law it is possible to lose a case. But they cannot seriously imagine this happening to them in the case of Orestes, so to show how far-fetched that would be, they picture for the audience what would happen if they were defeated (A1-B1). Then (B2-C2) they proceed to

Eumenides 203

supplement the account in Choros 3, stating how useful they, and the values which they enforce, are to individuals and to society.[18] Finally, they revert to their power to destroy the wicked, closing the ode in the D stanzas with a direct and terrifying attack on people like Orestes.

The second section of this ode is one of the most wide-ranging portions of the play. It refers back to *Ag* Choroses 2 and 3; the goddesses of the underworld confirm all that the Elders feared about the dangers of impiety and violence, and they use the same imagery (NB especially 537ff.). Even more importantly, the Furies' picture of their own role prepares for the final resolution of their conflict with the Athenians, through the parallel between their values and Athena's ideal for the Areopagos, which like the Furies will provide the essential element of fear in both individual citizens and the *polis* as a whole (681ff.).[19]

In choreography and music, this ode must begin to foreshadow the harmonious patterns which will dominate the concluding part of the Finale. The Furies' movements – in our production sinister, complex but steady circling patterns which gradually became more stately to match the developing mood of the C stanzas – at first bypassed Orestes almost completely. Abandoned to a degree of independence near the edge of the playing space, he was then suddenly but almost imperceptibly drawn back in towards the image, to become the centre of the circular dances in the C stanzas. But even after his return to the centre, he was ignored, as the patterns continued to flow away from him, out to the perimeter, to match the way in which the text is directed outwards as well.

Then, shockingly, the Furies revert in the D stanzas to savagery, perhaps even suddenly turning on Orestes, pursuing and surrounding him, so absorbed in their persecution that only Athena's re-entry into the playing space to begin the trial rescues him.

Scene 5

Preliminaries

A Herald (trumpeter) follows Athena into the edge of the playing area. He probably entered before 570 and sounded his fanfare to summon the jurors before 570 and/or immediately after 573.

Each juror has two pebbles, one black and one white. Some of them must bring benches to sit on, and others must bring two urns, one an 'active' urn for the actual casting of votes and another, 'passive' urn into which each juror discards his unused pebble to maintain the privacy of his vote. A table, onto which the votes are counted out of the active urn, is also useful in production. The acquittal of Orestes is the climactic moment in the drama, so the props for the voting must be placed in a central position (i.e. just in front of the image of Athena).[20]

The jurors must plainly take up a neutral position from which they can follow the arguments of Apollo and the Furies without being visually

204   *Theatrical Commentary*

predominant until they come to cast their votes. This position, in an arena staging, must be a portion of the perimeter. But which portion? Hammond (1972: 441) would arrange them round the rear in a semicircle, so they face towards the main section of the audience; this was actually done in Peter Hall's production and in Peter Stein's.

In the Greek theatre shape, speaking characters often turn their backs to some of the audience, but never for very long, and they almost always avoid facing away from the bulk of the audience. Apollo and the Furies must clearly direct their arguments against each other and forwards to the audience. If the jurors are at the back of the playing space, the litigants (and Athena) face away from them for most of the trial. This seems unnecessarily antirealistic and stylized; the closeness with which the jurors are involved in the trial – especially towards the climax, where the prosecution and defence subject them to bribes and threats – makes it very much preferable for them to be seated just in front of the first row of audience seats EFR-EFC-EFL, facing back across the space at the action. (This is unfortunately very difficult in most end-on theatres without steep rakes.[21]) Then the arguments can make their full impact simultaneously on the jurors and the theatre audience.

Placing the jurors at the front for the trial also helps with the Finale. They are, so to speak, protected during the trial by the comforting presence of thousands of fellow-Athenians above and behind them. If they do not resume their seats after voting, but stand towards the back of the space, the blocking captures their isolation when they and their goddess must face the anger of the Furies alone.

Apollo's Entry

Apollo's appearance is abrupt, unannounced and disruptive. Entrances in the Greek theatre were, with this exception, invariably significant, conspicuous and marked in the words. Apollo's sudden entry here (like his even more sudden exit after the verdict) is unparalleled in the extant plays. It can be made to work today (e.g., with a reprise of his music to mark his entrance), but it remains a breach of Greek dramatic convention. Taplin (1977a: 395ff.) may even be right to suspect that some lines may have been lost from the text before 574, though I doubt this.

The Prosecution

The positions at 583 are virtually dictated by the text. Athena must be near C, by or behind the urns and the voting table, Apollo and Orestes between FR and R, and the Furies in a group FL to L.

The democratic nature of the Athenian scenes can be disregarded. Three productions, in Epidaurus (Karolos Koun), Christchurch (Robin Bond) and Sydney, placed both Athena and Apollo on pedestals or on the roof of the *skēnē* for the rest of the drama, as if they as Olympians can talk down to the

Eumenides 205

Furies and the human beings. This completely misunderstands the relationship between the characters (especially in implying that Apollo has as much power and authority as Athena) as well as inflicting a static blocking which cannot do justice to the ebb and flow of the trial and the Finale. It is a terrible mistake.[22]

Apollo first goes near Orestes for 579 and then crosses to a position nearer to Athena. The cross-examination of Orestes then becomes a perfect example of adversarial *stichomythia*; he will step towards the Furies boldly on 588 (arriving near FC); but then they advance towards him one by one, attacking with ever-increasing vehemence on each successive line. Finally, they can surround Orestes on three sides, so that at 609 he beats a hasty retreat FR, turning to Apollo for assistance.

Apollo brushes Orestes magisterially aside, ignores the Furies, and steps in front of them to a point FC from which he can address the jury. From here on, Apollo attempts to dominate the trial, moving around freely in front of the jury, over most of the front half of the playing space, to add force to his arguments.

The Defence

The Furies will have retreated to L/BL to hear the god do his best. With three perfectly phrased, deferential interventions, they provoke Apollo into putting forward more and more flamboyant and increasingly less convincing arguments. Each intervention should be played by an individual emerging from the group, coming forward behind Apollo's back, as he attempts to dominate over the jury by commanding the sweep from FL via FC to FR. This forces him to round on each of the Furies, and now his possession of the front of the space is a hindrance rather than a help. He is trapped between the Furies and the jury and has to swing right round from one to the other; this brings out the bluster which is very obviously one aspect of his text in this scene.

Equally clearly, the issues in the trial are serious and are intended to be taken seriously. These four speeches present the clinching arguments in Orestes' defence, and they will secure the freedom from pursuit which Apollo had promised Orestes before he did the deed. However, they are not decisive arguments for matricide; *pace* Apollo, nothing could vindicate the son who had to take his loyalty to one parent to the extreme of murdering the other. Apollo's sophistry, evasiveness, specious rhetoric and final resort to bribery are designed to make us realize this. Since the verdict will show that the majority of the human jurors appreciate this fact and vote for the condemnation of Orestes, no actor can succeed if he either plays Apollo's arguments totally straight or sends them up. Productions must reflect the double focus, showing how at the crux the key elements in the defence of Orestes are both significant and sophistic.

Apollo's opening moves are impressive; but as he plays 619ff, the actor must bring out the fact that Zeus' commands are not a powerful point *of law* at all but a barely concealed reminder that 'might is right' – followed in Apollo's second speech by a highly emotive appeal to the jurors' male prejudices (631ff.).

206   *Theatrical Commentary*

The Furies let that pass but question Zeus' consistency. This evokes a furious, exasperated diatribe from Apollo (644ff.), and their counterargument shows that they have trapped him (652ff.).

Apollo now (perhaps with difficulty?) recovers his cool tone. He is certain that he can meet this new challenge head on, and he proceeds to his final demonstration (658ff.), an argument which was not in agreement with contemporary medical and philosophical views. So even for the Athenians, whose culture had a heavy bias towards the male, there is an air of sophistry about it[23]; and this feeling can only be reinforced when, to support his case, Apollo produces Athena as evidence like a rabbit from a hat (in our production, she made her disapproval very clear). He proceeds, with hardly a pause for breath, to come in close to her and urge all the advantages which Athens stands to gain if Orestes is acquitted.

No convincing argument can be made for claiming that one parent is 'truer' than the other. Feminism gives no more justification to Klytaimestra's claim on Orestes than Apollo's theory gives to Agamemnon's. It takes two people to make a baby, and circumstances, or social priorities, can create a preference in only one direction or the other. In the ultimate reckoning, even Zeus and Apollo have been obliged to show simple male bias, and no universal solution to the predicament which Orestes' deed has created is possible.

However, this does not mean that a fair and appropriate verdict cannot be reached. Orestes had to make an impossible choice. His was a special predicament, and it is matched by the specialness of his judges. He stands before a court composed of goddess and men combined, and Athena herself is unique in a way which is directly relevant to the case. She was the virgin daughter of Zeus, sprung from his head and not delivered from the womb of a goddess, let alone that of a woman. So in a conflict, she may well feel more favour for the father's side than for that of her own sex. Apollo was presumably well aware of this when he dispatched his suppliant to her city.

The Foundation Speech

Just before the climactic deed, Athena displays the insight which will make us understand its consequences.[24] Kassandra's prophecy of the return of Orestes undermined Agamemnon's murderess in advance, and Klytaimestra's twice-repeated threat that her Furies will hound him blighted Orestes' vengeance. The dramatic structure of *Eumenides* has now reached a position parallel to that when Kassandra's prophecy and Klytaimestra's threat were spoken in the two previous plays, for the casting of the votes is the climactic moment of choice and action in this play. However, in this third drama, a hope for the future appears instead. Athena's speech shows that although she is Apollo's sister and shares his preference for the male, she is in far deeper ways aligned with the values of the Furies (cf. especially 517ff.). The common ground extends to the audience the hope that their goddess may be able to placate the Furies if they are defeated in the trial.

Eumenides 207

Athena also engages with the issues which had convulsed her city three years before the performance; in 461 BCE, Perikles' political mentor Ephialtes was assassinated during their campaign to reform the Areopagos, limiting its jurisdiction to cases of homicide and enlarging its membership. *Eumenides* reflects the extreme polarization between oligarchs and democrats in the years before its performance; both here and in the Finale, Aeschylus warns all his fellow-citizens against the danger that excess may lead to civil war and advises that strengths like those of the Areopagos must be conserved.[25]

The speech plays best if delivered from FC. Athena is, exceptionally, pitching her remarks past the litigants and literally over the heads of the jurors to Aeschylus' audience, in preparation for the second half of the Finale, which will bind the Athenians of the present into a deep relationship with these events from their past.

The Voting

Despite their element of sophistry, Apollo's arguments have seemed to make Orestes deserve victory, though the Furies' cross-examination has also been cogent. In Athenian courts, the material consequences of acquittal or condemnation were almost always brought out openly; and in Orestes' case, these are evenly balanced. Apollo, with prophetic authority, has promised a permanent alliance with Argos; the Athenian audience would expect the jurors to weigh the benefits of this against the Furies' threat to blight their land.

An intense controversy has raged over the voting. Attempts have been made to suggest that there was an even number of human jurors, whose votes were evenly divided, and Athena's was a casting vote which breaks their deadlock.[26] This view creates difficulties on every level: language, performance and interpretation.

The Greek text of 734–5 cannot be distorted into having Athena say that she will give either a non-voting decision or a casting vote; and Aeschylus is careful never to say that she holds a position, such as court president, which might disbar her from making an actual vote. The language clearly implies that Athena is a member of the jury.

In performance, the couplets 711ff. begin as intimidatory remarks. Apollo steps forward a little from FR, and the Furies from FL, to deliver the opening couplets at the jurors as they file back one by one between the contending parties to C to vote. (Apollo and the Furies then rapidly turn to mutual recriminations, hurled over the remaining jurors' heads.) Given the way in which actions are matched as far as possible to words in the Greek theatre, it is irresistible to conclude that one juror votes during each of the first ten couplets. A longer, three-line speech by a Fury during the last human vote then covers the additional time required for Athena to move into position and show that she too is going to vote. Either she places her white pebble in the urn at 735 or (better!) she exhibits it at 735 and casts it finally with a flourish on 740. After that, she must step back, so the selected jurors can come forward to empty the 'active' urn.

208   *Theatrical Commentary*

At 742–3, she orders that the votes be taken out of the urn, and at 748ff. the words of Apollo indicate that the votes are being counted. Athena has already announced at 741 that should the votes be equal, Orestes will be freed. The result of the counting is still unknown at 751; but then at 752–3, Athena announces that the votes are found to be equal and therefore Orestes is free. The implication is clearly that Athena is the last to vote of twelve jurors. She has cast her vote by 740 at latest; the votes are counted out between 742 and 752, and at that point they are seen to have been equally divided, 6–6. During this section, the issues are fully polarized in a short, tense four-line 1–1 *stichomythia* between Orestes and two of the Furies. The extreme suspense is intensified if the jurors who count the votes show black and white pebbles alternately, until finally, after Apollo has begged for care, the last pebble appears and is added to make the white pile equal with the black.

Line 741 has nothing to do with Athena's announcement of how she is going to vote. This is the first time the court has ever sat, and it would be dramatically absurd if, on arriving at the declaration in 753, the participants were convulsed by argument as to what verdict an equal vote was to be held to indicate. Athena here lays down in advance the required procedural rule, which is, of course, that later followed at Athens.[27] By that miraculous conjunction of prediction or expectation and succeeding event with which the trilogy has familiarized us ever since *Ag* Scene 1, the contingency envisaged by 741 in fact occurs at 752. Apollo, god of prophecy, was right when he pleaded for careful counting at 751. One vote *does* save the house.

The crucial point is that the verdict falls between the two alternatives rejected by Athena at the end of Scene 4 (471ff.): for the case of Orestes to be judged by humans alone, which would be an unexplained human verdict, or for it to be decided by Athena alone, which would be an arbitrary divine decision. We are given a collective decision by Athens, in which Athena's vote is explained because it turns out to be decisive, since the human jurors have found 6–5 in favour of the Furies (though this fact does not dissuade them from subsequently threatening the Athenians). Facing up to the fundamental issues of the drama, Athena aligns herself with Apollo and accepts his arguments (739–40). Her vote has converted a verdict against Orestes into a technical acquittal, giving Orestes the benefit not of the doubt but of the deadlock.

The result precisely mirrors Orestes' position now. He deserves to be freed but not vindicated; if he were, Athena could not later placate the Furies in the terms which she uses at 794ff. Apollo wins no victory; a majority of the human jurors found in favour of the Furies' view that Orestes, since he murdered his mother Klytaimestra, deserves to be punished for it; the verdict of the court as a whole is therefore precisely equitable.

After the Verdict

The anger of the Furies is so great that they say nothing. (In our production, they wheeled away and collapsed into a motionless heap at BL, gathering their

Eumenides 209

powers ready for the onslaught which will begin the Finale.) Even more extraordinarily, Apollo (it would appear) leaves the playing area in silence at this point. Like his unannounced entry, his sudden exit, presumably at the end of 753, is totally unparalleled in extant Greek tragedy. A formal mime of curt, abrupt farewell will yield a smooth departure in the modern theatre; but if the text is sound, Aeschylus has adopted a striking way of conveying how Apollo's whole purpose and function in the trilogy vanish as soon as he has achieved his aim. 'His partial vision of the place of the Furies, his low abuse and tricky rhetoric at the trial – these might be taken to reduce [Apollo's] stature low enough for Aeschylus to push him from the stage without any attempt to justify him or to integrate him into the final scheme of things' (Taplin 1978:39). [28]

These moves leave the main focus on Orestes, who must now be written out of the play, to clear the playing space for the final confrontation. Orestes first thanks his saviours and then inaugurates (762ff.) an alliance of Athens with Argos (cf. 289ff., 670ff.). These words refer forward from the world of the drama to the thirty-year treaty with Argos which the Athenians had signed in 461 BCE, signalling a major shift in their foreign policy away from alignment with Sparta and its allies towards alliance with a fellow democratic state – an alliance which had led in 459, a year before the performance of the trilogy, to the outbreak of the First Peloponnesian War.[29]

The playing style must match the mood of 'secure strength and confident elation' (Taplin 1977a: 402). Clearly, Orestes approaches Athena on the first two and a half lines; but the rhetoric then opens up, and he can face forward from 756–61, ranging around the front half of the playing space. The second section from 762 needs to be played facing back towards Athena and the Athenians, who are now, after casting their votes, on the rear perimeter. Then the last three lines will be delivered from EBR before a crisp, sudden departure.

Finale

The emotions unleashed by the judgement must be discharged. After the spoken arguments of the trial scene, the playing space is once again filled with vigorous dance and song. Aeschylus contrasts the close of the whole trilogy in three ways with the bitter outcome of *Agamemnon*: a confrontation between lone female protagonist and hostile choros (cf. *Ag* Scene 7) now ends not in exhausted bitterness but in ecstatic resolution; extras come on to bring not male violence (*Ag* Scene 8) but female gifts of honour; and crimson robes are used not recklessly to honour one man but in proper moderation to honour goddesses.

In their resentment, the Furies revert temporarily to the imagery and the vehemence with which they complained at Delphi about Apollo. Once again, their ancient laws have been overridden by the younger gods. They are the senior, and they have been 'dishonoured' (780 etc.).

Or so we say, since it is hard to give adequate English expression to the Greek concept of *timē*, which dominates in the closing section of the trilogy.[30]

210   *Theatrical Commentary*

'Honour', 'dignity' and Oriental 'face' are abstract and intangible. *Timē* was not; and it was central to Greek values, since it was essential to self-respect and even to existence. The possessions and rights which give tangible, visible expression to status and prestige in modern society were for the Greeks themselves part of a person's *timē*. To be deprived of your appropriate degree of *timē* is to be without all that we commend by the separate ideas of power, status, credibility, material possessions and a defined and respected function and role in society.

Athena counters the Furies' feelings from two directions. First, she turns to the past (793ff.); then she turns to the future, offering them a positive *timē* at Athens to make up for their injuries. At last, for the first time in the trilogy, here is a clash of perspectives which can be resolved. The Furies' felt injuries in the case of Orestes belong entirely to the past; for the future, Athena promises them a *timē* which will be self-increasing. If they come into residence at Athens, their powers will help the Athenians to become more prosperous, and in return the Athenians will be able to pay them more *timē*.

As she proceeds with her task, Athena unfolds aspects of her city and its jurors' verdict which make plain that they do not deserve any retribution; in doing this, she takes up once again the ideals of the foundation-speech and shows how greatly her city values the Furies' own most fundamental concerns. From negative to positive, from past to future, gradually Athena comes to establish a concord of mutual respect between herself and the Furies. This takes time, persistence and the help of the goddess Persuasion.[31]

Subtly, Athena returns to full female power. Persuasion is now used without deception; and when the Furies yield, the drama flows into a coda of unrivalled lyric reciprocity and concord – for these goddesses can bestow a wealth of blessings on the Athenians in return for the residence, and the *timē* in the form of offerings, which the Athenians offer them.

Female fertility and creativity, balked at the outset in Klytaimestra by the sacrifice of Iphigenia, now come into their own to end the cycle. At last, the balance is restored; male intellect has, in the outcome, secured only a token victory by the acquittal of Orestes; and so the values of femininity can at last achieve the full strength, both intellectual and emotional, which has been their due ever since Aeschylus' cogent, deeply etched portraits of Klytaimestra, Kassandra and Elektra. The Furies, being goddesses of the earth, are powers of fecundity, who can blight – but also make fertile. In their concord with the Athenians, a true harmony will be reached, in which the images of creation and generation, so often perverted into metaphors of violence in *Agamemnon* and *Libation Bearers*, at last regain their literal force for good. Crimson robes now become a symbol not of bloodshed but of integration and acceptance; and blazing light signals a victory which will bring no consequent destruction.

As the Finale opens, the Furies sing violent lyrics, best divided between many individuals (and in the highly emotional dochmiac metre in the original Greek), against Athena's calmly spoken persuasion; and Aeschylus marks their unique position here with a unique device. They repeat both their first lyric outburst and their second *verbatim*; this seems to symbolize the absolute

Eumenides 211

sterility of their anger, in contrast with the consistency of Athena's patience and persistence as she first balances past with future, and then turns in her third and fourth speeches entirely away from the past. But here our loss of the original music and choreography are even more damaging than elsewhere, for perhaps in the interaction between his three media Aeschylus was able to communicate both the static, backwards- and inward-looking character of the Furies' anger and the underlying aspects of their nature which will soon make the resolution of the trilogy's last conflict possible.

These lyrics are structured in the form of an arch. The Furies rise up into their attack over the first three lines, and the song reaches a pitch of expressionist intensity at 784ff. But then, over the last five lines, the Furies turn from attack and rage to introspection; and the last three lines should be played as a quiet collapse back into despair. It is essential for the music and dance to capture this sequence, partly because the Furies must not be reduced to simple caricatures as monstrous demons but also because below their anger lies a real grief. The basis for a settlement is contained in this alteration of attitude. (The choreography must also reflect the fact that the metrical patterns of the first four stanzas are violently irregular, in designed contrast to 916ff.)

The movement in this first part of the Finale must reflect the ebb and flow of the Furies' attack and Athena's counterbalancing attempts to persuade them. It is, of course, possible for the Athenian jurors to simply stand helpless as well as silent, rooted to their positions throughout; but here movement by the jurors, responding to the power of the Furies' attack and the gradual success of Athena's persuasion, is valuable; their involved presence gives reality to Athena's repeated references to her countrymen and to her people. So in our production, the Furies rose up from BL and drove Athena and the Athenians (cowering behind their goddess for protection) back into EBR; the Furies fell away again only towards the end of the first stanza, as they moved during the last few lines of the song into postures of grief (some kneeling, some drooping), scattered around the playing space.

Athena comes to C or FC as her first speech opens (the jurors can then also advance a little forward from the rear perimeter); the difficulty of her task is immediately conveyed by the total *verbatim* reprise of the Furies' rising up, then closing in (perhaps even closer to Athena, surrounding her and threatening to overwhelm her), before they once more pull back (819ff.) and collapse into postures of grief.

So Athena can and must begin again. Heavy weather must not be made of the veiled threat in 826ff.; a relatively quiet, light tone allows for the contrasts which are needed between this speech and what precedes and follows. For Athena's Persuasion does not persuade. Twice she has emphasized that the trial was no defeat for the Furies – and even if they have been slighted, she and her city can make it up to them; but now they explode once again into another paranoid, irrational outburst. This second onslaught is even more emotional than the first; the Furies do almost nothing but express the intensity of their suffering in fragmentary, explosive individual outcries. Once again, Athena

212 *Theatrical Commentary*

and her citizens are thrust back to the perimeter, though this time not so much by the conscious efforts of the Furies (who are now wholly self-involved) but by the sheer terror inspired by their text, music and dance.

There is a hope of resolution. The last three lines, though powerful and angry, are a solid, lucid summary of how the Furies feel; and they give Athena a foundation on which she can build. Determinedly avoiding the past, Athena turns to the future; she is going to make them replace one emotion with another. She now begins the attempt to link up the Furies with the Athenians and their land, associating herself closely with the Athenians in 852ff., and gesturing vehemently towards the earthen floor of the Greek playing space at 858ff., as she confronts the Furies from in front of her jurors, in what can best be played as a passionate appeal.

There is still a reprise of the second outburst. Athena perhaps even mimes near-despair, turning away for a few moments from the scene of a conflict which threatens to become endless. After that, she can return and advance determinedly at 881ff. upon the Furies (who remain in control of the whole central section of the playing space) – accompanied, of course, by the jurors.

This speech must be played with great intensity. It is her last and most powerful attempt to use 'the glorious goddess of Persuasion' to win the Furies over. And finally, after the burnout of their emotion in the reprise of the second furious lyric, they are ready to listen.[32] One by one, the Furies come closer to Athena, and each of them can make a movement as she speaks her line. With these movements and a slow but vital change of body posture (on 900 and 902), they are preparing for – but not signalling fully in advance – the sudden outburst of ecstasy as they accept Athena's offer.

The second and last part of the Finale begins at 916. This is one of those passages where the modern director's instinct may be to cut; but it must be resisted. The sheer vehemence of the dance and song of attack and fury in the first part demands that it be counterbalanced now by the contrasting vigour and energy of the dance and song of love and benediction. Only in this way can the trilogy be properly ended, with enough dramatic time and space devoted to celebrating the concord between Athena from Olympos above, the Furies from the Night below, and the Athenians who own and inhabit this part of the earth. The *Oresteia* closes only when the image of this reciprocal and mutually favourable interaction is firmly established; Aeschylus extends to his fellow-citizens the hope that it will be valid for the rest of time.

The Furies do not change their powers or their nature; directors must not reveal some underlying goodness by visual means, as in John Bell's Sydney production in 1980, where the players removed their horrific masks early in this final section to reveal the human faces underneath. On the contrary, it is insisted throughout the Finale that Athens welcomes the Furies precisely because of their terrible punitive powers (cf. 930ff., 950ff. and especially 990ff.). Just as Athena, goddess of wisdom, can also deprive of their sanity mortals who offend her (cf. Sophocles' *Aias*), so too the Furies, goddesses of blight, can also be goddesses of fecundity. That is what Athena begs them to confer, and

Eumenides 213

that is what they give in the lyric final part of the play. Their conversion from opponents of Athens to its closest allies is shown as a conversion not from anger to passivity but from active anger to active blessing.

In an arena staging, there is one powerful way to convey this transformation. Circularity symbolizes completeness, and so the Furies can become placed, as the last of them move slowly and hesitantly towards Athena during the *stichomythia*, in such a way that they can suddenly and effortlessly complete a circle at 916. The jurors fall back to watch in wonder the spectacle of the hideous Furies turned from their rage to graceful dances of invocation and incantation. If the jurors retreat into a pattern which is itself a segment of another circle, then after Athena has drawn them back into the action at 948ff. to witness the Furies' conversion, a complete large circle can be formed in which Athena, the citizens and the Furies all take part. In our production, this was achieved at 968 – to be echoed, of course, at 989 and then reinforced by adding the Women and Girls of Athens to the pattern after 1003.

After B1 (957ff.), the Furies turn outward more and more to involve the audience. So too, Athena from 968 once again – as in the foundation speech – chants in a way which also invites playing out to the whole audience.

At 996, the drama enters its closing phase. The transition to departure should be marked by an acceleration of the musical tempo and an intensification of the dance in these last two stanzas; but by a fascinating strategy, Aeschylus takes Athena (whose part has risen since 928 to the greater intensity of chant)[33] back to spoken words for 1021ff., her final speech of acceptance and farewell.

Headlam argued convincingly (1906: 268–77) that the end of the trilogy echoes the procession to the statue of Athena in the Panathenaic Festival, in which the Athenians were joined by resident aliens cloaked in crimson. But how many people came on for the close? The assumption has so often been in favour of Hollywood-scale extravaganza that Taplin[34] rightly protested against crowds of extras and additional singing citizens; but he still felt that the 'sacrificial victims, flaming torches, red robes and female attendants' of the cult must be present for the final procession. He is right.

Women and girls (cf. 1025) arrive in procession during 1003ff. They are attendants of Athena's temple, and one of them should probably be costumed as the Priestess of Athena Polias. Twelve of them carry the robes, which they place around the Furies' shoulders after 1031. These crimson cloaks turn at last to positive use the colour of the robes which Klytaimestra used to destroy her husband; also, they both demonstrate the Furies' new status as resident aliens and perfectly symbolize their new role; the cloaks, the first *timē* to the Solemn Goddesses,[35] overlay but do not fully conceal the revolting garments of the terrible Furies. Others carry torches, to make real in the theatre this final appearance of the image of light out of darkness which has permeated the trilogy.[36] There may even be a sacrificial animal (cf. 1007), probably a cow.[37]

In the final procession, Athena (first, cf. 1003ff.) and the eleven human jurors escort the twelve Solemn Goddesses. They form up and begin to leave

214   *Theatrical Commentary*

during the B stanzas, followed by the singing supplementary choros of females. Those who brought the cloaks in probably now carry out the image of Athena (see 1025); the rest bear torches in their hands.

Notes

1 In Euripides' *Iphigenia among the Taurians*, after the events of *Eu* a splinter group of Furies refuses to accept the verdict of the Athenian court and pursues Orestes to Tauria (the modern Crimea), where he is finally relieved of their pursuit. The Furies' onslaught is recounted in a messenger speech by a cowherd who is convinced that Orestes is seeing phantoms.
2 Details in Sommerstein 1989: 1–6.
3 Anon. *Life of Aeschylus*, 9.
4 Neither Aeschylus nor the older members of his audience would have forgotten the expediency and cowardice of Delphi during the Persian invasion.
5 There are only two extant parallels for choral entry from the *skēnē*: Euripides' *Trojan Women* and the fragments of his *Phaethon*.
6 'Cancelled entry'; Rosenmeyer 1982: 67ff., Scott 1984: 107, and Rehm 1988: 290–301, 2002: 88–91 and 2017: 143. Some Furies on *ekkuklēma* Arnott 1962: 82–3, Walton 1984: 98, Podlecki 1989: 12–3 and Ley 2007: 40 (+ Orestes and the *omphalos*). All Furies and so on Brown 1982: 28. Mitchell-Boyask 2009: 49–50 tries to have it both ways: some Furies, Orestes and Apollo on the *ekkuklēma* and the other Furies on chairs. But those other Furies would not be visible, being inside the *skēnē*.
7 Brief, agitated movements are appropriate for much of the section. However, directors should not miss the touch of pedantry which overcomes the Priestess' terror in 48ff.; it provides a moment of contrast before the build to the climax at 56.
8 Some scholars believe that Apollo entered on the roof of the *skēnē*. But this would completely spoil the intimate interaction that is needed in performance for 1 (b). Brown 1982: 29 and Wiles 1997: 180.
9 A degree of tension between Orestes and his divine advocate can also be used in the trial scene, to make theatre sense of 609ff.
10 Hermes was usually invisible to human beings (cf. *LB* 818). It would also look very strange if Orestes left Delphi escorted by a visible Hermes and arrived at Athens without him.
11 The directions for their moaning and groaning appear in the Greek text, as translated; they are among the very few 'stage directions' preserved in any of our manuscripts of Greek drama. There is no reason to doubt that they go back to Aeschylus himself, since they are not so much stage directions as instructions for actors to respond with their voices and therefore belong in a Greek script just as much as cries of pain, and so on, which are notated in other plays. Compare Taplin 1977b: 122–3.
12 For a more detailed analysis of this scene, compare Ewans 2023: 22ff.
13 Some commentators (e.g., Sommerstein 1989: 123–4) place it in front of the doors. This is, of course, theatrically weak (cf. Rehm 2017: 122); and Orestes needs to be supplicating the image while the Furies dance the 'binding song', Choros 3, around him. Unless the image is gigantic – as in Hall's production – there are no real difficulties in blocking the trial scene and Finale with a statue central at C. (It could even be removed at the start of Scene 5; but this is unlikely since 1024 probably implies that the Women and Girls of Athens take the image with them in procession at the end of the trilogy.)
14 Thomson 1966: II: 199.

Eumenides 215

15 Five of the surviving tragedies are focussed around an act of supplication: Aeschylus *Suppliants* and *Eumenides*, Sophocles *Oidipous at Kolonos*, and Euripides *Suppliants* and *Children of Herakles*; and several others make substantial use of it. Compare Lattimore 1964: 46ff.

16 At the opening of the scene, an alternative line (405: 'yoking this chariot to power-ful horses') appears in the manuscripts. It was clearly composed for a later produc-tion, so that Athena could make a more spectacular entry. In Aeschylus' production, she entered on foot, perhaps miming the movement of her aegis; see Taplin 1977a: 388–90 against Hammond 1972: 440 and Podlecki 1989: 164. She is not in a chariot, let alone on the *skēnē* roof, as in some productions. Athena is in no sense, physical or metaphorical, above the people and issues that confront her. Wiles, 1997: 180–1 would have her fly in on a chariot and then disembark in the *orchēstra*. But I doubt whether the *mēchanē* had been erected by 458; the first play in which it is likely to have been used is Euripides' *Medea* of 431. Mitchell-Boyask 2009: 61–2 would keep 405 and have her enter on a chariot to echo the arrival of Agamemnon and Cassandra; but what is the parallel with *Ag* Scene 4, and when would the chariot be removed?

17 From 426 to 430, the prospect of open antagonism threatens even more strongly. One effective way of staging this crisis is for the Furies to almost break off the dia-logue after 427 and turn away angrily back to BL. One Fury can then return more aggressively towards Athena on 429; the goddess manages to detain this one close to herself at FC and negotiate the final settlement with her – after which the Fury withdraws again, to join the rest at FL.

18 The fact that the transition is made in the middle of a strophic pair shows how closely the first and second parts of the ode are connected.

19 For the 'silent guardian' (518), Aeschylus used in Greek the technical term employed at Athens to describe the role of the Areopagos.

20 There were no extra citizens present apart from the jurors themselves; compare Taplin 1977a: 394–5 (*pace* e.g. Melchinger 1979: 134–5). The approximately 20-metre square *orchēstra* would not have had much room for movement in this scene even with only the 26 essential characters present: twelve choros members, three solo actors and eleven jurors.

21 Perhaps use only five human jurors and seat them at front left and front right?

22 Meineck 1998: 141 believes that Apollo could enter and exit on the *skēnē* roof. But this is to give him a position of dominance not only over the Furies but over Athena as well. In view of his conduct during the trial, this is totally inappropriate.

23 It is attributed to Anaxagoras but has no other support before Aristotle in the fourth century. For a balanced discussion, see Sommerstein 1989: 207–8. Compare Rehm 2017: 117–8. Burian 2023: 138–9 calls it an 'arcane idea'.

24 Athena does not set down laws of procedure, as promised at 571ff; witnesses are not called and registered, and the jurors do not swear an oath of office. This led Taplin 1977a: 395ff. to suspect corruption and omissions in the surviving text at the begin-ning of this scene; he revives as a partial remedy Kirchhoff's idea of transposing 681ff. to the opening of the trial. Most of these difficulties are more apparent in the study than in the theatre. Since this is an image of a trial created in a play, Aeschylus was not obliged to show every formal procedure of real trials. And the foundation speech is in the right place; it creates suspense, by a dramatic pause which separates the argument between the two sides from the voting and the climax.

25 Compare Introduction on *Politics*, p. 18.

26 Compare especially Hester 1981 and Conacher 1987: 164–70. For additional argu-ments against the 'casting vote', see Kitto 1956: 65ff., Vernant and Vidal-Nacquet 1981: 23–5 and Sommerstein 1989: 222ff.

216   *Theatrical Commentary*

27 [Aristotle] *Athenian Constitution* 69.1.
28 Compare also Neuburg 1981: 55.
29 Compare Introduction, *Politics*, p. 18.
30 Ewans 1980: 202ff. Compare Macleod 1982: 138ff. and Ewans 1982b: 233ff.
31 Compare Buxton 1982: 105ff.
32 The offer is strong and arresting; 'part-owner' is not adequate as a translation of *gamoros* (890), with its overtones of a share for all time in the ancestral, original division of Athenian land.
33 Perhaps in deliberate echo of *Ag* Scene 7 (cf. Taplin 1977a: 328, 410).
34 1977a: 410ff. (cf. 1978: 39).
35 Compare Macleod 1982: 139.
36 Compare *LB* 961ff.; on the imagery, see Peradotto 1964: 392–3.
37 Sommerstein 1989: 275ff.

Glossary

Proper Names

Where other surviving narratives conflict with the *Oresteia*, this Glossary presents only the version used by Aeschylus.

Achaians Aeschylus follows Homer in using Achaians as a synonym for Greeks, reflecting the Achaian pre-eminence, especially throughout the Peloponnese, in the time at which the trilogy is set.

Acheron A river in the underworld.

Agamemnon Son of Atreus, grandson of Pelops; joint ruler of Argos with Menelaos.

Aigeian Sea Named after Aigeus, this sea divides mainland Greece from Asia Minor.

Aigeus An early king of Athens; father of Theseus.

Aigisthos Third child of Thyestes; the only survivor of Atreus' massacre of Thyestes' children.

Alexander See Paris.

Althaia Wife of Oineus and mother of Meleager. When Meleager was born, the Moirai prophesied that he would live no longer than a brand then burning on the fire; she snatched it from the flames and kept it. The adult Meleager quarrelled with Althaia's brothers and killed them. In revenge, she deliberately burnt the brand and so killed her son.

Amazons Warrior women from the Black Sea coast. They attacked Athens during the reign of Theseus, camped on the hill later called the Areopagos, and sacrificed there to their patron god Ares. Theseus eventually defeated them and married their queen, Hippolyta.

Apollo Son of Zeus and Leto and brother of Artemis; a major Greek god, worshipped especially at Delos and Delphi. Sun-god, god of archery (and so particularly able to protect his friends and send sudden death on his enemies); music and painting; purification from *miasma*; healing from disease; and prophecy.

Arachneion See Beacons.

Areopagos 'Place of Ares', where Athens' aristocratic and most ancient court sat – a hill near the city centre.

218 *Glossary*

Ares The god of war.

Argos A principal city of the Peloponnese, royal residence of the descendants of Tantalos and Pelops and therefore the scene of the action in *Ag* and *LB. Eu* supports the major shift in Athenian foreign policy in 461, when the Athenians broke with oligarchic Sparta and concluded a treaty with democratic Argos.

Artemis Sister of Apollo; a virgin goddess, imaged as a huntress who protects wild creatures, especially young ones. Also goddess of childbirth.

Asopos See Beacons.

Athena Virgin goddess of wisdom, sprung fully armed from the head of her father Zeus. Patron goddess of Athens and a major supporter of the Greeks in the Trojan War (cf. *Eu* 397ff.).

Athos See Beacons.

Atreidai The sons of Atreus, Agamemnon and Menelaos.

Atreus Father of Agamemnon and Menelaos. He avenged himself on Thyestes, who had seduced his wife and fraudulently claimed the kingship, by murdering two of Thyestes' children and serving their flesh and innards to him at a banquet.

Aulis A port on the coast of Boiotia, from which the Greeks sailed to Troy after sacrificing Iphigenia to Artemis.

Bacchantes See Dionysos.

Beacons Klytaimestra's relay started at Mt. Ida near Troy and went (1) to the rock of Hermes, on Lemnos; (2) to Mt. Athos, the easternmost promontory of Chalkidike; (3) to Mt. Makistos, on the island of Euboia; (4) to Mt. Messapion, on the coast of Boiotia; (5) across the Asopos valley to Mt. Kithairon; (6) to 'the mountain of the roving goats', probably on the island of Aigina; and (7) across the Gulf of Saron, which separates Aigina from the Peloponnese, to Mt. Arachneion between Epidauros and Argos. The leap from (2) to (3) is impossibly far for visibility; either a line is missing from the text or Aeschylus was not fully familiar with the geography.

Chalkis A town on the south-west coast of Euboia.

Daulis A small town in Phokis.

Delos An island in the Aigeian Sea; birthplace of Apollo.

Delphi A town in Phokis, on the slopes of Mt. Kithairon, site of Apollo's principal oracle.

Delphos Legendary eponymous first king of Delphi.

Dionysos Son of Zeus and Semele; god of ecstatic possession, fertility and the life-force, both creative and destructive – especially as manifested through liquids, the sap of young trees, the blood of young animals and, above all, through wine. His female followers are called Bacchantes, after his cult-title Bacchos.

Elektra Second daughter of Agamemnon and Klytaimestra, sister of Iphigenia and Orestes.

Erectheus One of the earliest kings of Athens.

Glossary 219

Eumenides 'The Kindly Ones', a euphemistic name for the Furies.

Euripos The strait dividing Euboia from the mainland.

Fates See *moira* in the Greek Words Glossary.

Furies Goddesses of the underworld (Greek 'Erinyes'), who spring from the spilt blood of murder victims and pursue vengeance – normally working through natural forces (e.g. inflicting madness or disease) or spurring on the conscience of the nearest male relative until he acts as an avenger. For obvious reasons, Klytaimestra's Furies cannot do this; they therefore pursue Orestes themselves.

Geryon A three-bodied monster killed by Herakles.

Gorgons Three winged, female monsters with bronze claws and hissing serpents instead of hair. One of them, Medusa, turned to stone anyone who looked at her.

Hades Brother of Zeus and Poseidon and husband of Persephone. Zeus' counterpart below the earth; the ruler of the underworld to which human souls pass after death.

Harpies Foul winged female creatures, who seized and befouled the food of Phineus.

Helen Daughter of Zeus and Leda, half-sister of Klytaimestra and wife of Menelaos; she eloped to Troy and there married Paris.

Hephaistos The god of fire.

Hera Wife of Zeus and goddess of marriage.

Herakles The greatest Greek hero – the only one to receive the same worship as a god after his death – was the son of Zeus by Alkmene. He was once enslaved to Eurystheus, king of Tiryns, and required to perform twelve Labours at his command.

Hermes Son of Zeus and Maia; herald and messenger of the gods; the god who escorts travellers and conducts souls between the worlds of the living and the dead; also the guardian of paternal rights and the god of deception and trickery.

Ida A mountain near Troy; see Beacons.

Ilion Troy.

Inachos The main river of Argos.

Iphigenia Eldest daughter of Agamemnon and Klytaimestra, sacrificed at Aulis so the fleet could sail to Troy.

Ixion King of the Lapithai in Thessaly. He killed his father-in-law to avoid paying the bridal gifts he had promised and became the first suppliant for purification from the *miasma* of homicide. This was granted by Zeus; but Ixion then attempted to seduce Hera and was punished with eternal torment.

Kalchas The seer who accompanied the Greek expedition to Troy.

Kassandra A daughter of Priam and Hecuba. She promised her body to Apollo in return for the gift of prophecy but then broke her word. The god could not take back his gift; he therefore punished her by ensuring that her prophecies would never be believed.

220 *Glossary*

Kilissa Orestes' old nurse, named after the coastal region of Asia Minor opposite Kypros. Slaves were often named after their place of origin.

Kithairon See Beacons.

Klytaimestra Daughter of Tyndareus and Leda; half-sister of Helen and wife of Agamemnon.

Kokytos A river in the underworld; its name means wailing or lamentation.

Korykis A large cave high on Mt. Parnassos above Delphi, sacred to the local nymphs.

Kranaos An early, almost unknown ancestor of the Athenians.

Kronos A Titan, son and (by force) heir of the first supreme god, Ouranos; father of Zeus, who in turn overthrew him in the battle of the gods and giants on the plain of Phlegra.

Kypris Aphrodite, the goddess of love; she was born from the foam of waves on the coast of Kypros.

Leda Wife of Tyndareus, mother of Klytaimestra and (with Zeus as the father) of Helen.

Lemnos A large island in the Aigeian Sea. The Argonauts found it inhabited only by women; they had killed all their men in revenge (except that Hypsipyle saved her own father) when they imported concubines from Asia Minor.

Libya Traditional birthplace of Athena. In 458, the Athenians were providing military assistance to the Libyan warlord in his attempted revolt against Persian hegemony.

Loxias Probably 'the crooked one'; a cult title of Apollo, referring to the obscurity of many of his oracles.

Lykian From Lykia, now a region of southern Turkey.

Makistos See Beacons.

Menelaos Son of Atreus, husband of Helen; joint leader of the expedition to Troy with his brother Agamemnon.

Messapion See Beacons.

Minos See Skylla.

Nightingale Prokne killed her son Itys to take revenge on her husband Tereus for raping her sister Philomela. Prokne became a nightingale when she prayed to be changed into a bird to escape from Tereus' pursuit; the sad song of the nightingale is her lament for Itys' death.

Nisos King of Megara, father of Skylla.

Odysseus Son of Laertes, husband of Penelope and father of Telemachos; king of Ithaka. The cleverest hero to go to Troy, he went unwillingly (feigning madness in an attempt to avoid enlistment) and reached his homeland after the sack of Troy only after ten years of wanderings. His homecoming is the subject of Homer's *Odyssey*.

Orestes Only son of Agamemnon and Klytaimestra.

Orpheus A musician from Thrakia, whose songs were so sweet that trees and wild animals followed him.

Glossary 221

Pallas A cult-title of Athena, of unknown origin and meaning.

Pan A god of nature, fertility, and animals and birds.

Paris Second son of Priam and Hecuba, often called Alexander. His abduction of Menelaos' wife Helen caused the Trojan War.

Parnassos The mountain in Phokis which towers over the town and oracle at Delphi.

Pelops Founding father of the royal house of Argos; father of Atreus and grandfather of Agamemnon and Menelaos.

Pentheus King of Thebes, son of Echion and grandson of Kadmos; he denied that Dionysos is a god and was torn apart by maddened Bacchantes, including his own mother Agauë.

Perseus The hero, son of Zeus by Danaë, who killed the Gorgon Medusa, looking at her image in a mirror given to him by Athena.

Pheres Father of Admetos. Apollo made the Moirai drunk and persuaded them to let Admetos live beyond his *moira* if he found someone else to die in his place. Admetos' wife Alkestis offered herself but was then rescued from Death by Herakles.

Phineus King of Salmydessos, who blinded his sons after a false accusation by their stepmother; the gods punished him by sending the Harpies.

Phlegra The plain, probably on the promontory of Pallene in the north Aigeian, where Athena once took a prominent part in the battle of the gods and the giants.

Phoibe A Titan, mother of Leto and grandmother of Apollo and Artemis.

Phoibos Cult title of Apollo, meaning 'bright'.

Phokis The region of central Greece surrounding Mt. Parnassos.

Pleiades The 'doves', a constellation visible in Greece from May to November. The moment at which the constellation sets could be used to indicate a particular time of night.

Pleisthenidai The house of Atreus; from Pleisthenes, a relative of Atreus whose place in the family tree is uncertain in other sources and not specified in the *Oresteia*.

Pleistos The river which runs through the deep gorge below Delphi.

Pluto The god of the underworld; giver of wealth, since crops and minerals come from the earth.

Poseidon Brother of Zeus and god of the sea.

Priam King of Troy.

Proteus A sea-god, living on the island of Pharos off the coast of Egypt, whom Menelaos encountered and had to outwit on his way home from Troy (Homer, *Odyssey* 4.351ff.). This incident was the subject of the lost satyr-play *Proteus* which concluded the *Oresteia* tetralogy.

Pylades Son of Strophios king of Phokis; companion of Orestes since childhood.

Saronic Gulf See Beacons.

Simois A river of the Trojan plain.

222   *Glossary*

Skamander   The main river of the Trojan plain.

Skylla   (1) The dangerous female monster which preyed on ships opposite the whirlpool Charybdis, in the straits of Messina between Sicily and the Italian mainland.

(2) The daughter of Nisos; when Minos of Knossos was besieging Megara, she accepted his bribe to cut off the purple (or golden) lock of hair which grew on top of Nisos' head and gave him life; the Kretans were then able to capture the city.

Strophios   King of Phokis; Orestes grew up in his home together with his son Pylades.

Strymon   The large river, flowing into the north Aigeian, which formed the boundary between Makedonia and Thrakia.

Tantalos   Father of Pelops and founder of the house of Atreus.

Tartaros   A place of punishment in the underworld.

Themis   Right, the Titan daughter of the Earth whose main role is to see that crime is punished; first giver of oracles at Delphi.

Theseus   A great king of Athens in early times.

Thyestes   Son of Pelops, brother of Atreus. His seduction of Atreus' wife Airope is the 'first-beginning crime' (*Ag* 1192) in the house of Atreus.

Triton   A river in Libya (q.v.); traditional birthplace of Athena.

Troy   A city in Phrygia in the north-west of modern Turkey; sacked after a ten-year siege by the Greek expedition commanded by Agamemnon and Menelaos.

Tyndareus   King of Sparta before Menelaos; father of Klytaimestra.

Zeus   The most powerful god; son of Kronos and Rhea. He was originally a sky- and weather-god, and his weapon is the thunderbolt. He punished several kinds of wrongdoing, including oath-breaking; the table of hospitality (*xenia*) was sacred to him as the protector of strangers, beggars and suppliants and of hosts. However, Zeus did not make the world, and he was not omnipotent or omniscient. Despite his great and wide-ranging powers, both other gods and human beings could defy him (at their own risk).

Greek Words

aegis   Literally 'goat-skin'; the miraculous cloak worn by Athena.

agathos   A good or noble man; head of an *oikos* by virtue of a combination of birth, wealth and military ability.

Agōn   Contest.

amphisbaina   A mythical snake with a head at each end.

anapaests   The metre of the chanted sections of a Greek tragedy, midway in intensity between speech and lyric song. Often used, as in *Ag*, for the entrance of the *choros*.

antistrophe   See *strophe*.

choros   Lit. song (and dance); denotes either the group of twelve choros members or the odes (songs) that they perform.

Glossary 223

daemon A god or godlike power; daemons are often what we would call personifications of abstract forces (e.g. Madness, Fear, Persuasion).

drama Lit. 'thing done/enacted'; the normal term in Athens for the combination of speech and song, movement and dance which comprises a tragedy or comedy.

eisodos One of the two entrance ways on either side of the playing space. By a convention reflecting the reality of the theatre's location, the actor left *eisodos* was imagined as leading 'downtown' from the place where the action was located; the actor right *eisodos* led to the countryside, the sea, and other cities.

ekkuklēma The rolling-out machine, used in tragedy when the pressure of events inside the building represented by the *skēnē* has such implications for the public forum outside that they must be seen (as they could not if simply displayed inside the entrance, because of shadows).

ephymnion A lyric refrain added between the responding *strophic* stanzas of a *choros*.

epode A non-strophic stanza used sometimes to conclude a sequence of stanzas after the alternation of *strophe* and *antistrophe*.

iambic trimeter The standard metre of dialogue in tragedy; six feet consisting of a short syllable followed by a long one or occasionally of three shorts.

kommos A lyric lamentation sung by the choros and one or more solo actors.

maenads Followers of the god Dionysos, possessed by the bacchic frenzy – a trance-like state in which superhuman feats of strength are possible.

mesode A non-responding lyric stanza inserted between a metrically responding *strophe* and *antistrophe*.

miasma Pollution; the word embraces both literal dirt and what we would call psychic pollution automatically incurred by breaches of taboo.

moira A person's share or lot in life; the 'destiny' which is not a predetermined fate but gradually takes shape as a human life unfolds under the guidance of three ancient goddesses, the Moirai.

oikos The great household, consisting of an *agathos'* family and the slaves who work for them, which was the basic unit of Greek society.

omphalos Lit. 'navel'; the sacred stone, in Apollo's temple at Delphi, believed to mark the centre of the earth.

orchēstra 'dance-floor'; the playing space.

philos Friend and ally, bound by loyalty or blood-relationship; especially relatives and members of one's own household.

poiētes Lit. 'maker'/'creator'; the man who was writer, composer, choreographer, dramaturg and director of a *drama* (also, until Sophocles, often the leading actor).

polis A city which, with its surrounding territory, was also an independent state; the largest social unit in ancient Greece.

prosōpon Lit. 'face'; the slightly larger-than-life, but realistic, whole-head masks which ensured that the age, gender and status of characters were visible even to distant members of the audience.

224 *Glossary*

skēnē The building where the solo actors changed costumes and masks, with a pair of double doors, one or two windows and a practicable roof.

skēnographia Painted panels on the front wall of the *skēnē*, showing the place that it represents – a palace, a temple, a tent, a cave, open countryside and so on.

stēlē A column erected beside the grave of an honoured deceased person.

stichomythia Lit. 'step-speech'; a dialogue sequence of rapid cut and thrust, in which the speaker changes with every line spoken.

strophe, antistrophe Lit. 'turn' and 'counter-turn'; corresponding stanzas in solo and choral lyrics, with different textual content but written in identical verse metre.

theatron 'Seeing-place'; the part of the theatre in which the audience sat.

theios Divine; marvellous.

timē 'Honour'; status, measured in material terms of position, possessions and power.

tragōidia Literally 'song for a goat'; the Greek term for the genre is of wider application than modern 'tragedy' since it includes dramas (e.g. *Eumenides*, Sophocles' *Oidipous at Kolonos*, and Euripides' *Iphigenia among the Taurians*) in which catastrophe is avoided or survived and plays which modern critics would regard as nearer to melodrama (e.g. Euripides' *Helen* and *Orestes*).

trochaic tetrameter A dialogue line of eight feet, consisting of trochees (long syllable followed by short); used when tension is heightened.

xenia Abstract noun denoting the act of hospitality and exchange of gifts and/or the consequent *xenos* relationship between members of two different households, often from different cities. *Xenia* is guaranteed by Zeus himself, who will punish breaches (such as Paris' elopement with Helen).

xenos A person who has contracted or inherited a relationship with the head of an *oikos* or who has arrived and is about to contract a relationship by exchange of gifts, which binds them and their descendants whenever they visit each other's territory. The relationship is reciprocal, regardless of which person is acting as 'guest' or 'host' at any one time, and it transcends any regional grievances or enmities.

Works Cited

Adkins, A.W.H. (1960) *Merit and Responsibility: A Study in Greek Values*. Oxford: Clarendon Press.

Adkins, A.W.H. (1970) *From the Many to the One*. London: Chatto and Windus.

Arnott, P. (1962) *Greek Scenic Conventions in the Fifth Century BC*. Westport, CT: Greenwood Press.

Arnott, P. (1989) *Public and Performance in the Greek Theatre*. London: Routledge.

Bain, D. (1981) *Masters, Servants and Orders in Greek Tragedy*. Manchester: Manchester University Press.

Bakola, E. (2018) 'Textile Symbolism and the "Wealth of the Earth": Creation, Production and Destruction in the "Tapestry Scene" of Aeschylus' *Oresteia* (*Ag.* 905–78)' in M. Harlow, M.-L. Nosch and G. Fanfani (eds.) *Spinning Fates and the Song of the Loom*. Abingdon: Taylor and Francis, 115–136.

Baldry, H.G. (1971) *The Greek Tragic Theatre*. London: Chatto and Windus.

Belina, A. and Ewans, M. (2010) 'Taneyev: *Oresteia*' in P. Brown and S. Ograjenšek (eds.) *Ancient Drama in Music for the Modern Stage*. Oxford: Oxford University Press, 258–284.

Besson, J-L. (2013) 'Translator and Director: At Daggers Drawn?' in S. Bigliazzi, P. Kofler and P. Ambrosi (eds.) *Theatre Translation in Performance*. New York: Routledge, 150–157.

Bowen, A. (ed.) (1986) *Aeschylus: Choephoroi*. Bristol: Bristol Classical Press.

Brown, A. (1982) 'Some Problems in the *Eumenides* of Aeschylus'. *Journal of Hellenic Studies* 102: 26–32.

Brown, A. (ed.)(2018) *Aeschylus: Libation Bearers*. Liverpool: Liverpool University Press.

Burian, P. (2023) '*Eumenides*: Justice, Gender, the Gods and the City' in P. Burian and J. Bromberg (eds.) *A Companion to Aeschylus*. Hoboken, NJ: John Wiley and Sons, 130–144.

Burian, P. and Shapiro, A. (2003) *The Complete Aeschylus: Volume 1, The Oresteia*. New York: Oxford University Press.

Buxton, R.G. (1982) *Persuasion in Greek Tragedy*. Cambridge: Cambridge University Press.

Calame, C. (2013) 'Choral Polyphony and the Ritual Functions of Tragic Songs' in R. Gagné and M. Hopman (eds.) *Choral Mediations in Greek Tragedy*. Cambridge: Cambridge University Press, 35–57.

Cohen, D. (1986) 'The Theodicy of Aeschylus: Justice and Tyranny in the "Oresteia"'. *Greece and Rome* 33.2: 129–141.

226 Works Cited

Conacher, D.J. (1987) *Aeschylus' Oresteia: A Literary Commentary*. Toronto: Toronto University Press.

Conington, J. (ed.) (1857) *Aeschylus: Choephori*. London: Parker and Son.

Connor, W.J. (1990) 'City Dionysia and Athenian Democracy' in W.J. Connor and J.R. Fears (eds.) *Aspects of Athenian Democracy*. Copenhagen: Museum Tusculum Press.

Coo, L. and Uhlig, A. (eds.) (2019) *'Aeschylus at Play: Studies in Aeschylean Satyr Drama'. Bulletin of the Institute of Classical Studies 62.2*. London: Institute of Classical Studies.

Csapo, E. and Wilson, P. (2021) *A Social and Economic History of the Theatre to 300 BC*. Cambridge: Cambridge University Press.

Dale, A. (1969) *Collected Papers of A.M. Dale* (Turner and Webster, eds.) Cambridge: Cambridge University Press.

Dunbar, Z. and Harrop, S. (2018) *Greek Tragedy and the Contemporary Actor*. Cham, Switzerland: Palgrave-Macmillan.

Easterling, P. (1973) 'Presentation of Character in Aeschylus'. *Greece and Rome* 20: 3–19.

Ewans, M. (1975) 'Agamemnon at Aulis: A Study in the *Oresteia'*. *Ramus* 4.1: 17–32.

Ewans, M. (1980 [1971]) *Aeschylean Inevitability: A Study of the* Oresteia. Ann Arbor: University Microfilms International.

Ewans, M. (1982a) 'The Dramatic Structure of *Agamemnon'*. *Ramus* 11.1: 1–15.

Ewans, M. (1982b) *Wagner and Aeschylus: The* Ring *and the* Oresteia. London; New York: Faber and Faber; Cambridge University Press.

Ewans, M. (1989) 'Aischylos; for Actors, in the Round' in R. Warren (ed.) *The Art of Translation: Voices from the Field*. Boston: Northeastern University Press, 120–124.

Ewans, M. (1995) 'Patterns of Tragedy in Sophokles and Shakespeare' in M. Silk (ed.) *Tragedy and the Tragic*. Oxford: Clarendon Press, 438–457.

Ewans, M. (ed. and tr.) (1996) *Aeschylus: Suppliants and Other Dramas*. London: J.M. Dent.

Ewans, M. (1999) *Sophocles; Four Dramas of Maturity* (ed. and trans., with G. Ley and G. McCart). London: J. M. Dent.

Ewans, M. (2000) *Sophocles; Three Dramas of Old Age* (ed. and trans., with G. Ley and G. McCart). London: J. M. Dent.

Ewans, M. (2002) 'Performance-Based Research into Greek Drama' DRAMA (Beiträge zum antiken Drama und seiner Rezeption) Band 12 in John Barsby (ed.) *Greek and Roman Drama: Translation and Performance*. Stuttgart: M&P Verlag für Wissenschaft und Forschung, 58–78.

Ewans, M. (2010) *Aristophanes: Lysistrata, The Women's Festival and Frogs*. Norman: Oklahoma University Press.

Ewans, M. (2011) *Aristophanes: Acharnians, Knights and Peace*. Norman: Oklahoma University Press.

Ewans, M. (2021) *Euripides: Medea. Translation and Theatrical Commentary*. Abingdon and New York: Routledge.

Ewans, M. (2023) *Staging Ancient Greek Plays: A Practical Guide*. London: Bloomsbury Methuen Drama.

Fagles, R. (tr.) (1977) *Aeschylus: The Oresteia*. Harmondsworth: Penguin.

Finglass, P.J. (2018) 'Stesichorus and Greek Tragedy' in R. Andújar, T. Coward, & T. Hadjimichael (eds.) *Paths of Song: The Lyric Dimension of Greek Tragedy*. Berlin and Boston: De Gruyter, 19–38.

Works Cited   227

Finglass, P.J. (2023) 'Aeschylus, Lyric and Epic' in P. Burian and J. Bromberg (eds.) *A Companion to Aeschylus*. Hoboken, NJ: John Wiley and Sons, 27–39.

Fischer-Lichte, E. (2017) *Tragedy's Endurance: Performances of Greek Tragedies and Cultural Identity in Germany since 1800*. Oxford: Oxford University Press.

Foley, H. (1998) 'Introduction to Aeschylus' *Oresteia*' in P. Meineck (tr.) *Aeschylus: Oresteia*. Indianapolis: Hackett.

Forrest, G. (1966/1978) *The Emergence of Greek Democracy*. London: Weidenfeld and Nicholson.

Fraenkel, E. (ed.) (1950) *Aeschylus: Agamemnon* (3 vols.). Oxford: Oxford University Press.

Gagné, R. and Hopman, M. (eds.) (2013) *Choral Mediations in Greek Tragedy*. Cambridge: Cambridge University Press.

Garvie, A.F. (ed.) (1986) *Aeschylus: Choephoroi*. Oxford: Oxford University Press.

Goette, H.R. (2007) 'An Archaeological Appendix' in P. Wilson (ed.) *The Greek Theatre and Festivals: Documentary Studies*. Oxford: Oxford University Press, 116–121.

Goheen, R. (1955) 'Aspects of Dramatic Symbolism in *Agamemnon*'. *American Journal of Philology* 76: 113–137.

Goldhill, S. (1986) *Reading Greek Tragedy*. Cambridge: Cambridge University Press.

Goldhill, S. (1992) *Aeschylus: The Oresteia*. Cambridge: Cambridge University Press.

Goldhill, S. (2007) *How to Stage Greek Tragedy Today*. Chicago: Chicago University Press.

Goward, B. (2005) *Aeschylus: Agamemnon*. London: Bloomsbury.

Griffith (2023) 'Critical Approaches to Aeschylus, from the Nineteenth Century to the Present' in P. Burian and J. Bromberg (eds.) *A Companion to Aeschylus*. Hoboken, NJ: John Wiley and Sons, 389–411.

Griffith, M. (1977) *The Authenticity of 'Prometheus Bound'*. Cambridge: Cambridge University Press.

Griffith, M. (1995) 'Brilliant Dynasts: Power and Politics in the "Oresteia"'. *Classical Antiquity* 14.1: 62–129.

Griffith, M. (1999) 'The King and Eye: The Role of the Father in Greek Tragedy'. *The Cambridge Classical Journal: Proceedings of the Cambridge Philological Society* 40: 20–84.

Griffith, M. (2002) 'Slaves of Dionysos: Satyrs, Audience, and the Ends of the *Oresteia*'. *Classical Antiquity* 21: 195–258.

Hall, E. (2010) *Greek Tragedy: Suffering under the Sun*. Oxford: Oxford University Press.

Hammond, N.G.L. (1972) 'The Conditions of Dramatic Production to the Death of Aeschylus'. *Greek, Roman and Byzantine Studies* 13: 387–450.

Headlam, W. (1906) 'The Last Scene of the *Eumenides*'. *Journal of Hellenic Studies* 26: 268–277.

Heinrichs, A. (2012) 'Dionysus' in S. Hornblower, A. Spawforth and E. Eidinow (eds.) *Oxford Classical Dictionary* (Fourth edition). Oxford: Oxford University Press.

Henderson, J. (1991) 'Women and the Athenian Dramatic Festivals'. *Transactions of the American Philological Association* 122: 133–147.

Herington, J. (1986) *Aeschylus*. New Haven: Yale University Press.

Hester, D. (1981) 'The Casting Vote'. *American Journal of Philology* 202: 265–274.

Hinds, A. with M. Cuypers (tr.) (2017) *Aeschylus' The Oresteia*. London: Oberon Books.

Hornby, R. (1977) *Script into Performance: A Structuralist View of Play Production*. Austin: University of Texas Press.

Housman, A.E. (1989) *Collected Poems and Selected Prose*. Harmondsworth: Penguin.

Hughes, A. (2011), *Performing Greek Comedy*. Cambridge: Cambridge University Press.

228 Works Cited

Hunningher, B. (1956) 'Acoustics and Acting in the Theatre of Dionysus Eleutherius'. *Mededelingen der Kon. Nederl. Acad. von Wetenschappen, Afd. Letterkunde* 198: 303–338.

Jones, J. (1962) *On Aristotle and Greek Tragedy*. London: Chatto and Windus.

Kaimio, M. (1970) *The Chorus of Greek Drama within the Light of the Person and Number Used*. Helsinki: Societas scientiaru Fennica.

Kells, J. (ed.) (1973) *Sophocles: Electra*. Cambridge: Cambridge University Press.

Kovacs, D. (1987) 'The Way of a God with a Maid in Aeschylus' *Agamemnon*'. *Classical Philology* 82.4: 326–334.

Kranz, W. (1933/1988) *Stasimon: Untersuchungen ze Form und Gehalt der Griechischen Tragödie*. Hildesheim, Berlin: Wiedmann.

Lattimore, R. (1964) *Story-Patterns in Greek Tragedy*. Ann Arbor: University of Michigan Press.

Lebeck, A. (1971) *The Oresteia: A Study in Language and Structure*. Cambridge, MA: Harvard University Press.

Lee, M. (2004) '"Evil Wealth of Raiment": Deadly Πέπλοι in Greek Tragedy'. *Classical Journal* 99.3: 253–279.

Lehmann, H.T. (2016) *Tragedy and Dramatic Theatre*. London: Routledge.

Ley, G. (1989) 'Agatharchos, Aeschylus and the Construction of a Skene'. *Maia*, N.S. 1.1: 35–38.

Ley, G. (2006) *A Short Introduction to the Greek Theater* (2nd ed.). Chicago: Chicago University Press.

Ley, G. (2007) *The Theatricality of Greek Tragedy: Playing Space and Chorus*. Chicago and London: Chicago University Press.

Ley, G. and Ewans, M. (1985) 'The Orchestra as Acting Area in Greek Tragedy'. *Ramus* 14.2: 75–84.

Lloyd-Jones, H. (1961) 'Interpolations in *Choephoroi* and *Electra*'. *Classical Quarterly* 11: 171–184.

Lloyd-Jones, H. (1971) *The Justice of Zeus*. Berkeley: University of California Press.

Lloyd-Jones, H. (tr.) (1979) *Aeschylus: Eumenides* (Second edition). London: Duckworth.

Macintosh, F. (1997) 'Tragedy in Performance: Nineteenth- and Twentieth-Century Productions' in P. Easterling (ed.) *The Cambridge Companion to Greek Tragedy*, Cambridge: Cambridge University Press, 284–323.

Macleod, C. (1982) 'Morals and Politics in the *Oresteia*'. *Journal of Hellenic Studies* 102: 124–144 or *Collected Papers*. Oxford: Oxford University Press, 1983, 20–40.

Marinetti, C. (2013) 'Transnational, Multilingual and Post-dramatic: Rethinking the Location of Translation in Contemporary Theatre', in S. Bigliazzi, P. Kofler and P. Ambrosi (eds.) *Theatre Translation in Performance*. New York: Routledge.

Marshall, C.W. (2017) *Aeschylus: Libation Bearers*. London: Bloomsbury.

Marshall, H. R. (2023) '*Oresteia* on Stage: Koun, Stein, Hall and Mnouchkine' in P. Burian and J. Bromberg (eds.) *A Companion to Aeschylus*. Hoboken, NJ: John Wiley and Sons, 491–504.

Mastronade, D. (1979) *Contact and Discontinuity: Some Conventions of Speech and Action on the Greek Tragic Stage*. Berkeley: University of California Press.

Mastronade, D. (1990) 'Actors on High: The Skene Roof, the Crane and the Gods in Attic Drama'. *Classical Antiquity* 9.2: 247–294.

Meineck, P. (tr.) (1998) *Aeschylus: Oresteia*. Indianapolis: Hackett.

Meineck, P. (2017) *Theatrocracy: Greek Drama, Cognition and the Imperative for Theatre*. Abingdon: Routledge.

Works Cited 229

Melchinger, S. (1979) *Die Welt als Tragödie* (Vol. 1). Munich: Beck.
Mitchell, K. (2009) *The Director's Craft: A handbook for the theatre.* Abingdon: Routledge.
Mitchell-Boyask, R. (2013) *Aeschylus: Eumenides.* London: Bloomsbury.
Murnaghan, S. (2013) 'The Nostalgia of the Male Tragic Chorus' in F. Macintosh, F. Budelmann and J. Billings (eds.) *Choruses, Ancient and Modern,* Oxford: Oxford University Press, 173–188.
Naiden, F.S. (2023) 'Aeschylus and Athenian Law' in P. Burian and J. Bromberg (eds.) *A Companion to Aeschylus.* Hoboken, NJ: John Wiley and Sons, 361–372.
Neuburg, M. (1981) *An Aeschylean Universe.* Ann Arbor: University Microfilms International.
Nigri, L. (2013) 'From the Peninsula Westward: A Journey among Translations' in S. Bigliazzi, P. Kofler and P. Ambrosi (eds.) *Theatre Translation in Performance.* New York: Routledge, 97–119.
Olson, S.D. (ed.) (1998) *Aristophanes: Peace.* Oxford: Oxford University Press.
Osborne, R. (1993) 'Competitive Festivals and the Polis: A Context for Dramatic Festivals at Athens' in A. Sommerstein, et al. (eds.) *Tragedy, Comedy and the Polis.* Bari: Levanti Editori.
Padel, R. (1990) 'Making Space Speak' in J. Winkler and F. Zeitlin (eds.) *Nothing to Do with Dionysos? Athenian Drama in its Social Context.* Princeton: Princeton University Press, 336–365.
Papastamati-von Mook, C. (2014) 'The Theatre of Dionysus Eleuthereus in Athens' in Eric Csapo, Hans R. Goette, J. Richard Green and Peter Wilson (eds.) *Greek Theatre in the Fourth Century BC.* Berlin and Boston: De Gruyter.
Papastamati-von Mook, C. (2015) 'The Wooden Theatre of Dionysos Eleutherios in Athens: Old Issues, New Research' in Frederiksen, Gebhard and Sokolicek (eds.) *The Architecture of the Ancient Greek Theatre* (Monographs of the Danish Institute at Athens, vol. 17). Aarhus: Aarhus University Press.
Peradotto, J. (1964) 'Some Patterns of Nature Imagery in the *Oresteia'. American Journal of Philology* 85: 378–383.
Pickard, J. (1893) 'The Relative Positions of Actors and Chorus in the Greek Theatre of the Fifth Century BC'. *American Journal of Philology* 14: 68–89, 199–225 and 273–304.
Pickard-Cambridge, A.W. (1968) *The Dramatic Festivals of Athens* (Second Edition). Oxford: Oxford University Press.
Podlecki, A. (1966) *The Political Background of Aeschylean Tragedy.* Ann Arbor: University of Michigan Press.
Podlecki, A. (ed.) (1989) *Aeschylus: Eumenides.* Warminster: Aris and Phillips.
Pool, E.H. (1983) 'Clytemnestra's First Entrance in Aeschylus' *Agamemnon'. Mnemosyne* 36: 71–116.
Postgate, R. (ed. and tr.) (1969) *The Agamemnon of Aeschylus.* Cambridge: Rampant Lions Press.
Raeburn, D. (2016), *Greek Tragedies as Plays for Performance.* Hoboken, NJ: Wiley and Sons.
Rehm, R. (1985) 'Aeschylus and Performance: A Review of the National Theatre's *Oresteia'.* in J. Redmond (ed.) *Themes in Drama* (Seventh edition). Cambridge: Cambridge University Press.
Rehm, R. (1988) 'The Staging of Suppliant Plays'. *Greek, Roman and Byzantine Studies* 29: 263–307.

230   *Works Cited*

Rehm, R. (2002) *The Play of Space: Spatial Transformation in Greek Tragedy*. Princeton: Princeton University Press.

Rehm, R. (2017) *Understanding Greek Tragic Theatre*. Abingdon: Routledge.

Reinhardt, K. (1949) *Aischylos als Regisseur und Theologe*. Bern: Franke.

Rosenbloom, D. (2023) 'Aeschylus' Athens between Hegemony and Empire' in P. Burian and J. Bromberg (eds.) *A Companion to Aeschylus*. Hoboken, NJ: John Wiley and Sons.

Rosenmeyer, T.G. (1982) *The Art of Aeschylus*. Berkeley: University of California Press.

Rudkin, D. (tr.) (1980) *Euripides: Hippolytus. A Version*. London: Heinemann.

Scott, W.C. (1984) *Musical Design in Aeschylean Theatre*. Hanover and London: University Press of New England.

Seaford, R. (1989) 'The Attribution of Aeschylus *Choephoroi* 691–9'. *Classical Quarterly* 39: 302–306.

Seale, D. (1982) *Vision and Stagecraft in Sophocles*. London: Croom Helm.

Segal, C. (1981) *Tragedy and Civilisation*. Cambridge, MA: Harvard University Press.

Sommerstein, A. (1980) 'Notes on the *Oresteia*'. *Bulletin of the Institute of Classical Studies, Supplement* 27: 63–75.

Sommerstein, A. (ed.) (1989) *Aeschylus: Eumenides*. Cambridge: Cambridge University Press.

Sommerstein, A. (ed. and tr.) (2008) *Aeschylus: Oresteia*. Cambridge, MA and London: Harvard University Press.

Sommerstein, A. (2010) *Aeschylean Tragedy*. London: Bristol Classical Press 2012.

Sourvinou-Inwood, C. (1994) 'Something to Do with Athens: Tragedy and Ritual' in S. Hornblower and R. Osborne (eds.) *Ritual, Finance, Politics: Athenian Democratic Accounts Presented to David Lewis*. Oxford: Clarendon Press, 269–290.

Steiner, G. (1961) *The Death of Tragedy*. London: Faber and Faber.

Steiner, G. (1975) *After Babel*. Oxford: Oxford University Press.

Storey, I. and Allan, A. (2013) *A Guide to Ancient Greek Drama* (Second edition). Oxford: Blackwell.

Swift. L. (2010) *The Hidden Chorus: Echoes of Genre in Tragic Lyric*. Oxford: Oxford University Press.

Swift, L. (2015) 'Stesichorus on Stage' in P.J. Finglass and Adrian Kelly (eds.) *Stesichorus in Context*. Cambridge: Cambridge University Press, 125–144.

Taplin, O. (1972) 'Aeschylean Silences and Silences in Aeschylus'. *Harvard Studies in Classical Philology* 76: 57–98.

Taplin, O. (1977a) *The Stagecraft of Aeschylus: The Dramatic Use of Exits and Entrances in Greek Tragedy*. Oxford: Clarendon Press.

Taplin, O. (1977b) 'Did Greek Dramatists Write Stage Instructions?' *Proceedings of the Cambridge Philological Society* 203: 121–133.

Taplin, O. (1978) *Greek Tragedy in Action*. London: Methuen.

Taplin, O. (2005) 'The Harrison Version' in F. Macintosh, P. Michelakis, E. Hall and O. Taplin (eds.) *Agamemnon in Performance 458 BC to AD 2004*. Oxford: Oxford University Press, 235–254.

Thomson, G. (ed.) (1966) *The Oresteia of Aeschylus* (Second edition). Amsterdam; Prague: Adolf M. Hakkert; Academia.

Vernant, J.P. and Vidal-Nacquet, P. (1981) *Tragedy and Myth in Ancient Greece*. Sussex; New Jersey: Harvester Press; Humanities Press.

Vickers, B. (1973) *Towards Greek Tragedy*. London: Longman.

Works Cited 231

Walcot, P. (1976) *Greek Drama in Its Theatrical and Social Context*. Cardiff: University of Wales Press.

Wallace, R. (2023) 'Democracy's Age of Bronze: Aeschylus's Play and Athenian History, 508/7 to 454 BCE' in P. Burian and J. Bromberg (eds.) *A Companion to Aeschylus*. Hoboken, NJ: John Wiley and Sons, 13–26.

Walton, J.M. (1980) *Greek Theatre Practice*. Westport, CT: Greenwood Press.

Walton, J.M. (1984) *The Greek Sense of Theatre: Tragedy Reviewed*. London: Routledge.

West, D. (ed.) (1990) *Aeschylus: Tragoediae*. Stuttgart: Teubner.

Whallon, W. (1980) *Problem and Spectacle: Studies in the* Oresteia. Heidelberg: Winter.

Wiles, D. (1997) *Tragedy in Athens: Performance Space and Theatrical Meaning*. Cambridge: Cambridge University Press.

Wiles, D. (2000) *Greek Theatre Performance: An Introduction*. Cambridge: Cambridge University Press.

Wilson, P. (2000) *The Athenian Institution of the Choregia: The Chorus, the City and the Stage*. Cambridge: Cambridge University Press.

Winnington-Ingram, R.P. (1980) *Sophocles: An Interpretation*. Cambridge: Cambridge University Press.

Winnington-Ingram, R.P. (1983) *Studies in Aeschylus*. Cambridge: Cambridge University Press.

Zeitlin, F. (1965) 'The Motif of the Corrupted Sacrifice in Aeschylus' *Oresteia*'. *Transactions of the American Philological Association* 96: 463–508.

Index

Aegina 18
Aeschylus *passim*: *Agamemnon* 7, 8, 10,
12–3, 15–7, 141–71, 178, 180, 183,
185, 186, 188, 191, 193, 194, 203, 209;
Eumenides 7–9, 13, 14, 15, 17–9, 22–3,
168, 181, 185, 188, 192–216; *Libation
Bearers* 7, 12, 13, 15, 17, 156, 161,
168–91, 193, 194, 199, 200; *Oresteia* 1,
2, 4, 7, 9, 11–6, 18–9, 23, 24, 144;
Persians 4; *Proteus* 1; *Suppliants* 7;
Women of Aitna 4
Apollo 17, 157, 158, 177, 187, 189,
192–9, 201–9
Areopagos 192, 203, 207
Ares 17
Argos 17, 149, 150, 160, 163, 171–3,
207, 209
Aristophanes 6; *Frogs* 18, 172
Aristotle: *Poetics* 32
Arnott, P. 11
Artemis 17, 146–7
Athena 7, 17, 192, 195, 198, 199, 200–14
Athens 17, 192, 195, 197, 199,
202, 208–14

Bell, John 212
Birtwistle, Harrison 22
Bond, Robin 204
Brook, Peter 144

Chekhov, Anton 11
Clever, Edith 22, 185
Cohen, D. 14
Corinth 18

Dale, A.M. 10, 177
Delphi 187, 192, 194, 195, 196, 199, 209
Dionysos 1; Festivals of 2, 3, 4; Theatre
of 3, 4; *Ekkuklēma* 4–6, 10, 142, 143,

160, 161, 165, 169, 170, 186–8, 196;
Orchēstra 4–6, 9–11; *Theatron* 4–6;
Skēnē 2, 4–6, 9–11, 142, 144, 178, 195

Ephialtes 18, 207
Epidaurus 21, 22, 205
Euripides 16; *Alkestis* 192; *Bacchae* 3;
Elektra 174; *Herakles* 144; *Iphigenia
at Aulis* 19–21
Ewans, M. 6, 11, 13, 30, 178

Forrest, G. 18

Gagné, R. 7
Garvie, A.F. 177
Goethe, J. W. von 18
Goldhill, S.: *Aeschylus: the Oresteia* 30
Goward, B.: *Aeschylus: Agamemnon* 30
Griffith, M. 7–8

Hall, E.: *Suffering under the Sun* 30
Hall, Peter: *Oresteia* 21–2, 204
Hammond, N.G.L. 204
Harrison, Tony 22
Headlam, W. 213
Hermes 197
Homer 6, 12, 143; *Iliad* 14, 193; *Odyssey*
151, 193
Hopman, M. 7
Hornby, R. 2–3
Hughes, Ted: *Oresteia* 19, 23

Ibsen, H. 11
Icke, Robert: *Oresteia* 23–4

Jones, J. 14

Kimon 18
Koun, Karolos: *Oresteia* 18, 155, 204

Index 233

Ley, G. 6
Lloyd-Jones, H. 14

Marshall, C.: *Aeschylus: Agamemnon* 30
Marshall, H.R. 23
McLaughlin, Ellen 23
Megara 18
Mitchell, Katie 23; *Agamemnon* 23
Mitchell-Boysak, R.: *Aeschylus: Eumenides* 30
Mnouchkine, Ariane: *Les Atrides* 21–2, 24

Naiden, F.S. 14
Nauplion 149

Padel, R. 9
Perikles 18, 207
Persia 18
Pickard, J. 6
Pindar 6
Plutarch: *Life of Solon* 5
Power, Ben: *Medea* 19

Rehm, R.: *Understanding Greek Tragic Theatre* 30
Reinhardt, K. 154
Rosenbloom, D. 18

Schlegel, F. 7
Scott, W.C. 177
Shakespeare, William: *Hamlet* 1, 168; *King Lear* 1
Sommerstein, A. 8, 31; *Aeschylean Tragedy* 30
Sophocles 6, 16; *Aias* (*Ajax*) 212
Sparta 18, 209
Stein, Peter: *Oresteia* 21–2, 187, 204
Steiner, G. 24; *After Babel* 19
Stesichoros 12
Storey, I. and Allan, A.: *A Guide to Ancient Greek Drama* 30
Swift, L. 7

Taplin, O. 10, 22, 153, 177, 195, 204, 209, 213; *The Stagecraft of Aeschylus* 22

Vickers, B. 11; *Towards Greek Tragedy* 31

Walcot, P. 11
Wallace, R. 14
Wiles, D. 6, 10, 18, 20; *Greek Theatre Performance* 30
Wilson, P. 8

Zeus 147, 149, 155, 188, 192, 199, 205–6, 207

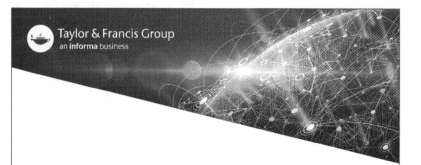

Printed in the United States
by Baker & Taylor Publisher Services